# Redux
## The Arts & Crafts Revival

---

## 1972-2012

Judith Budwig
Jeffrey Preston

**Mercer Oak Publishing**

Princeton • New Jersey

# Acknowledgements

*We are deeply grateful to everyone who helped us, from interviews, to loans of photographs and ephemera, to honest feedback. Special thanks to Maria Cicchino for her patience and long hours, and to Rosalie for inspiration, counsel, and for being Rosalie. To Bruce Johnson, who helped us get started and was there at every turn, and to the Arts and Crafts Research Fund for their support. A huge thanks to Bill and Patsy Porter for opening their archives, sharing ideas, and their warm hospitality. To A. Patricia Bartinique for her expertise and help in a myriad of ways, and to Judy Jordan for anything and everything—she was there for us. To Dave Rago and Suzanne Perrault for your help in so many ways and being 10 seconds away by e-mail. For the support and patience of Robert Kaplan, Ted Lytwyn, and Cara Corbo. And thanks to Heather Stivison and Bernadette Rubbo at Craftsman Farms for all the research, photos, and endless e-mails. To Aminy Audi, whose warmth and authenticity touched us. David Smith's wonderful support, his sensitivity, and photos made this project possible, and thank you to Art Accardi for his wit, wisdom, and artistic sensibility. And to Don Nelson, Mary Ann Davis, and Jeff Wood for their herculean efforts on this project. Also to Mandy and Duncan MacTavish—you deserve extra catnip and attention. And to many others—thank you.*

| | | | |
|---|---|---|---|
| John Bryan | Wadsworth Atheneum | American Bungalow | Tod Volpe |
| Crab Tree Farm | Jennifer Strauss/Style 1900 | Kitty Turgeon | Isak Lindenauer |
| Tom Gleason | David Rudd and | Boice Lydell | Derek Danton |
| Alyce Englund | Debbie Goldwein | Nancy McClelland | Peter Smorto |
| Allan Phillips | Rudy Ciccarello | Linda Hubbard Brady | Richie Savoia |
| Don Magner | Two Red Roses | Marilee Meyer | David Watson |
| Paul Rocheleau | Tom Magoulis | Ray Stubblebine | Christie's New York |
| Jerry Cohen | Andrea Valluzzo | Nancy Clark and BAHA | Grand Rapids Art Museum |
| Michael Adams | David Cathers | Princeton University | Everson Museum of Art |
| Dawn Hopkins | Don Marek | Art Museum | Jill Thomas-Clark |
| Benoit Cortet | Eliane Talec | Linda Myers | (Michael Clark) |
| Beth Cathers | Penelope Whitney | Martha Augat | Antiques and |
| Peter and Janet Copeland | Don Treadway | Richard Caggiano | The Arts Weekly |
| Ed and Kathy Friedman | John Toomey | Stephen Fletcher | David Kornacki |
| Laura Harris (Stephen Gray) | John Brickmann | Kathryn Gargolinski | (photos p. 157) |

Cover© 2013 by Jeffrey Preston and Judith Budwig

Cover designed by Bowhaus

Designer: Maria Cicchino

Mercer Oak Publishing

Suite 3274

213 Carnegie Center

Princeton, NJ 08543

First Edition

ISBN 978-0-578-11806-2

*Printed in the United States of America*

*[Handwritten note:] Dear Lois + Ed. Hope you enjoy this book friends of mine wrote and I put together. xo Maria*

# Redux
The Arts & Crafts Revival
**1972-2012**

## CONTENTS

## Revival Redux

John Crosby Freeman studied Gustav Stickley, largely unknown to people in the mid-20th century, because his thesis advisor at Winterthur suggested the subject. Freeman based his research on interviews, furniture catalogs, *The Craftsman* magazine, which he indexed by author and subject, and Craftsman Farms, where he cataloged Gustav Stickley's personal library (Freeman 1966). While his resources were primitive in some instances, his research was valuable if not always accurate, and it opened the door for further research into the fascinating man, Gustav Stickley.

A few years earlier, Robert Judson Clark was avidly reading *The Craftsman* and developing his own Stickley library. Although Clark's familiarity with Stickley predated Freeman's, it was John Crosby Freeman's 1966 *Forgotten Rebel: Gustav Stickley and His Craftsman Mission Furniture* that provided the first published research on Stickley in the second half of the 20th century.

In his introduction, Freeman expresses his hope of creating an awareness of an important period in American design and saving mission furniture from wanton destruction "out of ignorance and unwarranted prejudice. Craftsman was the first popular modern furniture that the United States produced. As such it deserves preservation and appreciation" (Freeman 1965).

It was only four years later that professor Robert Judson Clark began planning *The Arts and Crafts Movement in America, 1876–1916* at Princeton University, which many view as the event that launched the American Arts and Crafts revival. Freeman and Clark both established important benchmarks at a time of national awakening. In the early 1970s the country was reflecting on itself in light of the Vietnam War, the sexual revolution, the *Whole Earth Catalog,* and individual magical mystery tours.

Jordan-Volpe roared onto the New York arts scene in 1976 with a big vision of creating a market for Arts and Crafts design. They also recognized its potential for yielding huge profits in return for audacious and innovative marketing. They played every angle and presented a fabulous show to a receptive New York crowd. They were so effective at creating drama and mystique around the Arts and Crafts movement that the excitement and titillation attracted Hollywood celebrities.

That drove the market and sent prices to dizzying levels at auction. People were intoxicated by the possibilities of so much money flying around.

Beth Cathers, buying for Jordan-Volpe, had an impressive knowledge of Gustav Stickley's furniture. One memorable early auction, 1979, was the "snowstorm auction" at Oliver's in Maine, famous for what it sold and the prices it brought. Beth bought a Gustav Stickley inlaid Harvey Ellis desk and chair for $14,500, a heady price for the time, and Don Magner was the underbidder.

At Christie's, Nancy McClelland took charge of the Arts and Crafts sales in 1981, and the auction house began to dominate the market. As the 1980s progressed, smaller auctions started getting into the Arts and Crafts as pieces were becoming more available to them. It was an exciting time as people were learning with every new piece that came their way, and in addition to the beauty and sensuality of the pieces, many held the potential for bringing record prices at auction.

Meanwhile, Bill Porter was showing his Gustav Stickley collection at the Detroit Historical Society and not long after, in 1981, David Cathers issued his *Furniture of the American Arts and Crafts Movement.* Now dealers and collectors had a reference in hand that pivoted on truth, and within the year, Stephen Gray jumped in to add his important reprints of Gustav Stickley furniture catalogs.

Adding a stabilizing dimension to the Arts and Crafts maelstrom, Robert Edwards began publishing *Tiller* in 1982. Printed on carefully selected paper and with typeface evocative of the early twentieth-century, articles were by respected experts and investigated serious topics. Edwards, a prolific writer with a piercing wit, has frequently contributed to exhibition catalogs, journals, and *Maine Antiques Digest.*

Since 1976, Vance Jordan and Tod Volpe had been doing everything they could to raise the stock on the period—donating pieces to museums, giving lectures at the New School, executing joint projects with experts and museums, and pulling out all the stops with their cataloged exhibitions of Grueby, Fulper, Rookwood, Stickley, Harvey Ellis, and their final extravaganza, the bizarre work of the Martin Brothers. Jordan-Volpe closed in 1986, but some important Arts and Crafts galleries, such as Michael Carey, had opened throughout the eighties on Spring Street in SoHo.

The Phillips sale in 1987 set a record with a Gustav Stickley ebonized crib settle for $66,000. A few months later, Skinner set a new record with a Gustav Stickley inlaid Harvey Ellis fall-front desk that Jim Bakker bought for $102,300. And in December 1988, Christie's sold the sideboard from Gustav Stickley's Columbus Avenue home in Syracuse for $363,000 to Barbra Streisand. David Rago, Treadway-Toomey, Savoia, and Skinner were ramping up Arts and Crafts sales. People were responsive, the market was reacting, and it seemed money was everywhere. Major collectors like John Bryan, Jovan Lombardo, and Max Palevsky were emerging, pushing prices at auction higher on premium pieces.

*"The Art That Is Life": The Arts and Crafts Movement in America, 1875–1920,* curated by Wendy Kaplan, opened at the Boston Museum of Fine Arts in 1987 and presented an exhaustive display of furniture and decorative arts that were both lived with and spectacular. It was the first major Arts and Crafts exhibition since the 1972 Princeton exhibition. Coincidentally, in the exact same months it was showing in Boston, March to May, *Arts and Crafts Furniture Design: The Grand Rapids Contribution 1895-1915,* curated by Don Marek, exhibited at the Grand Rapids Art Museum and highlighted, in particular, the work of Charles Limbert. Because of these exhibitions, some people were viewing the Arts and Crafts for the first time and found themselves drawn to the uniquely holistic phenomenon that was the Arts and Crafts movement.

In 1988, Bruce Johnson transplanted Boice Lydell's idea from the Roycroft campus, which was closing for long-term renovations, and created an Arts and Crafts splash with his first Grove Park Inn conference. People were thirsting to talk with other collectors, to see what dealers had to sell, and to hear what experts had to share. Attendance tripled within two years.

In 1992, Craftsman Farms put itself on the map through widespread publicity of the first major exhibition—ever—of exclusively Gustav Stickley's work. *Gustav Stickley: His Craft* was attended by people from all over the country. Where there had been very few exhibitions through the eighties, a rash of major exhibitions took place on the heels of *His Craft,* such as *The Ideal Home* at the American Crafts Museum in 1993; *Head, Heart and Hand: Elbert Hubbard and the Roycrofters* in 1994; and *Inspiring Reform: Boston's Arts and Crafts Movement* at Wellesley College in 1997. The pace of

the revival slowed down in the late nineties. There were no major exhibitions until 2005 when LACMA presented *The Arts and Crafts Movement in Europe and America: 1880–1920.*

In this post-911 world, premium Arts and Crafts pieces are still setting records, and major exhibitions happen every few years, such as the Wadsworth Atheneum's 2008 *At Home With Gustav Stickley* and the 2010 Dallas exhibition, *Gustav Stickley and the American Arts and Crafts Movement.* Scholarship is still vigorous and supported by institutions such as Winterthur, Craftsman Farms, and the Arts and Crafts Research Fund; and Bruce Johnson's Grove Park Inn Arts and Crafts Conference still attracts a large crowd.

Robert Judson Clark initiated the Arts and Crafts revival with his 1972 exhibition, and Jordan-Volpe lit the fire. Bruce Johnson has sustained it, enriched it, and undoubtedly prolonged it, but behind all of it was David Smith of *The Bee.* He was everywhere documenting the twists and turns, the events, and the people, and broadcasting the stories across the country. His quiet influence was powerful, and we maintain that he was one of the important drivers of the Arts and Crafts revival.

Our intention was to capture the story of dealers, collectors, scholars, and auction houses that were involved in the Arts and Crafts revival and to tell these stories in a cohesive manner. A good deal of the text in *Redux* is based on interviews we conducted. We selected individuals to highlight, and we focused on the unique stories of their involvement in the Arts and Crafts and how it shaped their lives and how they, in turn, influenced it. There are personal histories to record and photographs to preserve before they are lost. This, in a modest way, is what we have attempted to do.

Our view is east coast centric because we feel the east coast was the central radiating point for the revival. It is an enormous subject, and there are important people, exhibitions, and institutions we could not include. There are other points of view about the revival—what it is and what it means—and it is our hope that this book sets the stage for debate and argument and inspires research into this fascinating period that will ultimately add to the body of scholarship. That is the intention of this book.

Judith Budwig

Jeffrey Preston

Don Magner at a café in Paestum, Italy during filming of The Sailor From Gibraltar

LES AVANTS
sur MONTREUX

18th September 1962.

Dear Don,

    I have just returned from London to find your letter waiting.

    I am afraid this will be too late to get to you before you leave for Lausanne, but just in case it isn't - yes, do give me a ring when you get there.

    My number here is 6. 62. 3I.

    I hope you have been enjoying your visit to Europe - I saw Arthur when he was here and he seemed to have had a very good time.

    Yours sincerely,

Letter to Don Magner from Noel Coward, 1962

# 1. Don Magner

*Don Magner is one of the great dealers, and was the first Arts and Crafts dealer actively selling in the 1960s, before anyone could even name the style. The first Arts and Crafts galleries all bought inventory from him. Few people know that Don was not only a gifted painter, exhibiting in Manhattan, but also a natural dramatist and storyteller who was a scriptwriter in the film industry. Anyone who has experienced the pleasure of Don's colorful company, his artistry, his ability to entertain, and his intellect, should be delighted—but not surprised—at his life in the celebrity world of film.*

Maybe because he was such a visual person, Don Magner, a young man in the late 1940s, chose the alternative path by not acting on his acceptance to Columbia University but instead attended film school in New York. He was always outstanding in everything that interested him and was awarded best screenwriter upon his graduation from college in 1953.

Teeming with the physical energy of an attractive young man, the amazingly multiskilled Don joined the Riggers and Derrickman Number 197 and began working on skyscrapers in New York, but that vocation soon morphed into something more along the lines of his visual nature and artistic bent. He became friends with Tennessee Williams in the late 1950s. Williams was mercurial and moody, and he often needed the physical presence of Don in order to write, to actually put words on the page. Don kept him company in his New York apartment and, sometimes, even Key West.

An opportunity presented itself in 1964, and Don began working in Europe on a movie script with Christopher Isherwood for *Sailor from Gibraltar*, directed by Tony Richardson and starring Vanessa Redgrave, Jeanne Moreau, and Orson Wells (IMDb 2012). In addition to screenwriting, Don was production manager and found the *Xarifa*, a large three-masted schooner in the Mediterranean—securing it for six months of filming in Italy, Spain, Morocco, and Tunisia (Magner July 2012).

Intoxicated by the protean existentialism of the sixties, Don was caught up in highly charged friendships with the likes of Jean Genet and Noel Coward, but he tore himself away from the European lifestyle he savored and returned to New York for the 1967 cinematic premier of *Sailor* in Manhattan. The reviews were unkind but were overshadowed by

the bigger story of Vanessa Redgrave's divorce from director Tony Richardson because of his affair with Jeanne Moreau during *Sailor* filming in Ethiopia (Crowther 1967).

Don ached to get back to his art, so he rented a studio in New York. His intensely creative energies were directed into his painting, and his strong abstract expressionist canvases held their own next to the works of Willem de Kooning, Franz Kline, and Arshile Gorky. Don's paintings were shown at the Charles Alan Gallery on Madison Avenue and the Martha Jackson Gallery on East 69th Street (Magner July 2012).

**THE**

**YOUNG PLAYERS THEATRE**

*presents*

**Quality Street**

*by*

**JAMES M. BARRIE**

—▫—

**NASH'S BARN – KINGS HIGHWAY**

**Westport, Connecticut**

Head shot of Magner and program for Quality Street by James M. Barrie. Don acted and assisted in scene design, 1950

In his first year back from Europe, Don was asked to take over an antiques shop on Second Avenue in Manhattan. It belonged to a very wealthy friend of his who "thought that the millions his family was making in the clothing business was not a good way to make a living, even though they were making millions and supporting their family and lots of other people" (Magner August 2012). The shop was full of Biedermeyers and eighteenth-century English furniture, as well as some Arts and Crafts. Decorators were the mainstay of his business, but he also sold to people who would come in off the street.

Don in Zurich on his 1966 BSA Lightning

*They'd walk in and I'd show them an Art Nouveau inkwell, and they'd say, "What's an inkwell?" And to get them interested, I'd have to say something like, "Well, that's where you stash your pot." Of course young people then had no idea what things were. (Magner August 2012)*

*When boutiques and discos gained popularity and began opening in his neighborhood, rents skyrocketed. Don moved to Brooklyn Heights. His shop was open only on weekends because he spent the rest of the week collecting stuff, driving to places like Montclair, New Jersey, which yielded a lot of Arts and Crafts (as well as Victorian and Deco). According to Don, this was before the Montclair dealers "discovered Sotheby's and Christie's"* (Magner August 2012).

u.l. and above: Don, at 32, aboard the *Xarifa*, 1964

Don on location in Ethiopia for Sailor, 1964

Don in Ethiopia

Tony Richardson directing
Ian Bannen and Jeanne Moreau aboard the *Xarifa*

New York Times ad and Daily News review of Sailor

In the 1960s, no one in New York, except Paul Morrissey, seemed to know what Arts and Crafts was, however Don Magner had been blithely finding it, liking it, and buying it.

*I had seen it . . . but I had no idea what Arts and Crafts or Mission oak was. I don't remember who broke the news to me who Gustav Stickley was or that he was going to dominate my life for the next thirty or forty years. I got that book, "Forgotten Rebel" (1966), which was the only book about him—it was the only information available. (Magner August 2012)*

Don was enthralled with "these wonderful old geometrical-shaped pieces" and was simultaneously learning about Stickley and collecting pieces by him. But selling it was almost impossible. The main draw of these pieces was that they were both useful and cheap, but not everyone liked the style. There was only one Stickley collector on the east coast at that time, according to Don Magner, and that was Paul Morrissey, who was famous for being Andy Warhol's film-

maker. But Morrissey wasn't willing to pay anything because his outstanding collection, developed over many years, was made up of pieces he had found for almost nothing in antique shops or from sidewalk curbs.

*Paul Morrissey had a pretty large Arts and Crafts collection. It was the look he wanted. I never really had anything to do with him except through Warhol. I started doing business with Warhol sometime later, but I never saw his collection, and I never got to be friendly with him, so I guess I wasn't his Joe Dallesandro or some hunk like that. My relationship with Warhol was very strange and remote. He had forgotten—or didn't want to remember—that I had been at the Factory with Tony Richardson, and that we had been showing films by Warhol and Morrissey at the Factory. At that point I had no idea that such a thing as Stickley existed. This was before I went into the antiques business, so there was some reason why he was not warm to me.*

*But Jed Johnson and his brother often bought things from me when I first opened my shop in Brooklyn. They shopped for themselves and sometimes they bought for Warhol while he was on the sidewalk outside waiting for them. He would not come in. (Magner August 2012)*

*When the Johnson brothers left the shop with something for Warhol, I would have to go to Andy to get paid. I would ring the bell of his mansion on the Upper East Side, and he—I always expected a servant to be there to hand me a check, but no!—he would come down the stairs and open the door for himself and invite me into the hallway— but never upstairs—and I would wait in that hallway at the foot of the stairs until he came back with a check for the piece that the Johnsons had bought. (Magner August 2012)*

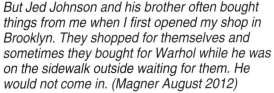

By 1969, Don had a booth in an important show at the Park Avenue Armory, displaying a mixture of design styles, including Arts and Crafts.

In the spring of 1972, Don Magner went to Stratford, Canada, to see an Art Deco exhibit curated by Mario Amaya that included eight of Don's pieces. On his way back, he stopped for the night in Syracuse. The next morning he walked by the public library and saw a placard announcing a special exhibit, "Gustav Stickley: Books and Other Information," so he went in looking for Stickley books. The curator suggested he go to Fayetteville, a suburb of Syracuse and where the L. & J.G. Stickley factory was located. Hopelessly lost to one-way streets on his way, he passed a house sale jammed with people.

Don found an L. & J.G. footstool in one of the upstairs bedrooms. He asked the price and then asked where he might find some other Stickley furniture for sale. "If you're interested in Stickley," the woman in charge said, "this is Louise Stickley right here." There she was sitting at the checkout. They were introduced and became friendly. She complained she had been badly treated by some dealers who had come up early and bought some inlaid L. & J.G. Stickley from her, but Don had never seen such a thing and wondered if she was perhaps mistaken, and it was really Harvey Ellis or Gustav Stickley, or someone like that. She was Leopold's second wife, who was quite young when she married him, and she greatly outlived him. She was of the generation that loved reproduction cherry furniture, and that was her preference.

Sometime after his return home, Louise invited Don to come visit her, so he took his two great big dogs, Henrietta and Hemingway, with him. Louise had a big old dog, and everybody, dogs included, got along and had a terrific time. Don and Louise became good friends. He never asked to buy anything from her, but she did introduce him to a few other people who worked for her at the factory and had some things to sell. This was before her sale of L. & J.G. Stickley to Alfred and Aminy Audi in 1974.

Little by little, Louise began showing Don the other houses she had that were in the area and were in the Gustav Stickley style and, slowly, she offered things to him. In time, she brought pieces for him to look at out of her main storage house, which was Victorian with some Arts and Crafts things inside. She had stored lots of things from the L. & J.G. Stickley showroom at the Merchandise Mart in Chicago, which they had for a long time after Gustav had gone out of business.

In the 1970s, house sales were common in upstate New York, and Don discovered that many of the houses filled with traditional furniture in them would have one room—the gentleman's study or the library—where the gentlemen went after dinner to smoke their cigars, while the women sat around the dining table to talk. There was a house not too far outside of Fayetteville where there was a room that was all Stickley, including andirons, and nobody noticed them except for Don Magner. He waited all day for them to come up for sale.

Anything could turn up at any time. An antiques shop had gone out of business and was going to be demolished, so Don went to the sale. All the furniture was gone, and hundreds of objects were just sitting all over the floor, which was very uneven. The guy in charge yelled to be careful. It was so bad, they even had this thing covered with neckties blocking a door.

*It took me a while to realize that this thing blocking the door was a Gus Stickley dinner gong. I asked him how much it was and he said "That's not for sale." So I held my breath, then I said, "Oh, you could put something else here to keep people from going in that room. That chair over there would keep people out—how much is this?" I thought he was going to repeat, "That's not for sale," but instead he said, "That's five dollars." I don't think I've ever gotten five dollars out of my pocket so fast. Anyway, there were a lot of fun times like that—and surprises. You never knew what you were going to come up with.*
*(Magner September 2012)*

Niedecken serving table for Irving house in Decatur, Illinois, now owned by Baltimore Art Museum, collection of Don Magner, 1979

l. r: Margaret Macdonald wall sconce, collection of Don Magner

*Prior to Robert Judson Clark's 1972 Princeton exhibition, Don Magner had never seen Rohlfs and didn't even know who he was. The Arts and Crafts Movement in America: 1876–1916 was the first all inclusive survey, and Don found the "visual aspects of the exhibition to be overwhelmingly interesting" Magner September 2012).*

As a result of the exhibition, a few collectors began appearing, people looking for individual pieces. Don's sales improved a bit. At that time he had one shop, a mixture of Victorian, Deco, Art Nouveau, and Arts and Crafts, but he acquired so many pieces of Stickley and other Arts and Crafts designers, that he opened American Arts and Crafts Warehouse around the corner from his other shop. It was unheated and by appointment only. On a cold, rainy December day in 1975, art critic Rita Reif of the *New York Times* came from Manhattan, looked at everything and then went back and wrote "Lagging Style: Interest in Furniture by Gustave [sic] Stickley and Elbert Hubbard Is Growing," a favorable review of Don's new shop.

*Fortunately this dealer makes no inflated claims for the pieces he offers. The designs he identifies as Gustave Stickley all bear paper labels or the burned-in mark, "Als ik kan/ Stickley" . . . and Mr. Magner readily turns pieces over to show the proof. . . . Mr. Magner welcomes visitors to the unheated premises by appointment. (Reif 1975)*

As a result of the review, his business picked up. He developed a working relationship with the serious Arts and Crafts collector couple, Terence and Ethel Leichti, who started buying from Don after they relocated to New Jersey from Los Angeles (Magner August 2012). What Don wasn't prepared for was that

*publicity would bring all the kooks out of the woodwork. Any kind of article or publicity you get in the paper brings you a small amount of business, but it also brings you all the nuts who surround any kind of emerging, new style of anything. So I was very surprised at the reaction that came from that article, that most of the people I heard from were people who were a little bit unbalanced (Magner August 2012).*

Magner developed clients in California but found them more difficult "than all the rest of my customers together— flaky and crazy" (August 2012). He had some problems when he drove out to California in 1975 to deliver furniture in person. Some people stopped payment on their checks once he made the delivery and left, and it was difficult to resolve some of those situations.

*Even one big Hollywood movie mogul never sent me the check I asked for in advance before I drove all the way across the country. I finally got to San Francisco, and I kept calling New York and the check hadn't arrived. I went to his Beverly Hills house, a fancy house, it was Halloween and the place was all decked out with candy and decorations all over the place, and I had to help him carry the stuff in. Everything went up to the second story, and the whole time I was there—I did get my check—he never offered me a glass of water or something to eat or even thanked me for helping him carry stuff upstairs. (Magner August 2012)*

The drive across the country was punctuated with the pleasure of finding Arts and Crafts pieces tucked away in odd shops in Denver and Salt Lake City, and great pieces in San Francisco.

Back in New York, at a shop on Madison Avenue, Don found an elegant Gustav Stickley director's table labeled "French Provincial," and it was expensive. It took a lot to convince them it wasn't French Provincial, that they were ruining their reputation by selling a mismarked Gustav Stickley table, and that they would be in a lot of trouble with their customers. He ended up buying it and still had to pay quite a bit. As late as the 1980s, Don would find shops specializing in Americana but unaware of Gustav Stickley.

Of course by that time there were more articles out— *New York* magazine published, "Move Over, Deco—Here Comes Mission," that brought a lot of attention to the Arts and Crafts and Jordan-Volpe Gallery, in particular (Brener 1977). Tod Volpe and Vance Jordan had started buying pieces from Don a year in advance of their gallery opening. Jordan-Volpe had the resources to mark prices high and simply wait for someone to buy at that price. Being an upscale SoHo gallery, they could get clients Don could not.

*That was just the beginning of the parade of people who joined in the excitement of living and dealing with Gustav Stickley. There were many other dealers, some very, very enjoyable and people of good character, and many who were not that way, who joined the soon-to-be crowd of people*

u.l.: Detail of Rohlfs tea table, 1905, collection of Don Magner

r.: Charles Rohlfs armchair, 1901, collection of Don Magner

*selling these things. Plus, dealers were cropping up in California, upstate New York, Massachusetts, and other places, a lot of them encouraged by the Princeton show. (Magner August 2012)*

Little by little, people were willing to pay a bit more, and then a bit more. In 1980, Sotheby Parke-Bernet had an Arts and Crafts auction, but pieces still did not bring a lot of money. It was hard for Don to make a living. He kept his business in Brooklyn Heights for a number of years, but he could not get the prices of a Manhattan gallery. Dealers like Michael Carey and Tod Volpe would often take pieces on consignment and sell them for far more than a Brooklyn shop could get.

New Yorkers were reluctant to cross the Brooklyn Bridge. Don could get customers from Europe and from California to come to his shop, but he couldn't get customers like Richard Gere. He did get Jerry and Willy Brandt, big collectors early on, who bought pieces for their house in Vail, Colorado—*the* house in Vail, which they shared with Andy Warhol. And he did get Jed Johnson, Andy Warhol's buyer, and Barbra Streisand came once. Michael Carey and Jordan-Volpe were getting big prices for Don's consignments, so in 1982, Don opened a shop in Manhattan.

l: Detail of worn seat, Charles Rennie Mackintosh, c. 1900, from Mrs. Cranston's billiard room, Glasgow, collection of Don Magner

r: Detail of hand grip from Mackintosh chair, above

o.p.: Don, at home, sitting in Gustav Stickley built-in inglenook taken from New Jersey farmhouse; 1907. Red decal in drawer

He found an empty store on Lafayette Street, which was in horrible condition. It had a balcony inside, like a loft, which was hidden from down below, and he set it up as an office and a bedroom. At that time, it was common for shops in that area to get robbed by men with big garbage trucks at 3 o'clock in the morning. They'd have someone scout the shop out in advance, then bring their garbage trucks up at 2 or 3 in the morning, and push them up on the sidewalk right to the security gate and put chains into the gate. Then with the motor grinding, so nobody would notice the noise (in the city nobody pays any attention to garbage trucks at 2 or 3 in the morning, grinding up the garbage), they would turn on the grinder to cover the noise and rip the security gates off, and they'd go in and grab what they wanted in a hurry and get out of there before the alarm would call the police.

*I had no insurance there, so I would spend the night there with my big German shepherd and my other large dogs. I would take them over there. In the morning I would get up early and take them back to Brooklyn, then go back to Manhattan, then go back in the evening to get them and take them back to the shop. So I was worn out all the time going back and forth with my dogs, and it got to be quite a hassle, and my health was suffering. But I did get Richard Gere as a customer and other people who would not come to Brooklyn. The person who took the shop after me had a serious robbery. (Magner August 2012)*

Adding to his exhaustion, Don also had a booth in Sanford Smith's first two Modernism shows at the Park Avenue Armory. The second one was in1983, right after the 1980–82 recession, and it was a financial disaster for him. In 1988, Don gave up his Manhattan shop and sold Arts and Crafts by appointment from a storage area.

As much as Don admired many of the things Stickley did, he wondered how much of it was actually his work. He had no doubt Gustav was the driving force, and the furniture never would have existed without him. But whether they were his designs or not was another matter. Besides Harvey Ellis, he believed there must have been many other people making the furniture or designing the furniture for him.

Don also raised questions as to who designed the Gustav Stickley metalwork and the wicker furniture. He thought the wicker designs were superb, possibly the best of Gustav Stickley, and very similar to many German designs. The question Don posed was whether they were designed in-house. If they were designed by someone working for Gustav, none of this would have existed without him, so Gustav should get the credit.

> When it comes to comparisons like Limbert, some of the designs are identical to European designs. I have a Josef Hoffman settle with spindles that looks exactly like a Gus settle with spindles. Which came first? There was a lot of cross-fertilization, and a lot, I suppose, of outright theft— stealing other people's designs. And if you print that, it'll probably outrage a lot of Gus fanatics, but I don't see any way out of it. There were certainly a lot of fantastically beautiful pieces of design in his name. (Magner August 2012)

In spite of loving much of Stickley's furniture, Don believes some of his designs should be thrown away, and he feels the same way about Rohlfs. He notes that Beth Cathers, antiques dealer and buyer for Jordan-Volpe after the gallery opened, managed to get a lot of Rohlfs. She had a connection with one particular dealer in the Buffalo area. Since Rohlfs was from Buffalo, that's where a lot of his work was to be found. But Don could never break into the pipeline between Beth and this dealer, who sold everything and anything, had no particular taste in any direction, and turned over anything he could profit from.

In an effort to try to get this dealer away from Beth, Don bought a piece of Rohlfs that nobody else wanted, an interesting piece of furniture, but not very good looking.

> It's useful, it's signed, it's mahogany, and it looks like a combination of Tudor and Empire, if you can imagine. Nobody but Rohlfs would do a combination of Tudor and Empire in the same piece. It's a little bit strange in other ways, but I bought that from him at his price in order to wean him away from Beth, but he stuck with her, and I was never able to get anything from him. (Magner August 2012)

Don slowly wound down his business activity, and the last exhibition he participated in was the Pier show in New York, in 1992.

For my interviews with Don, he sat comfortably in a Gus Stickley built-in inglenook that came from an old New Jersey farmhouse whose entrance had been converted to a Gus Stickley room. The piece had been extracted from the house and put into auction. Don bought it and, instead of building it into the walls of his house, he had a back made with

the same lumber the inglenook came from, so that the piece became freestanding.

Due to severe arthritis, Don Magner is semiretired and has returned to his guilty pleasure of living as a Luddite. He now has time to paint and enjoy nature. Curators from Sotheby's, Christie's, the Metropolitan Museum of Art, and Museum of Modern Art are familiar and friendly with Don. They occasionally go visit him to see his magnificent collection that doubles as a study collection, full of the rare and the exquisite.

### References

Brener, Carol. 1977. "Move Over, Deco—Here Comes Mission." *New York Magazine*. January 27, 1977.

IMDb. *Sailor from Gibraltar*. http://www.imdb.com/title/tt0062225. (accessed September16, 2012).

Magner, Don. Interviewed (phone) by authors. July 17, 2012.

———. In interview with Jeffrey Preston. Brooklyn, New York. August 17, 2012.

———. In interview with Jeffrey Preston. Brooklyn, New York. September 3, 2012.

Reif, Rita. 1975. Lagging Style: Interest in Furniture by Gustave Stickley and Elbert Hubbard Is Growing. *New York Times*. December 20, 1975. http://query.nytimes.com/mem/archive/

Crowther, Bosley. 1967. Vanessa Redgrave Divorced. *New York Times*. April 29, 1967.

# 2. Rosalie Berberian

*A diminutive dynamo, Rosalie Berberian, radiates wit, intelligence, and humor when she engages in conversation with anyone about the Arts and Crafts or when she gives one of her beautifully crafted lectures with an entire slideshow of Arts and Crafts pieces to die for. It would be difficult to find anyone who knows more about the Arts and Crafts movement and the pottery, silver, and jewelry of that period than Rosalie. She is a collector, dealer, and scholar, and she has done it all.*

Rosalie, "girl reporter," after graduation from college

Rosalie Berberian as tap-dancing highlander

She has always been passionate about design and beauty. A child of Armenian immigrants, Rosalie and her brother were always surrounded by beauty that their mother had to create from nothing—because they had nothing. But Rosalie longed so much for what she saw around her and knew she could never have, that when she grew up, she became a collector (Berberian 2012). She didn't plan it—it just happened.

Rosalie always excelled at everything she took on—from tap dancing as a young child to being a successful newspaper reporter after college, or "girl reporter," as she puts it. Her collecting began in 1967 with a piece of Weller pottery she found for fifty cents. She became a regular at the local thrift shops, and once the different owners became familiar with her tastes, they started calling her when a piece of art pottery would come in. Rosalie was now on the path to becoming collector extraordinaire (Berberian 2012).

Imagine Rosalie's outrage when she was rejected by the first graduate program she applied to at Yale, because she was (1) a woman, (2) married, and (3) too old (she was in her early thirties). And imagine her satisfaction when she was admitted to a different department at Yale and ended up with a similar course of study to the one she had wanted in the first place and—the best part of the story—after all that, when she graduated, she was appointed to the faculty at Yale! (Berberian 2011).

When Rosalie first started collecting pottery in 1969, she hadn't heard of the Arts and Crafts movement. She had no art or art history background, and now believes most people who collected art pottery then, like her, had little awareness of the Arts and Crafts movement. There were some excep-

Curtsy

Rosalie reporting on Ballet Russe—Mary Ellen Moylan, Leon Danielian, and Alexandra Danilova in 1950

tions, like Don Magner, who knew about the furniture, the lamps, and the movement itself, but gradually, as the American Arts and Crafts revival took hold, art pottery began to be appreciated in its proper context—as part of the Arts and Crafts movement.

Over the years, Rosalie developed a daunting expertise in pottery. She collected what she loved but, like many serious collectors, she found as her tastes evolved, she had pieces she wanted to sell. "I was very much a collector, but then I had to support my habit, so I became a part-time dealer, establishing ARK antiques in 1971. I retired from my real job in 1981, and became a full-time dealer" (Berberian 2011).

Rosalie had a friend who was a PhD candidate in art history at Yale, who had loved Robert Judson Clark's 1972 Princeton University exhibition, *The Arts and Crafts Movement in America: 1876-1916.* So he went to see it again at the Smithsonian in Washington, DC. While there, he bought three George Ohr pieces in their gift shop, of all places, and brought them back and showed them to Rosalie. She went out of her mind; she thought they were so beautiful.

When it came to pottery, it was the clay and the form of the clay that interested Rosalie, and how the fire changed it, and how the glaze developed. These things fascinated her. To her, this was what pottery was all about (David Rago 1993, 8).

Rosalie at 25

Remembering one of her first George Ohr pieces, Rosalie wrote in David Rago's catalog:

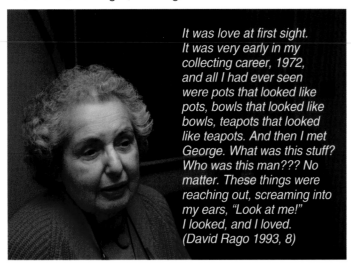

*It was love at first sight. It was very early in my collecting career, 1972, and all I had ever seen were pots that looked like pots, bowls that looked like bowls, teapots that looked like teapots. And then I met George. What was this stuff? Who was this man??? No matter. These things were reaching out, screaming into my ears, "Look at me!" I looked, and I loved.*
*(David Rago 1993, 8)*

The vase amazed Rosalie by its beauty—its thinness, its color. It spurred her to read *The Unknown Ohr* (1986) by Robert W. Blasberg, plunging her even more deeply in love with the maker of this marvelous pottery, and demanding more (David Rago 1993, 8).

Then Rosalie heard about Jim Carpenter, who had bought the entire George Ohr collection from the Ohr family in Biloxi, Mississippi, and in February 1973, she and her husband, Karnig, arranged to see him. Her plan was to buy two or three pieces for herself and a few for resale. They went in and Carpenter had a few pieces on his desk. Rosalie asked if there were more, and he took them upstairs.

*He's got this big, big space and this loft has walls all lined with shelves and tables full of George Ohr. And I said, "How much are these?" He said, "Pick out what you like, and then I'll price them for you."*
*(Berberian 2012)*

So the plan was for her to go around the room and pick out maybe nine or ten. When Jim started pricing, Karnig would keep track, and when they reached their limit (twenty-five hundred dollars), he would tell her.

*So we went around the room, and we're taking one of these, and one of those. And then, when we're finally done, I started picking out the ones I liked the best. And the most I paid for anything was a hundred bucks. By the time we got through, including a couple of things I found in the wastebasket (one with a little chip, and I thought it was wonderful), I had sixty pieces of George Ohr. (Berberian 2012)*

Even in 1973, with the wonderful Ohr pieces she had acquired, most of the "multi-handled, twisted, and collapsed stuff was already gone" (Berberian 2012).

Rosalie tells a collector's heartbreak story of true love. It was 1975, and she had one George Ohr pot that was her absolute favorite. She and Karnig never had a lot of money,

but he loved computers and desperately wanted one. He had taught himself how to program and do other things, but they couldn't afford the three thousand dollars.

So Rosalie decided to sell her favorite George Ohr piece to Tod Volpe, who was always after her to sell it to him, and it was the only one worth that kind of money to him. She called him up, he paid a visit to buy the piece, and she bought Karnig the computer. Rosalie laughs at what that computer is now worth—and what that vase is now worth!

*At one point in the life of this particular vase, it was sold for $250,000, I think, to Jasper Johns. It was very expensive. My husband was out of his mind, he was so happy with that computer. That's my true-love story (Berberian 2012).*

Art pottery lovers had been gathering annually in Zanesville, Ohio, where a group of local devotees of their native pottery had begun an assemblage that eventually attracted art pottery collectors and dealers from across the country. Out of this, a desire for a formal organization grew, and in 1980, became the American Art Pottery Association. As second president of the American Art Pottery Association from 1981 to 1983, Rosalie thought about the future of the association. Rosalie canvassed the membership, which voted to hold the association's meeting in various cities around the country, rather than in Zanesville every year. But changing traditions creates controversy, and it was heated. Since then, the AAPA has conducted its annual meeting and show in different metropolitan areas.

More and more, Rosalie felt that, as a pottery dealer, she was playing on a field dominated by men with large territorial needs. She did not like the way they treated her, and she did not like what was going on. With great soul-searching, Rosalie decided to leave the pottery business entirely and sell her complete inventory. To do that, she ran an auction in 1982 with Dick Blacher, a collector friend of hers, who also had a lot of pottery to sell. Rosalie ended up successfully selling all of her inventory.

Following that success, Rosalie held two auctions a year for three years from 1984 to 1986, in Darien, Connecticut, because of the proximity to New York. They took place on Sundays at the Holiday Inn and attracted the intended New Jersey-New York crowd. They were very successful and people loved them. She claims she had all kinds of Arts and Crafts stuff in the auctions and didn't care how humble it was or what it sold for, as long as she also had the "good stuff," some of which came from a pottery collection that a friend and her husband had built over the years in Hartford. They had invested a lot of money into very good pottery but were now at a place in life where they wanted to sell it.

As her auctions continued, however, fewer interesting pieces were being consigned. Rosalie felt some of the big dealers were deflecting quality items from her auctions. She didn't mind handling small things, but to keep her auction viable, she also needed really good pieces. Once she had sold her friend's collection, there was little else significant coming through.

There was so much competition among dealers and auction houses for valuable inventory, it seemed to Rosalie there were forces monopolizing the market. She had taken enough and was tired of the constant struggle. The auctions had been a transition period between the end of Rosalie as a pottery dealer and the beginning of something else, but it took her a while to figure out just what would replace pottery in her life.

In the meantime, Rosalie had put her focus on silver because it was a new thing for her to learn, and it could be found at auctions and shops because nobody was buying it. One day, the curator from the Chicago Art Institute, Milo Naeve, called her and asked,

Rosalie Berberian
(203) 387-3754

ARK ANTIQUES

Box 3133
New Haven, CT 06515

**AMERICAN ART POTTERY AND THE ARTS & CRAFTS MOVEMENT**

Inspection
from 10 A.M.

Auction
12:30 P.M.

**AUCTION: Sunday, March 23, 1986**

**Holiday Inn - Darien, CT**

Price $5.00

$7.00 by mail

o.p.: George Ohr barrel-shaped vase, The Berberian Collection auction, 1993. 7½" x 5½";

u.r.: ARK Antiques auction catalog, 1986

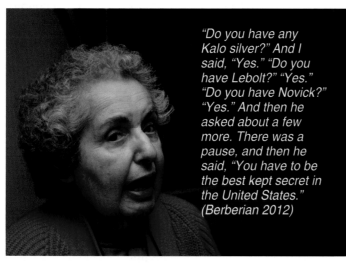

*"Do you have any Kalo silver?" And I said, "Yes." "Do you have Lebolt?" "Yes." "Do you have Novick?" "Yes." And then he asked about a few more. There was a pause, and then he said, "You have to be the best kept secret in the United States." (Berberian 2012)*

As she sat in her home basement office and mulled over this conversation, she knew she did not want be a secret. However, Rosalie had no interest in opening a shop. She knew she could manage a mail-order business as she had been successful with it in pottery, so she "decided to go for broke" (Berberian 2012). In September of 1986, after being nudged to the sidelines too many times, Rosalie Berberian came up out of her basement and introduced herself to the world. She had signed a twelve-month contract for full- and half-page ads with the magazine, *The Magazine Antiques.*

Rosalie had settled on a new field for her collecting focus—metalwork—which encompassed silver, copper, and jewelry, and she started learning about the metalsmiths. She initially concentrated all her attention on the silver. The jewelry came along gradually because she didn't know anything about that area of the Arts and Crafts. Nor did anyone else.

She began running her ads in *Antiques* at the end of 1986 and got no response. The second and third months of advertising passed, with again no response. Maybe she had acquired no business from the ads, but *Antiques* did send her mounted display posters.

Rosalie took these posters she had been sent and displayed them on top of her showcases. Twenty-five years ago, antiques shows were essential to dealers, especially those who had no shop. These shows were the bread-and-butter for many of the antiques dealers, where they made sales, and where the public could meet them and connect a face with a name they may have seen over and over, such as in *Antiques* magazine.

*People are walking by and saying, "Oh, I've seen your ad," and they'd walk into the booth. And all of a sudden I realized it was because I'd advertised in Antiques. Everyone decided that I was real and important and that they were going to pay attention. I began to develop a clientele—and it wasn't people interested in Arts and Crafts. (Berberian 2012)*

People who liked nice silver had discovered Rosalie. She had always confined herself to the Arts and Crafts world, but she soon realized that her market was elsewhere.

Several years earlier Rosalie had auctioned off her pottery business inventory, but now that she was getting established in the world of silver and jewelry, she was ready to let go of her previous life in pottery by putting her personal collection up for auction. David Rago held The Berberian Collection Auction at the Puck building in New York in February 1993.

In the exhibition catalog, David Rago praised Rosalie, "By trusting what she loved, and what stirred her, Rosalie has built one of the most focused and sophisticated collections of American art pottery in the country. Certainly no better collection of esoteric art ware has been sold in the last twenty-five years." In addition to David Rago's (1993) warm introduction to her, the catalog features color photographs of each piece and is annotated by Rosalie's very personal reflections, revealing her passion for these extraordinary pieces of pottery that she collected piece by piece, and with a great deal of sacrifice, over two decades. On seeing a Grueby at Carol Ferranti's on Madison Avenue, for example, she wrote,

*. . . such a robust gourd-like shape, such wonderfully thick and thin running glazes which had bubbled up in the fire, such beautiful streaking from grey to light blue. And then, to discover it was Grueby. Grueby? No! How perfectly sensational! I loved it, yearned for it, coveted it, but left it behind. A few months later I visited her shop again. Still there. Left it behind. Another few months, still there,*

*tantalizing, calling to me. I took it home. (David Rago 1993, 22)*

And describing a Wheatley vase, she wrote,

*And here's the whole Atlantic Ocean wrapped up in a piece of clay from Ohio. The seaweed, the clam shells, the scallop shells, and . . . the lobster . . . sitting there on the top of the heap . . . In the early 1970s I had seen a small Wheatley piece with a lobster in a collection. I kept looking and looking for another. I found Wheatley vases with shells and seaweed, but no lobster, no crab, no skittering crustacean. I bought, and kept upgrading. And then one day in 1979 came a call from Dave Rago. He had it! He wheeled and dealed, I sighed*

*and moaned. He was asking for more than money. He was asking me to give up the one I had which was quite magnificent—a tall bottle-shaped vase in brilliant color with seaweed and shells cascading down the front of it. . . . Dave, that master trader/player of the art pottery world, was going to keep everyone happy. I had to do it. I did it. Have never regretted it. Here's to you, Dave. (David Rago 1993, 46)*

The Berberian Collection auction successfully closed the chapter on Rosalie Berberian, Pottery Dealer.

In her new area of specialization, Rosalie taught her clientele that the beauty and interest held by a piece of jewelry is about the craftsmanship, not about the diamonds. Her clients did, in fact, prefer unusual and different silver and were not looking for jewelry dominated by diamonds. They liked fine silver and simplicity of design, appreciated the Arts and Crafts aesthetic, and loved the story of the Arts and Crafts movement, but they were not Arts and Crafts collectors, nor did they live in Arts and Crafts homes.

Aram, Rosalie's son, became her business partner in 1991, and was instrumental in strengthening and developing the jewelry part of the business. Arts and Crafts jewelry was not something most collectors were familiar with, but Aram learned it quickly and better than anyone else. He would go through big antiques shows where there were lots of jewelry dealers and pull out of the cases Arts and Crafts pieces that no one had spotted. This gave Rosalie and Aram a larger

o.p., l.l.: Grueby gourd-shaped vase, 13" x 8½";

o.p., u.r.: Wheatley vase, 13¼" x 9¼";

o.p., l. r: Tiffany three-handled vase, 6¼" x 6";

l: Rosalie with Arum Berberian;

r.: ARK ad in The Magazine Antiques

variety to present to the public. They were creating catalogs with their business contact information, and people were starting to recognize the ARK Antiques and the Berberian name. As a result of word of mouth and all of the printed advertising, when people had something to sell, they would often give Rosalie or Aram a call.

Having worked with collectors for decades, Rosalie has seen all types. When she started out, she was just a collector, and she didn't understand why dealers did the things they did. As she gained experience as a dealer, she began to understand, and realized how little collectors, in general, do understand. Some are meant to be auction buyers, because they need the competition and the feeling of out-besting someone else, or they need the security of knowing that the item has value to another person. That's why some things do so well at auction.

At the other end of the spectrum is the collector who really understands how things work and is willing to pay the dealers to go out and find the rare and appealing pieces for the collector to buy. And, of course, they expect the dealers to make money in the process. The collector pays for the knowledge and the time and effort the dealer spent on cultivating relationships and building up contacts—they understand that this took some effort. These are the collectors who have the potential to build really great collections because they collaborate with the dealer.

One of the most aggravating and naive kinds of collectors that antique dealers have to put up with at antique shows and exhibitions is described succinctly by Rosalie:

> I've seen 'em all. There are people who would walk into your booth and ask you what the price of something is, and then say, "but what did you pay for it?"

In terms of the Arts and Crafts movement, Rosalie often hears the assertion that the style is just a fad. She insists that the Arts and Crafts movement was all about design reform, and she maintains that

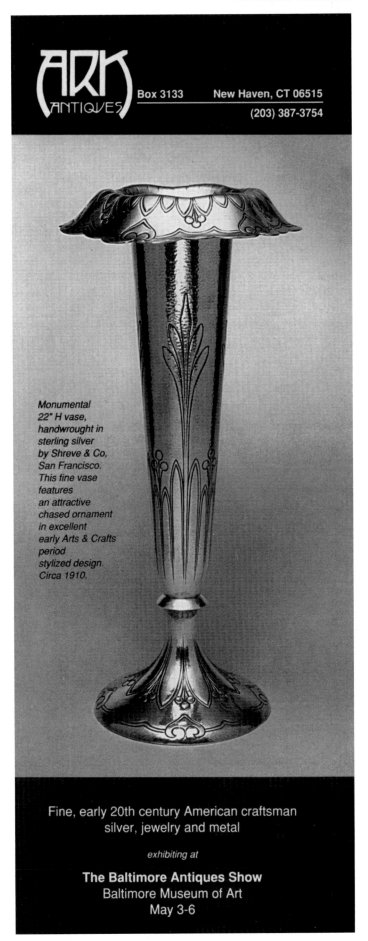

Horace Potter bracelet, private collection.

All jewelry shown is included in Berberian's forthcoming reference book on American Arts and Crafts jewelry. All pieces are handcrafted and extant, and there will be no archival images shown. The pieces are currently in private or museum collections.

*as long as museums are collecting something and putting it out there, it'll be alive, and it'll keep on going, giving it legitimacy and keeping it in front of the public. It is not a fad, but a legitimate aspect of our material culture. All of the museums recognize this now, and they're all very busy acquiring American Arts and Crafts things for their own collections. (Berberian 2012)*

Throughout the years, what guided Rosalie's decisions as a collector, whether of pottery, silver, or jewelry, was her own instincts, independent of what everyone else was saying and doing. She brought a freshness to her collections based on her knowledge, experience, and discerning eye, but primarily based on her visceral response to the beauty of a piece.

Rosalie is creating a reference book for collectors on the jewelry and enamelwork of the American Arts and Crafts movement. It will include approximately fifty-five craftspeople from the east coast to the west coast and will feature about four hundred photos of extant jewelry and enamelwork. This is groundbreaking, as there is very little written on the jewelry of the Arts and Crafts. She expects it to be published in 2013.

In 2010, Rosalie Berberian was awarded the prestigious Arts & Crafts Lifetime Achievement Award from the national Arts and Crafts Conference at the Grove Park Inn. Rosalie actively pursues knowledge in all her activities. She is insatiably curious about any number of areas, questions everything, and is diligent and exhaustive in her search for information.

Through her collecting alone, Rosalie has spent her lifetime in service to others—as a mentor; a teacher; a compassionate, knowledgeable, and honest dealer; and a lecturer, freely sharing the findings and conclusions that result from her research. Rosalie is detail-oriented, yet she keeps it all within the larger perspective. She is the rare person involved in the Arts and Crafts who is engaged in all three areas of activity, and she has set the bar very high. As a scholar, collector, and dealer, Rosalie Berberian is truly one of the treasures of the Arts and Crafts revival, a gift to all of us.

### References

Clark, Robert Judson. *The Arts and Crafts Movement in America: 1876-1916*. Princeton: The Art Museum, Princeton University, and The Art Institute of Chicago, 1972. Also curated by Martin Eidelberg, David A. Hanks, Susan Otis Thompson, and others. November 1972–January 1973.

Berberian, Rosalie. In interview with authors in New Haven, Connecticut. July 15, 2011.

———, Rosalie. In interview with authors in New Haven, Connecticut. February 4, 2012.

Blasberg, Robert W. 1986. *The Unknown Ohr*. Milford, PA: Peaceable Press.

Clark, Garth, Robert Ellison, and Gene Hecht. 1989. *Mad Potter of Biloxi: The Art and Life of George E. Ohr*. New York, New York: Abbeville Press.

Rago, David. February 1993. David Rago Presents *The Berberian Collection*. Lambertville, New Jersey: Rago Arts and Auction Center.

Frank Gardner Hale, pendant, private collection

Wilhelmina Stephan bracelet, private collection

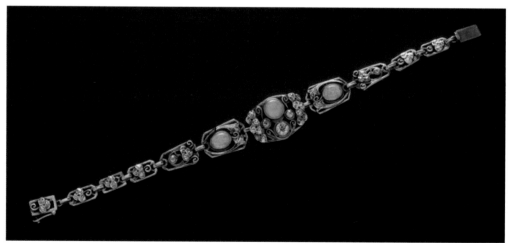

Josephine H. Shaw necklace,
private collection

Carence Crafters brooches, acid-etched base
metals, private collection

The Rokesley Shop brooch and
watch fob, private collection

Margaret W. Vant necklace, private collection

The Kalo Shop necklace,
private collection

Edward E. Oakes bracelet, private collection

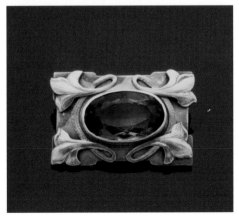

The Kalo Shop brooch

In living room

Surrounded by plants and light on her sunporch

Rosalie at "Women's Table" by Maya Lin (1993),
Yale University

Showing her 2010 Arts and Crafts
Lifetime Achievement Award

Bill and Patsy Porter finding a place in their new home for their Gustav Stickley leather-topped hexagonal table. The table was on loan to Craftsman Farms from 1992 until 2012.

# 3. Bill and Patsy Porter

*Bill and Patsy Porter infuse the Arts and Crafts world with energy and joy, and always offer a critical eye and valuable commentary based on years of learning, observing, and collecting.*

When you hear Bill Porter speak, his creativity, passion, and originality are palpable, and his warmth and zest for life are contagious. Bill and Patsy are a small-framed couple, short in stature but with outsized artistic vision. They began collecting early, in the 1960s, and have been collectors of various artists and time periods their entire married life, but none of their interests have consumed as much of their mutual time as collecting Arts and Crafts. Bill Porter designed cars for General Motors and is passionate about good design—the driving force behind his collecting.

Bill has long been intrigued by what he calls the virus (the contagious condition of being obsessed with the Arts and Crafts) and how it spread across the country early on. One seminal moment in the revival occurred at the University of Michigan, where Ethel and Terence Leichti were students in the early sixties. The couple started collecting Gustav Stickley in the mid 1960s and by 1974 had built a formidable collection.

The Porters in front of their "farm industrial" home

Terence and Ethel were passionate about Gustav Stickley and Dirk Van Erp and were among the earliest collectors of Arts and Crafts. They began collecting as students at the University of Michigan in Ann Arbor, where they lived in the same complex with some architecture students. The story Bill tells is that they all caught the virus from an unnamed architecture professor. With Terence accepted to a PhD program, he and Ethel moved to Pasadena, California in 1968, and became even more obsessed with collecting Arts and Crafts. On the west coast, there were new possibilities for collecting, and they continued to focus on Gustav Stickley and Dirk Van Erp, spreading the contagion to others.

In a few short years the Leichtis had gathered a remarkable collection of Stickley furniture, Dirk Van Erp lamps, Jarvie candlesticks, and painted Marblehead pottery. In 1974, Terence Leichti joined the philosophy faculty at Rutgers University in New Jersey and he and Ethel took their collection back East with them. According to Bill Porter, who, with his wife Pat, visited the Leichtis around 1974, their collection "almost defined what the great pieces were." It included such gems as Gustav Stickley tables with Grueby tile tops and numerous inlaid Harvey Ellis pieces.

In the California Bay Area, there was another intense, dedicated collecting couple, the Mattisons whom the Leichtis had encountered in their relentless coverage of shops, swap meets, and auctions. Rumor had it that the two rival couples worked out a territorial arrangement—the Mattisons would buy Arts and Crafts only north of Fresno and the Leichtis would buy only south of Fresno.

A third pair of serious Arts and Crafts collectors in California, during the late sixties, were the Marrins, Jim and Janeen, who lived next door to the Leichtis in Pasadena and had picked up the bug from them. Bill Porter, swiping an idea from the Leichtis, began running ads in Hobbies magazine, a publication for home crafts people, "folks who wove baskets and ladies who embroidered and made crocheted things" (Porter September 2011). Janeen Marrin saw Bill's ad and contacted him in hopes of obtaining a copy of Craftsman Homes. In fact, Bill did have an extra copy he sold to her for what he had paid for it, six dollars. As it happened,

Bill traveled to Los Angeles regularly to recruit young designers from Art Center College of Design in Pasadena for General Motors, so he was able to meet the Marrins in person, and, naturally, they became good friends. They were a valuable resource in many ways, but Bill insists they were a goldmine because they were great gossipers who knew everybody, what they were up to, what they collected, and what they had just bought. They were also more than willing to trade Xerox copies of what were, at the time, extremely rare catalogs of Arts and Crafts makers.

Janeen wrote the Porters in September 1974 about an upcoming exhibition, *California Design: 1910*, at the Pasadena Conference Center, for which she and Jim had been asked to design two rooms typical of California bungalows at the time. While they included a wide range of California decorative artifacts, the furniture they selected for the two rooms was all Stickley (Marrin 1974).

Collectors in the early 1970s had to be creative to find pieces. Writing in a breezy and informal style to the Blue Swan Gallery in San Francisco, Porter, clearly in a comfortable relationship with the gallery, suggested the following:

In conversation with Bill

> The idea occurred to us that we might locate a Dirk Van Erp lamp by advertising in a San Francisco Sunday newspaper's want ads under "Antiques." If this idea sounds at all promising to you, we might use your phone number in the ad. If anyone called, you could perhaps handle it for us on a cost-plus-commission basis or something. Maybe worth a try?
>
> (September 21, 1974)

Porter designed a flyer in 1970, a *Wanted* poster with sketches of key pieces of Gustav Stickley furniture he wanted to acquire, and he sent it out by the hundreds to dealers and posted it in antique centers and flea markets.

Bill's 1970 "Wanted" poster

It became an important supplement to his ads in *Hobbies* magazine. It was so successful, in fact, that it was plagiarized from Cincinnati to New England.

The Leichtis noticed Bill Porter's ubiquitous ads and contacted him in January 1974:

> I have for some time been seeing your ads for mission furniture in various publications. My husband and I have an extensive collection of Gustav Stickley furniture—every piece of furniture in our home is from the Gustav Stickley Craftsman workshops, and we have a floor-to-ceiling collection in our garage . . . . As with other collections, we have over the years had a number of unneeded duplicates, pieces no longer needed because of narrowing interest (we used to have lots of L. & J.G. Stickley, Stickley Brothers, Limbert, etc., before we narrowed down to just the Gustav Stickley pieces) or upgrading, etc. Therefore we have sold many pieces of good mission furniture to acquaintances both here on the west coast and in the East, too (Leichti 1974).

In his response letter, Porter mentioned a mutual acquaintance who sold the Leichtis a small Gus Stickley desk that Bill and Patsy had admired at her house. He went on to say that sometime after that, he visited the Gamble house, where he picked up a May 1972 catalog from the Sweeney Art Gallery (University of California at Riverside), with pictures of furniture. The pieces Bill was most drawn to were all on loan from the Leichtis: "By coincidence, your collection played a part in the formation of our own interest in Mission style furniture" (January 1974). Porter explained that they were learning and honing their tastes, generally preferring Gus Stickley to Roycroft, but finding an occasional Roycroft piece to be exceptional (January 1974).

In the world of automobiles, Bill Porter is one of the great car designers, as evidenced by the Pontiac GTO, the Firebird, and the Buick Riviera. During a long career he headed a number of GM Design Studios, both production and advanced. Regardless, the auto industry had its ups and downs, poignantly expressed by Bill in one letter, in an indefatigable effort to build his collection. He wrote New York architect Roy Frangiamore, explaining, in a way that is particularly resonant to us in these times, his tardy reply to an information-packed letter he had received in 1974:

> *It may not be in the foreground in New York, but the American automobile industry here in Detroit is in the throes of a terrible economic crisis. It is even worse than expected, and that was bad. It is, after all, difficult to indulge one's taste in antiques, no matter how avid you are, when you know that your income may be drastically reduced or even terminated any day. If things look a little better in a few weeks or months, I would certainly be interested in the Dedham pieces especially, but they will no doubt be long gone by then. C'est la vie. (Porter November 20, 1974)*

Birmingham home until 2012

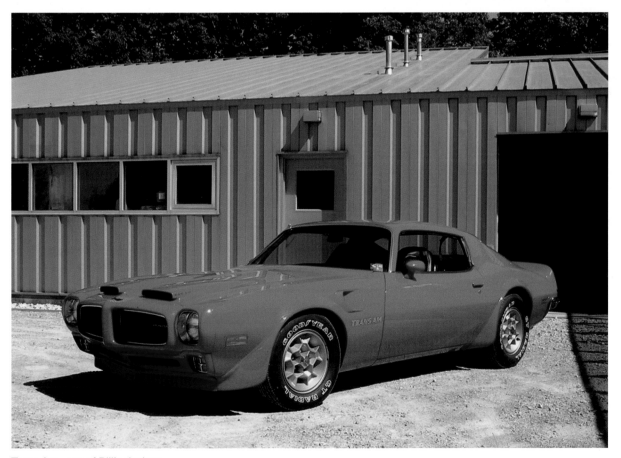

Trans Am, one of Bill's designs

Characteristically leaving no stone unturned, Bill pressed Roy further:

Incidentally, pursuant to my eternal search for Gustav Stickley furniture catalogs, I have located two at the Department of Prints at the Metropolitan Museum. However, as usual, there is a snag. They will not lend them or allow them to be Xeroxed! They charge $12.50 per negative and the negatives remain their property. They say that one or two negatives already exist, and I suspect that they are the ones Charles [sic] Freeman used in his book *Forgotten Rebel*, since the catalogs are 1909 and 1913—the two years he lists in his bibliography. Can either you or your wife think of some way I can obtain a copy of one or both of these catalogs without spending a fortune for negatives which would remain the property of the Met? If so, I am open to suggestions . . . short of violence, that is. (November 20, 1974)

For Arts and Crafts collectors of this time, there was very little information available. It had been only two years since Robert Judson Clark's exhibition, *The Arts and Crafts Movement in America, 1876-1916,* at Princeton University. The exhibition catalog and *Forgotten Rebel* were essentially the only information available to collectors, and people knew relatively little about specific craftspeople.

Correspondence among collectors often involved sharing detailed information and descriptions of pieces very few had seen or would recognize, and created an important body of knowledge. For example, Bill Porter offered this description of one of their favorite pieces in their collection: ". . . a small Gustav Stickley settee, presumably by Harvey Ellis,

inlaid with small oval yellow brick road scenes surrounded by pewter pincers and topped by pewter spear points. Back and arms are the same height, and the overall effect is surprisingly plain and modern" (January 19, 1974). As seen in the Roy Frangiamore letter to Bill, drawings were often used to describe more effectively than words.

The following excerpt from Mrs. Rhodes, who sold Bill a pair of Roycroft bookends, referred to shop marks he had drawn by hand in a previous letter to her:

Am mailing your "R" set today, . . . also I will file your letter so that I can look for the marks you drew. I think that in general I recognize the Mission Style but it is helpful to know where to look for marks (Rhodes October 21, 1974).

In a response letter, Bill offered a Roycroft lesson on the matching brass bookends:

We think that this design has a sort of art deco look about it, dating it probably from the late twenties or early thirties. This is borne out by the fact that the word ROYCROFT appears below the mark—a feature that we are almost certain belongs to later Roycroft production. (Porter November 2, 1974)

Bill had actively been seeking Gustav Stickley furniture catalogs, with a flurry of correspondence, in the fall of 1974. He wrote Joseph T. Rankin, Chief of the Art and Architecture Division of the New York Public Library,

. . . in the hope that you have one or more catalogs of Gustav Stickley 'Craftsman' furniture, manufactured circa 1900

---

FRANGIAMORE ASSOCIATES
ARCHITECTS/PLANNERS
95 FIFTH AVENUE
NEW YORK, NEW YORK
10003/212·691·2770

11/11/74

DEAR BILL,

THIS IS A COMBINATION THANK-YOU NOTE & OFFER. THANK YOU FOR YOUR HOSPITALITY WHEN WE WERE IN DETROIT LAST MONTH. I ENJOYED SEEING YOUR COLLECTION VERY MUCH. YOU'VE BEEN VERY ASTUTE AND FORTUNATE IN FINDING SOME WONDERFUL THINGS.

A WOMAN HERE HAS SOME PEWABIC FOR SALE. I CAN'T ALLOW MYSELF TO BUY IT SINCE I'VE ALREADY GONE OVER BUDGET ON SOME OTHER POTTERY I BOUGHT LAST WEEK, PLUS THE EXPENSES OF OUR MOVE TO ATLANTA HAVE PUT ME INTO SHOCK. I HAVEN'T EVEN MENTIONED THEM TO ERIC BECAUSE I KNOW HE'S CRYING POOR ALSO. SHE'S AGREED TO HOLD THE POTS FOR A WEEK SO IF YOU'RE INTERESTED, BELOW IS A DESCRIPTION AND PRICES WHICH INCLUDE A 10% COMMISSION. SHIPPING IS EXTRA.

① ±6" HIGH
SIGNED, LIGHT
BLUE/GREEN AND
COPPER IRRID. GLAZE
$93.50

② ± 7" WIDE x ±4" HIGH
DARK BLUE + LIGHT BLUE
HEAVY IRRID. GLAZES
MARK IS COVERED BY GLAZE
BUT, IT'S PEWABIC
$165.00

③ ±6" WIDE x ±5" HIGH
DARK BLUE + LIGHT BLUE
MARK PARTLY HIDDEN BY
GLAZE. REAL BEAUTY!
$198.00

SHE ALSO HAS SOME DEDHAM VOLCANIC GLAZE VASES, EXPENSIVE BUT HARD TO FIND. I'VE SEEN THE RED IRRIDESCENT ONES PRICED AS HIGH AS $1600.00. THESE ARE: ① A HUGE (± 14") IN DARK BROWNS FOR $335⁻; ② AN 8" IN BROWNS FOR $247.50 AND ③ A 12" GREENS + BROWNS FOR $286.00; ALL ARE SIGNED DEDHAM AND HAVE HUGH C. ROBERTSON'S DEVICE INCISED. ALSO A VERY GOOD PIECE OF GRUEBY ± 12" HIGH VERY GOOD SHAPE AND PROPORTIONS, HAS A KILICK THIS BIG → ☐ IN THE UNDER EDGE OF THE LIP. I'D BUY IT IN A MINUTE IF I HAD THE EXTRA MONEY. IT'S PRICE WOULD BE $467.50. A NEARLY IDENTICAL PIECE IS COMING UP AT PARKE-BERNET LATER THIS MONTH AND IS ESTIMATED AT $600 TO 700.

SHE'LL HOLD THE PEWABIC BUT NOT THE OTHERS SO IF ANYTHING INTERESTS YOU GIVE ME A CALL. MY OFFICE # IS ON THE LETTERHEAD & MY HOME # IS (212) 348-8889.

AGAIN, MANY THANKS FOR BEING SO NICE ON OUR DETROIT TRIP. HOPE TO HEAR FROM YOU HERE OR IN ATLANTA.

SINCERELY,

Roy Frangiamore

through 1916 in Eastwood (Syracuse), New York. During much of this period he had his main office in New York City. (September 6, 1974)

He wrote similar letters in that time period to the Cooper-Hewitt Museum of Design (October 11, 1974) and to the Rare Book Division of the Library of Congress (October 1, 1974).

Arts and Crafts devotees were on a common journey of discovery—sharing, teaching, and learning—and Bill and Patsy were the archetypal collectors from this period, contributing to the revival and infusing it with energy. As they gained expertise, they began sharing their knowledge in a more formal way, and establishing relationships in the process. In addition to their interactions with some California collectors, by the mid-1970s, Bill was trading information with a few east coast collectors, such as Jane and Chuck Kaufmann in Maine.

In 1980, Bill curated an exhibition, *The Craftsman in Detroit 1900–1916* at the Detroit Historical Museum, featuring the furniture of Gustav Stickley and the art and architecture of the craftsman era in room settings put together from the Porter's collection. Just after its opening reception, coincidentally, Stephen Gray contacted Bill because he had seen his flyer, and wanted to know if he had any Gustav Stickley catalogs to sell him. He had plans to issue Stickley catalog reprints through his publishing house, Turn of the Century Editions. They introduced themselves over the phone, and Bill told Stephen about the show that had opened. So Ste-

phen made the trip to Detroit to see it. This was eight years before the Grove Park Inn conferences began, so there was not yet a national venue where collectors and dealers could get together.

Other friendships were forged at the Detroit show. Bill met Tom Maher, collector and scholar; Randy and Pat Reed, collectors; and Bruce Szopo, an antiques dealer. A decade later, in the *Arts and Crafts Quarterly,* Suzanne Perrault published an interview with Bruce Szopo of Duke Gallery in Birmingham, Michigan, who spoke of the important role Bill had played in his learning about the Arts and Crafts movement.

In 1980, I met Bill Porter who was then one of the most significant collectors in the country. For the next ten years, he was nice enough to let me study his collection. I would go there every Saturday, and we would just talk about furniture, look at this incredible accumulation of Arts and Crafts pieces, discuss the seat constructions, the different designs, the finishes. His collection spanned from some more common pieces to some extraordinary rare items. Through Bill I was able to develop a hands-on expertise in the Arts and Crafts at a time when few people had that opportunity. (Perrault 1990)

In 1988, Bill and Patsy began attending the annual Arts and Crafts Conference at the Grove Park Inn in Asheville, North Carolina. They belong to the steadfast group that has attended every single conference. Bill gave a presentation at the Grove Park Inn in February 1990, and distributed an informative handout, "Gustav Stickley Furniture: A Brief Design Analysis," clarifying Gustav Stickley's different periods of design.

Bill retired from General Motors in 1996, although one could hardly say he retired. After he left GM, Bill and Patsy wanted to move to a larger house, ideally built between 1900 and 1915, something big enough to accommodate their collections—but they could not find anything that was suitable. So they decided to buy a piece of land and build their own house.

GUSTAV STICKLEY FURNITURE:
A BRIEF DESIGN ANALYSIS

GROVE PARK INN - 1990
WILLIAM L. PORTER

TIME LINE

1897
PRE
1898 ARTS & CRAFTS
1899
1900 EARLY
EXPERIMENTAL
1901
1902 FIRST
MISSION PERIOD
1903
1904 HARVEY ELLIS
1905
1906
1907
MATURE
1908 MISSION PERIOD
1909
1910
1911
1912 LATE
MISSION PERIOD
1913
1914
1915 LATE ECLECTIC
1916

( Example of post & beam construction.)

( Example of slab-sided constuction.)

© William L. Porter, 1990

o.p.: illustration of one way collecting information was exchanged before the Internet;

l: handout for Bill's talk at Grove Park Inn on Gustav Stickley's furniture

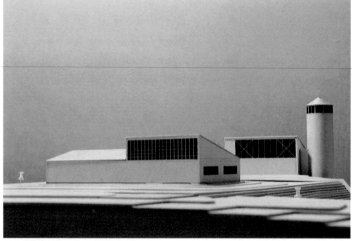
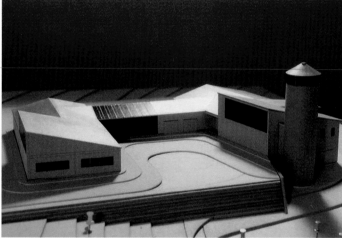

Bill designed a house that would both warehouse and display their enormous and various collections. Bill Porter coined the term farm industrial to refer to the architectural style of the house, which is a low sprawling structure with the exterior walls and roof made of corrugated steel panels. The entire house has a heavy steel frame, which is visible in the interior. While very modern, the house looks like what it is. Bill's farm industrial house exemplifies the honesty of design and materials integral to the Arts and Crafts movement, but in a twenty-first century interpretation. It's not wood, it's metal and glass, but what you see is what is there. The seams, the joints, the frame and bolts are the keys and tenons of Porter's design—everything is there in plain sight. This house is, indeed, one of Bill's great achievements.

This is not just any house put up in a year or two. Arguably, it is the raison d'être of Bill and Patsy in the twenty-first century. Once designed and mocked-up in a three-dimensional model, the project began in 2000 with the creation of a pond on the twenty-acre tract of land, and the ground-breaking took place in the summer of 2001. The house includes a gallery for changing displays of paintings selected from their collection, a silo where Bill's collection of model airplanes can be suspended and, most stunningly, a set of period rooms—one based on Frank Lloyd Wright and several based on Gustav Stickley, true down to the smallest architectural and decorative detail that can be replicated in 2012.

Porter designed the pre-engineered house (early on in collaboration with a structural engineer), and has done much of the work himself, acting as foreman to the various workers involved. The authors witnessed firsthand the power of Bill's congenial and personable nature. He takes an active interest in the craftsmanship of his workers. Just as he both learned and taught as a collector early on with his colleagues, he respectfully both learns from and teaches his workers and, in the end, gets the results he wants.

Bill arrived at his final design after considering several possible styles, including modern, craftsman, prairie, and even shingle style. He studied various construction methods and attended night school to obtain his Michigan builder's license. But since he had collected objects over the years from several eras, in addition to Arts and Crafts, and because the house is located on rural acreage, he decided to abandon the external eclectic approach and build an anonymous farm industrial shell with contemporary functional areas, such as the kitchen, bathroom, and laundry room, and eclectic living areas, such as the living room, dining room, and bedrooms. Patsy refers to their home as a "warehouse with period rooms."

Bill canvassed manufacturers of warehouses and farm buildings, and American Buildings Corporation, a very large national outfit, agreed to work with him, using their pre-en-

gineered, all-steel type of structure. All parts were precut in the factory, shipped to the site, and erected. It is a ranging 13,400 square foot structure that, in addition to the main house, includes a spacious north-lit studio for both Bill and Patsy, a sizeable workshop, a large storage area, a greenhouse, and two generous garages that house examples of some of Bill's outstanding car designs. Having been an auto designer, Bill knows materials, construction methods, and industrial processes. One interesting manifestation of his professional background in the design of this house is the exhaust hood over the kitchen island. Only someone with Bill's industrial background could imagine and know how to realize such a design.

The house is a work in progress and has been for over ten years. Bill has the complete design overview constantly in mind but is attentive to the smallest detail. He makes certain everything is done exactly right, just as it must have been in his car design and production. Meanwhile, after more than ten years, the Porters now officially live in the house they are building, sharing it with the Gustav Stickley furniture that stands sentry at the

o.p.: models of new Porter home designed by Bill; top: nearly finished home in 2011;

above: Bill working out details of Gustav Stickley period rooms

doors to what will be the finished period rooms. The master bedroom, presently under way, will have burlap-paneled walls similar to those presented in *The Craftsman* magazine in July, 1905, p.538 (see also *Craftsman Homes*, 1909, p. 18). The burlap on the wall will be painted "a blue that is just breathtaking, like a nocturnal fog—just exquisite," according to Bill, and the wood trim will be "a gray-tan brown, like moondust."

Bill has the precision and artistry of the industrial designer he is, but it's the poetry and passion about him, and about Patsy, that make them remarkable. Who else would, through passion for beauty and detail, turn paint on burlap to nocturnal fog and wood trim to moondust?

### References

Leichti, Ethel. Letter to Bill Porter. January 2, 1974.

——. Letter to Bill Porter. September 4, 1974.

Marrin, Janeen. Letter to Bill and Patsy Porter. September 16, 1974.

Patton, Phil. 2012. Bill Porter, Designer of Pontiac GTO, Moves to a New Biorhythm. *New York Times*. April 17, 2012.

Perrault, Suzanne. Dealer Gallery: Bruce Szopo. *Arts and Crafts Quarterly*. 3(1): 23.

Porter, Bill. Letter to Blue Swan Gallery. September 21, 1974.

——. Letter to Edith Adams, Cooper Union Museum Library. October 1, 1974.

——. Letter to Ethel Leichti. January 19, 1974.

——. Letter to Fredrick Goff, Rare Book Division, Library of Congress. October 1, 1974.

——. Letter to Joan Rhodes. November 2, 1974.

——. Letter to Joseph T. Rankin, Art and Architecture Division, New York Public Library. September 6, 1974.

——. Letter to Roy Frangiamore. November 20, 1974.

Porter, Bill and Patsy. In interview with authors. September 21, 2011.

——. In interview with authors. July 15, 2012.

——. In phone conversation with authors. August 28, 2011.

——. In phone conversation with authors. November 28, 2012.

Porter, Bill. In an e-mail to authors. Jul 18, 2011.

Remembering Roy Frangiamore: http://royfrangiamore.blogspot.com/

Rhodes, Joan. Letter to Bill Porter. October 21, 1974.

o.p., top: checking for color;

o.p., bottom: leveling the ledge; below: checking against The Craftsman plans

u.l.: exhaust hood designed by Bill for stovetop;

u.r.: Patsy and friend beneath exhaust hood

below:
Gustav Stickley crib settle and daybed

u.l. and u.r.: Breakfast room, Charles Rohlfs hutch and fancy chair, both signed with Rohlfs' "R" in bucksaw, 1901 below and filled with coral red paint. Inside of drawers stained vivid olive green. Exhibited as Washburn-Crosby Mills "Dutch Kitchen" at 1902 Buffalo Pan American Exhibition; Breakfast room, Charles Rohlfs bench, part of "Dutch Kitchen" for Washburn-Crosby Mills at 1902 Buffalo Pan American Exposition. Bench signed with "R" inside bucksaw and dated 1901. Signature filled with bright coral red paint. Bench belongs to set with fancy chair and hutch. Original finish was flat black, as was hutch. Fancy chair has original finish, added shiny black paint carefully scraped off.

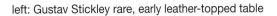

left: Gustav Stickley rare, early leather-topped table

l.l: Bill in makeshift office

l.r.: return of Porter's Gustav Stickley hexagonal table from 20-year loan to Craftsman Farms

above: Gustav Stickley sideboard returning from the 2010 Dallas exhibition, Gustav Stickley and the American Arts and Crafts Movement; r.: moving in, 2012

above: winter scene of house from across the pond created by Porters;

r.: dramatic view of farm industrial look; below: Patsy in the greenhouse

above: looking up, inside the silo;

r: landscape view from living room

above: view from living room; r: Bill and Patsy;

below: view of house from across the pond

The 1972 exhibition, *The Arts and Crafts Movement in America, 1876-1916*
Photo: courtesy of Princeton University Art Museum.

o.p.: Robert at work, 1982

# 4. Robert Judson Clark
## The Arts and Crafts Movement in America, 1876-1916

*In planning his exhibition, Robert Clark realized how little was known in 1970 of the American Arts and Crafts movement, and no public collection existed from the period except for the art pottery at Newark Museum (Clark 1992, 11).*

When asked about senior seminar ideas for the fall semester, Professor Robert Judson Clark of Princeton mentioned the American Arts and Crafts movement to associate chairman of the Department of Art and Archaeology, Jonathan Brown. Clark was not sure if Brown's response was positive, so he added the idea that "it would make a good exhibition." It was as though a contract had been signed because within two hours the exhibition had been added to the Princeton Art Museum's schedule (Clark 1992, 9).

A member of the department's advisory council, Joshua Taylor of the Smithsonian Institution, suggested a traveling exhibition because he felt it was important that the country know about this period in American cultural history. *The Arts and Crafts Movement in America, 1876-1916* opened in Princeton, New Jersey and traveled to Chicago and Washington, DC. David Hanks of the Art Institute of Chicago had been trying to put together an exhibition of Frank Lloyd Wright and the Prairie School, but the Art Institute was resistant to the idea. It was Joshua Taylor who suggested that Hanks and Robert Judson Clark co-curate the show (1992, 11). Clark and Hanks would combine their work and resources to create a richer show.

As an undergraduate at Berkeley from 1955-1960, Clark was "trying to figure out William Morris and CFA Voysey and their influences." There was a fraternity house Clark walked by daily that he found curious yet compelling. At first he didn't like the clinker bricks in the foundation and the shingled walls, but the more familiar he became with the house, the more he was taken in by the eclectic mix of materials and its aesthetic. In 1958 Clark attended an exhibit by the American Institute of Architects at the de Young Museum in San Francisco. Among photographs of works by Thomas Jefferson, Henry Hobson Richardson, and Louis Sullivan were three or four photos of structures that Clark was certain had been created by the same hands as the fraternity house. He was correct and the name was Greene and Greene (1992, 13).

At the same time he was intoxicated by the local architecture, Clark discovered *The Craftsman* magazine of Gustav Stickley. The magazine was a rich resource of architecture and design, and Clark began collecting the full run of the sixteen-year publication in four-volume increments, as his budget allowed.

Robert with architectural historian Betty Marvin in front of Allenoke Manor, Berkeley, 1982

While visiting the Victoria and Albert Museum on a 1963 trip to London, Clark observed that the English Arts and Crafts movement was indeed the prologue to Gustav Stickley. Robert Judson Clark had the idea that there must have been an American Arts and Crafts movement in this country, but had never heard the term or the concept (Clark 1992, 9).

In planning his exhibition, Robert Clark realized how little was known in 1970 of the American Arts and Crafts movement, and no public collection existed from the period except for the art pottery at Newark Museum (Clark 1992, 11).

There were few resources available. There was no list of Arts and Crafts designers or furniture makers, but Clark remembered seeing photos of Rohlfs works in European fine arts magazines. He managed to contact Charles Rohlfs' son, who was very glad to learn about the exhibition and said he had worshipped his father. Clark visited Roland Rohlfs at his home a few days later, and Clark convinced him to lend several pieces to the exhibition. Roland was so pleased to see his father's work receive the attention it deserved, that it was a small step to get him to donate his pieces to the Art Museum after the exhibition closed (1992, 12).

The Princeton exhibition was the groundbreaking event that launched the American Arts and Crafts revival. Many people were introduced to the American Arts and Crafts through Robert Judson Clark's exhibition, but far more were introduced through the excellent catalog that still stands as a valuable source of primary information. The exhibition and its catalog provided the foundation for much, if not all, of the ensuing scholarship on the Arts and Crafts in the United States, and it is the legacy of Robert Judson Clark.

*There were to be many interruptions and postponements in my professional career. The 1972 exhibition was one of the major interruptions. It took on a life of its own and derailed my plans, so that I am still known more for my American work than for my Austro-German researches which I have now resumed in early retirement—in California, where I was first fascinated by the turn of the century as it happened a century ago. (Clark 1992, 18)*

In the twenty-first century, when it is increasingly difficult for collectors to acquire the kinds of works that Clark exhibited in 1972, it is interesting to note that Robert Judson Clark did not distinguish between old crafts and new crafts. To his thinking, the Arts and Crafts movement was on a continuum, and there was no line separating the two (Accardi 2011).

### References

Accardi, Art. In interview with Jeffrey Preston. Woodstock, New York. July 17, 2011.

Clark, Robert Judson. 1998. "The Princeton Exhibition of 1972: Random Recollections of the Idea, the Event, and the Preludes." *The Tabby: A Chronicle of the Arts & Crafts Movement.* 1(4): 9-18.

The 1972 exhibition, *The Arts and Crafts Movement in America, 1876-1916*.
Photo: courtesy of Princeton University Art Museum.

Robert and Nancy Clark on the
2009 Berkeley Architectural Heritage
Association (BAHA) House Tour.

Tiffany Studios, covered bowl with decoration of Virginia creeper, H. 6", The Metropolitan Museum of Art, gift of Martin Eidelberg

# 5. Martin Eidelberg

*Martin Eidelberg, professor emeritus of art history at Rutgers University, embodies the wit and scholarship of the Arts and Crafts revival. His passion, knowledge, and intellect have significantly contributed to the recognition of the American Arts and Crafts movement as a legitimate period in art history.*

His first love was French eighteenth-century paintings, but then he was also seduced by Tiffany and the Arts and Crafts movement. He began collecting in the summer of 1964. As a lecturer at Rutgers University, he was only months away from receiving his PhD from Princeton University, and by the following year, he advanced to assistant professor. His latitude as collector was limited by his income, but he bought what he could afford. His first piece of Tiffany was a little candlestick with a globe he bought from a Victorian lighting dealer in Greenwich Village (Eidelberg November 2012).

Eidelberg had seen the Tiffany show as a seventeen-year old at the American Craft Museum and then saw the Art Nouveau show at the Museum of Modern Art. He always loved Tiffany glass. His grandmother had two vases she called Tiffany, but later on it became evident they were just middle-European imitations of Loetz. Discovering Lillian Nassau's 3rd Avenue gallery, full of Tiffany lamps, was revelatory for him. The doorway to the gallery was very narrow, and he started to go in but, as a 23-year-old, he lacked the courage to enter (November 2012).

A week or two later, Eidelberg returned to Lillian Nassau's with a friend who was twenty years older, but they were stopped at the door and asked about their interest. Eidelberg's friend pointed at a candlestick and they were told, "ninety-five." Did he mean ninety-five dollars or ninety-five hundred dollars? "So we took yet another trip. Looking back it's very funny, but we were pretty naive" (November 2012).

Eidelberg began collecting modestly and when he finally bought a decorated vase with an organic form for three hundred dollars, he knew he could not afford to collect at that level and made the decision, instead, to collect pottery. It was more affordable and, because he had made pottery as a teenager, he had a certain understanding of it. Gradually pottery consumed him, both European and American (November 2012).

Newcomb College Pottery, bowl with decoration of campanula flowers by Esther Huger Elliot, 1901, H. 7½". Collection of Martin Eidelberg

These were the 1960s, and he was learning fast. Eidelberg once saw a piece of Rookwood, very early on, and then went home and looked it up—he didn't know what the mark was and didn't yet know that the *xxiii* on the bottom meant 1923 (November 2012).

The same process happened when he began collecting Van Briggle pottery. Initially, he bought some little pieces of Van Briggle, not realizing they were from the twenties and thirties. But then he met Bob and Gladys Koch, who were friends of a friend. They recently had visited the Van Briggle pottery in Colorado Springs and showed him their early pieces, dated 1903 and 1904, made before Artus Van Briggle died. Eidelberg promptly bought all five of them—all that they had—for about thirty dollars each (November 2012).

Some collectors buy paintings by minor artists and gradually improve their collection or not, and then there are others who from the start buy only Rembrandt. But, at that time, at least in the world of Arts and Crafts pottery, there was enough to go around, and there were great shows—New Haven, and Torrington in Connecticut, and even down in Pennsylvania Dutch country—Renningers twice a year had spectacular ones (November 2012).

In those early years of the American Arts and Crafts revival, Eidelberg had no sense that the supply of pottery was finite, and would one day run out. He had started collecting as a lark, a diversion from his specialization in art history (November 2012).

Because he chose to live in New Brunswick where he taught, Eidelberg's rent was relatively low—certainly much lower than it would have been in New York—and it was for this reason that he could develop an exceptional collection of pottery on the limited salary of an academic. Of course, that alone did not make his collection outstanding. He researched and studied pottery and had a superior eye for recognizing a pot worth collecting (November 2012).

In the sixties, Eidelberg started going to auctions at Parke-Bernet, which was acquired by Sotheby's in 1967. The auctions became more sophisticated during this time. First they began developing specialized sales, then they introduced colored illustrations into their catalogs, and that led to all lots being pictured, which was a significant step forward (November 2012).

Eidelberg, who lived in New Brunswick, barely knew Robert Judson Clark when he received a phone call from him in 1971, telling him about an Arts and Crafts exhibition he would be doing at Princeton University the following year and

Martin Eidelberg claims to be almost un-American because he's never owned a car and cannot drive. He's made his way around "because of the kindness of others" (November 2012). Lillian Nassau took him to his first antiques show, which surprised him. He didn't know you could actually find interesting things to buy at an antiques show. The first ones he went to were at the old Madison Square Garden. There he would buy five, six, seven things at a show. It was there in great abundance. He could buy in New Jersey (he lived in New Brunswick at that time), or he could go into New York and find even more things to buy. Eidelberg says that, looking back, things were so available and affordable at that time, it was like a dream (November 2012).

Eidelberg remembers his excitement at discovering *The Studio* in the University of Pennsylvania library stacks. It was a London fine art magazine first published in 1893 and was very influential in broadening interest in the English Arts and Crafts movement.

> *Oh my god, I realized, there were magazines at the time, with images and sections about European—primarily European—pottery. That was now the last major barrier. I had discovered the field, had discovered antiques shows, and now had discovered literature—I was fully armed to begin! (November 2012).*

asking if he could visit Eidelberg and see his collection. At the end of his visit, Clark asked him to curate the pottery portion of the exhibition, *The Arts and Crafts Movement in America: 1876–1916* (November 2012).

In the end, most of the pottery in the show belonged to Eidelberg, but he went to great lengths to convince museums and private collectors to lend their pieces to the show. Some private collectors declined, of course, but to the benefit of all of us, many agreed to enrich the exhibition with their pieces. (Eidelberg Spring 2012). The 1972 Princeton exhibition was the singular event that began the American Arts and Crafts revival. This was the first exhibition entirely focused on American Arts and Crafts, and it created awareness and interest in the subject.

In the 2012 Spring issue of *Style 1900*, Eidelberg shared his rather surprising memories of how the 1972 Princeton exhibition came together. Clark and David Hanks of the Chicago Art Institute put the show together on a shoestring budget, thus the lack of color photography in the exhibition catalog. As curator, Eidelberg was given no budget or reimbursement for his travel expenses, postage, or long-distance phone calls, which were a considerable expense at that time, so his geographic reach was somewhat limited (Eidelberg Spring 2012).

Although Eidelberg finally did meet Hanks once when he came to New Jersey, there were no curatorial meetings.

Martin Eidelberg, 1975

Eidelberg had no idea what pieces the other curators were exhibiting, so it was not an integrated approach. His selections were not at all influenced by the rest of the show (Eidelberg Spring 2012). However, in the exhibition catalog, Clark praised Eidelberg for putting together "the first comprehensive display of American art pottery" (1972, 7).

In response to Eidelberg's requests for participation in the exhibit, the Everson Museum of Art in Syracuse generously lent pieces, as did museums in Cincinnati, Washington, and several in the New York-New Jersey area. One aspect working in Eidelberg's favor was the low market value of Arts and Crafts pieces at the time. The Everson Museum in Syracuse, for example, insured one loan piece for a mere three-hundred fifty dollars (Adelaide Alsop Robineau's *Viking*), easily worth a million dollars today (Eidelberg Spring 2012).

An academic respected throughout the art world for his expertise in both French painting and the Arts and Crafts, Dr. Martin Eidelberg, professor emeritus of art history at Rutgers University, is in demand for his knowledge and his eye. He has worked with several important collections and is frequently asked to curate catalogued exhibitions. Eidelberg is an accomplished researcher with in-depth knowledge of the subject, and his writing is intimate and compelling. He co-curated the exhibition and co-authored the catalog for the Two Red Roses Foundation's 2008 exhibition, *Beauty In Common Things: American Arts And Crafts Pottery* (Two Red Roses Foundation website. News. February 17, 2009).

In addition to his published works on French eighteenth-century painting, Eidelberg has published five books on Tiffany and been involved in several exhibition catalogs. He is currently co-cataloguing the pottery collection donated to the Metropolitan Museum of Art in 2009 by Robert A. Ellison, Jr. (November 2012).

**References**

Clark, Robert Judson, ed. 1972. *The Arts and Crafts Movement in America: 1876-1916*. Princeton: The Art Museum, Princeton University, and The Art Institute of Chicago, 1972. With texts by the editor and Martin Eidelberg, David A. Hanks, Susan Otis Thompson, and others.

Eidelberg, Martin. In phone interview with Jeffrey Preston. November 2, 2012.

———. 2012. "The Rocky Road to Princeton." *Style 1900*. Spring 2012, p. 54-58.

Two Red Roses Foundation website. News. *Beauty in Common Things: American Arts And Crafts Pottery*. February 17, 2009. http://tworedroses.com/News/news_021709.htm.

Vogel, Carol. 2009. Major Gift of Art Pottery to Adorn Met's Restyled American Wing. *New York Times*. January 14, 2009. http://www.nytimes.com/2009/01/15/arts/design/15muse.html.

Tod Volpe with ceramic art of the Martin Brothers, 1981

# 6. Jordan-Volpe Gallery

*If there was one singular act that created the revival of the early twentieth-century Arts and Crafts movement, it was the opening of Jordan-Volpe Gallery in 1976. The combination of Vance Jordan's business sense, financial backing, and academic interest in art and Tod Volpe's sense of theatre, marketing ability, and talent for presentational sleight of hand created a tour de force unseen in the Arts and Crafts since the days of Elbert Hubbard and his creative sales genius.*

**THE JORDAN·VOLPE GALLERY®**

457 WEST BROADWAY • NEW YORK, N.Y. 10012 • (212) 533-3900

Tod Volpe had no plans for college when he graduated from Yonkers high school in 1966, but he was determined to use his talents and ambitions to become a success. A year later he was working in a funeral home and attending mortuary college (Volpe 2002, 23–24).

Things changed for him over the next six years, and Tod was studying art history at New York University in 1972 while working for an uncle as a stagehand at Metropolitan Opera. With this odd background, Volpe was grooming himself to play one of the most pivotal roles of the Arts and Crafts revival. With his funeral background, he could convincingly offer comfort and a sympathetic ear to those in need, and as a stagecrafter, he was able to create settings, moods, and timeframes that seemed real (2002, 31–32).The art and the craft he learned in these disparate arenas prepared him for success.

In the early seventies, Volpe's only awareness of the Arts and Crafts was a Gustav Stickley Morris chair he had seen in a friend's apartment in New York. His cousin, Vance Jordan, was running a talent agency, buying art nouveau and Tiffany from Lillian Nassau, and had friends like Robert Judson Clark, Robert W. Blasberg, and James Carpenter (Volpe May 2012).

Tod and Vance were busy with their own lives and had lost contact with each other for a few years but when they were reunited, they discovered common interests, mainly centered around art. Tod was very impressed with both the quality of Vance's collection and how beautifully he displayed it (Volpe 2002, 43–44). Since high school, Tod had frequented thrift shops and flea markets and now decorated his own studio apartment in the style of a *salon*, creating an illusion of more than was really there, so he had particular appreciation for Vance's apartment (Volpe 2002, 27).

The Morris chair with its red joiner's compass had made a lasting impression on Tod and when he told Vance about it, Vance wanted to see it. Although they ended up buying it together for seventy-five dollars (Volpe May 2012), this was a moment of much larger investment for them. Vance "confirmed my belief that [Arts and Crafts] could become a vehicle for collecting on a scale that certain art forms, such as nouveau and deco, had achieved" (2002, 45).

In the mid-1970s, Tod began going to the 26th Street flea market every Sunday and was getting to know some of the dealers, like Beth Cathers. Vance and Tod had similar views on the way a dealer should handle art and developed a vi-

above: Grueby vase in a form of a gourd, H 15½"
impressed Grueby mark; above r: Grueby vase with daisies,
with stems and leaves, H. 16¼" W. 8½", faience mark with
artist's initials (Ruth Erickson); Everson Museum of Art
exhibition catalog, 1981, traveled to Jordan-Volpe Gallery

sion together for creating an Arts and Crafts market (2002, 44). They were both ready for something new in their lives.

Tod and Vance strategized and planned their gallery when Tod was in his last year at New York University, and they started acquiring and cramming Arts and Crafts pieces into their apartments and friends' and relatives' houses. They brought Beth Cathers into their business because she knew furniture and sometime after that, they brought in David Rago, whose specialty was pottery (2002, 50).

Tod was the charmer, the seducer, and the showman. Vance provided the business background, financial resources, and intellect (2002, 46). Six months after Tod finished the program at New York University, they burst onto the New York art scene with the opening of the Jordan-Volpe Gallery. At that time, SoHo was a mostly boarded-up neighborhood, but that didn't seem to keep anyone away (Volpe May 7, 2012).

The day Rita Reif walked through the gallery door for the first time, she became convinced that this gallery was an expression of Tod and Vance's lifelong love affair with the Arts and Crafts style (Volpe 2002, 50). Art critic for the New York Times, Reif (1976) wrote a review of the new gallery that attracted crowds of people waiting in line for the Jordan-Volpe experience. It turned the gallery into an overnight success (2002, 51):

> Now [the mission style] is back and booming. This week the revival of the style seemed headed for success with the opening in SoHo of the Jordan-Volpe Gallery . . . . This development marks the first time since Princeton University's pioneer exhibition

*Grueby*

Everson Museum of Art

in 1972 that the Arts and Crafts style . . . has been surveyed comprehensively and can be viewed in a proper setting. (Reif 1976)

The impact of Jordan-Volpe Gallery on public awareness of the Arts and Crafts was huge. Vance and Tod, well aware of consumer fads, created visual displays of Arts and Crafts pieces set in a modern context (2002, 49–50).

> By bathing objects in an illustrious light, I was able to make pieces with relatively little value seem as though they were worth their weight in gold. By incorporating skills developed at Havey's [funeral home] and the Met, I put an irresistible spin on things. (2002, 51)

The Arts and Crafts Desk:
A Study in Style and Function
1900-1915

JORDAN-
VOLPE
GALLERY

457 WEST BROADWAY
NEW YORK 10012
Tuesday through Saturday, 11:00 A.M. - 6:30 P.M.

1979 Jordan-Volpe exhibition catalog

Rosalie Berberian remembers Tod Volpe as a promoter.

*He got all of the art magazines, all of the decorators, and everybody excited about this stuff. He really promoted it. Every other month you'd see an article in one of the fine arts and antiques magazines. And he had shows and catalogs. What he did was make Arts and Crafts into something really serious in the larger world of the arts. I believe that he was the one.*

*And he was in New York, so he brought the attention of the architects, and the designers, and the decorators, and he presented it like it was really something. I don't know if you ever saw that gallery. You'd buzz your way in, and it had these oriental rugs on the floor, and the place was lit by Tiffany lamps, with this brown furniture and a vase here, not at all cluttered. It was just gorgeous.*

*I think he is the one, more than anybody—you know people like Don Magner were very knowledgeable, and they knew their stuff, but nobody did what [Tod] did. He made it. He presented it, in essence, to the world. And made it something that then everybody wanted (2011).*

below: Rookwood vase, Edward T. Hurley, decorator, 1922, H. 11½", D. 5"
rt: Rookwood artist, Edward T. Hurley

Tod Volpe's "influence was extremely important in escalating the interest, the prices, and the value of things in the Arts and Crafts movement. Tod was a very important cog in that machine—he was a visionary" (Treadway August 2012).

*The gallery has assembled superb examples of the period, and presented them in a style equal to any museum, a feat few dealers in the decorative arts ever trouble to attempt. No wonder, then, that the Philadelphia Museum of Art, the Newark Museum, the New Jersey State Museum at Trenton and the Hunterdon County Historical Society agreed to loan selections to the show. What's more, the catalog published by the gallery . . . represents the best in current scholarship, quality graphics and printing. . . . when the show is over it will travel to the Akron Art Institute.*

For all its visual sensitivity and beauty, the gallery was a carefully calculated business operation. Beth Cathers provided a steady stream of new inventory, mostly furniture (Volpe May 2012), and David Rago brought in pottery. Don Treadway and Don Magner also sold to the gallery, partnered on pieces, and provided consignment pieces.

Millions of eyes saw beautiful and cutting-edge ads (Volpe 2002, 52) in the pages of magazines such as *The Magazine Antiques*, costing the gallery over $100,000 per month (Volpe May 2012).

Jordan-Volpe also offered a series of gallery lectures by well-known curators and scholars in the field of Arts and Crafts, such as Robert Judson Clark, David Hanks, Gillian Moss, Robert W. Blasberg, Martin Schwarts, Susan Otis Thompson, Rowland Elzea, and Diane Pilgrim. The gallery extended its influence to museums such as the Metropolitan Museum of Art, the Brooklyn Museum, and the Cooper-Hewitt by developing relationships with curators and gifting generously, part of its strategic plan for creating a solid Arts and Crafts market (Volpe 2002, 131–134). As museums began developing these collections, the American Arts and Crafts gained importance and legitimacy as a significant period of art history in the United States.

> *Advertising in major magazines helped, as did a feature story on Stickley authored by me for a leading publication, conveniently timed to coincide with the opening of our gallery's doors.*
> *(Volpe 2002, 51)*

Once the business was underway, Jordan-Volpe presented catalog exhibitions in collaboration with museums. One example was "Fulper Art Pottery: An Esthetic Appreciation, 1909–1929," reviewed by Rita Reif in the *New York Times*, April 22, 1979:

> *Strolling through the American Wing, I picture all the people we had to persuade to trust the style before spending the mega dollars it took to get the Met's attention. . . . Rooms displaying masterpieces by Frank Lloyd Wright, Albert Herter, Stickley and Tiffany might never have existed if our gallery hadn't opened its doors. By arousing interest, we created enthusiasm that led to the support of philanthropic collectors such as Max Palevsky, Richard and Glory Manney, Edgar O. Smith and Sydney and Frances Lewis. (Volpe 2002, 129)*

TOWARD THE MODERN STYLE

ROOKWOOD POTTERY
THE LATER YEARS:
1915-1950

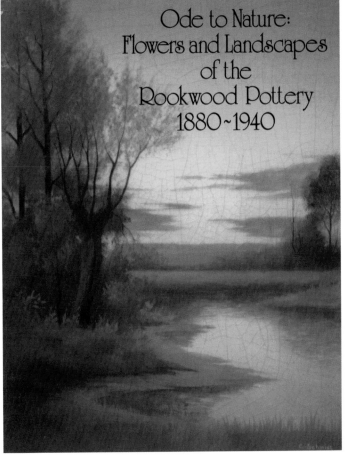

Ode to Nature:
Flowers and Landscapes
of the
Rookwood Pottery
1880~1940

Tod Volpe developed strong relationships with some of the curators at the Metropolitan Museum of Art in New York:

*Nonnie Frelinghuysen, curator of decorative arts in the American Wing of the Met, was one of the primary [Jordan-Volpe] supporters. As a connoisseur of turn-of-the-century decorative arts, she and fellow curator Craig Miller were aware of the gap in collecting that we were attempting to fill. After receiving calls from us, Nonnie and Craig would find ways of acquiring objects that were coming through our hands. If it hadn't been for their efforts, the wealth of the collections that now stand in the museum's nineteenth- and twentieth-century rooms may never have materialized. (2002, 131)*

The gallery exists to make money, however philanthropic its activities, and Tod Volpe described one aspect of the process:

Jordan-Volpe exhibition catalogs: 1983, "Toward the Modern Style: Rookwood Pottery, The Later Years 1915–1950"; 1980: "Ode to Nature"

*By putting an important art object on display in a major museum, I was able to draw old clients back to the gallery and take new ones to new heights. Doing more than just buying and selling art, we demonstrated to the general public that the gallery was making a commitment, which goes a long way*

with collectors. *We continued to donate art to the Met during the 1980s. Great examples of furniture bear our name as do objects and metal work. We were also able to sell to museums all over the country. For what seemed like a sizeable sacrifice to others, to me, what we were doing made total sense. We were able to sell millions of dollars in art as a result of those simple donations. (2002, 131)*

Volpe continued, explaining how museums gain from such gifts.

*The art is theirs for eternity. They use it to attract other donations from collectors who would be otherwise uninterested or dormant. Once the period rooms at the Met were opened, collectors ran to see examples similar to their own on display. We would sell to them and advise them where to offer gifts of their own. We helped push pieces back into the museum's hands. The museums, in turn, continued to stimulate interest. (2002, 132)*

Jordan-Volpe established relationships with museums all over the country and internationally, as well. "Placing a Stickley morris chair into the British Museum broke cardinal rules of collecting, but we attracted a lot of interest" (2002, 128).

Jordan-Volpe was a high-stakes project that involved a lot of risk. They took the concept of mission furniture and moved it "out of that realm of being antique, and into the realm of being design" (Volpe May 7, 2012). They wanted to develop a clientele beyond the city to people building modernist houses in the suburbs and exurbs who cared about the design of their furnishings and not about Stickley. Vance believed that if the Arts and Crafts style became fashionable, it could become collectible (Volpe May 7, 2012).

Tod wined and dined wealthy clients to encourage them to make more purchases. In *Framed: Tales of the Art Underworld*, Tod described one such evening:

*They were excited about being around a world that was fascinating to them, but their primary interests were the art and learning as much as they could from it. After fashionable dinners and piano recitals at the gallery held in their honor, [the couple] would hone their senses by soaking in the sights and sounds of sacred objects I showed them in my private chambers. By this time, their salivary glands were working on overtime and I knew what I had to do to stimulate them even more. By subjecting them to Mozart's Requiem in D Minor and a vintage bottle*

**FULPER POTTERY**

# Fulper Art Pottery:
## An Aesthetic Appreciation
### 1909~1929

opp. page: Tod Volpe and Beth Cathers at Jordan-Volpe Gallery;

above: catalog to Jordan-Volpe 1984 Fulper exhibition

u.r.: Tod Volpe at home on Castillian Drive in L.A., taken for Connoisseur Magazine's story on "Dealer To The Stars" (1990s);

r.t.: Vance Jordan with Tod Volpe's parents at 1976 premier of Jordan-Volpe Gallery

1981 Jordan-Volpe exhibition
catalog of Harvey Ellis designs

*of port, the eerie and surreal atmosphere would push collectors like [them] over the edge. By the time they finished filling their mansion in [New Jersey] with art, they had pretty much spent everything they had. (2002, 77–78)*

Celebrities jumped into the action, and soon auction prices started setting records. Barbra Streisand, Richard Gere, and Brad Pitt are just some of the famous celebrities who were willing to spend far more than most other people to get a Harvey Ellis inlaid desk or a Gustav Stickley early sideboard or a high-back spindle armchair. Auctioneer Don Treadway refered to Jordan-Volpe as the "bridge to the retail involvement of collectors." Before that, a lot of people were "stealth collectors, not visible, and once Tod opened the doors, it just launched things—it gave it importance" (Volpe May 7, 2012).

Many believe that Jordan-Volpe Gallery brought recognition and familiarity to the term *Arts and Crafts*. Don Treadway maintains that the gallery was a "major force behind the revival. . . . The only thing that really came close in terms of promoting the revival was the Princeton exhibition, and that was more from the academic side" (Treadway August 2012).

Certainly, the elegant atmosphere of the gallery allowed prices to climb over the ten years they were open, but as a result of their success in creating Arts and Crafts demand, the costs of acquiring inventory rose astronomically. Overhead was high, and bills accumulated over time until a breaking point was reached. As careful a business plan as they had, the ledger sheet simply did not balance (Volpe May 2012).

*We owed money to a lot of people and were losing hold of the client base it had taken forever to build. The arena was still under the impression we were the be all and end all, but behind closed doors our empire was crumbling. (Volpe 2002, 155)*

Ten years after it opened, Jordan-Volpe closed. It was 1986 (Volpe May 2012). Their impact on the Arts and Crafts world had been huge. Tod and Vance went their separate ways: Tod Volpe moved to Los Angeles to become "dealer to the stars," (Volpe 2012) and Vance Jordan opened a painting gallery on Madison Avenue within a year, Vance Jordan Fine Art (Vogel 2003), which he owned until his death at age 60 in 2003 (Sims 2003).

Trying to keep up the façade of being a multimillion dollar success as dealer to the stars, Tod Volpe ensnared himself in the debt trap. In 1998, he was convicted in a fraud scheme and sentenced to twenty-eight months in jail (Weiser 1998). Volpe is rebuilding his life and is currently working on a movie that will be based on his autobiography, *Framed: Tales of the Art Underworld* (Volpe May 6, 2012).

**References**

Berberian, Rosalie. Interview by authors in New Haven, Connecticut. July 15, 2011.

Lydell, Boice. Interview by authors in Lakewood, New York. March 18, 2012.

Rago, David. Interview by authors in Lambertville, NJ, July 26, 2011.

Reif, Rita. 1979. "American Pottery." *New York Times*, online, April 22, 1979.

———. "Antiques." *New York Times*, online, October 15, 1976.

Sims, Carol. 2003. "A Double Loss for the Art World: Dealer Vance Jordan, 60." *Antiques and the Arts Online*, October 28, 2003. (http://antiquesandthearts.com/TT-2003-10-28-12-24-17p1).

Treadway, Don. Interviewed (phone) by authors, August 1, 2012.

———. E-mail to authors, August 19, 2012.

Vogel, Carol. 2003. "Vance Jordan, 60, a Dealer in Turn-of-the-Century Art." *New York Times*, online, October 21, 2003.

Volpe, Tod. *Framed: Tales of the Art Underworld*. Edinburgh: Cutting Edge Press, 2002.

———. In a phone interview with authors. May 7, 2012.

———. In an e-mail to authors. May 6, 2012.

Weiser, Benjamin. 1998. "Art Dealer Receives Prison Term Of 28 Months in Fraud Scheme." N.Y./Region. *New York Times*. March 4, 1998. http://www.nytimes.com/1998/03/04/nyregion/art-dealer-receives-prison-term-of-28-months-in-fraud-scheme.html.

Robert Mapplethorpe photo of Tod Volpe, mid-1980s

# 7. David Cathers

*Arts and Crafts aficionados know, unfailingly, that the writer among us is David Cathers. His first publication, The Furniture of the American Arts and Crafts Movement was a watershed for Arts and Crafts collectors, dealers, and scholars. Cathers has written books that have illuminated the period and delighted our eyes, and he constantly has projects, whether articles for American Bungalow, an essay for an exhibition catalog, or giving the historian's eye to a unique work.*

Although very gentle in manner with soft brown eyes, David Cathers is a Jersey boy and intense about his interests. In high school in the 1950s, he was nearly obsessed with cars, even starting a high school newpaper column, "Under the Hood," about hot rods. His other passion was design.

Having grown up not far from the city, in Florham Park, David had access to the cultural offerings of New York and Princeton, where his brother studied architecture. As a high school student, he felt comfortable with the vocabulary of architecture because his brother was studying in the School of Architecture at Princeton University and they would have long discussions when his brother came home for the occasional weekend or for vacations. David developed an interest in modernism, which intensified after experiencing the innovative Lever House on Park Avenue, completed in 1952, and "one of the country's first glass-walled International Style office buildings" (Skidmore, Owings & Merrill Website 2012).

After finishing graduate school at Rutgers in the mid-sixties, and newly married, David and Beth Cathers moved into a small, very old, very empty house in the heart of Philadelphia. Their home was on Efreth's Alley, reputed to be the oldest residential street in the country and is now a National Historic Landmark District. The shoulder-to-shoulder narrow red-brick houses lining the alley were built between 1728 and 1836 and "form one of the last intact early American streetscapes in the nation" (Efreth's Alley website). On a mission to buy furniture that was appropriate for their new place, the Cathers went to Freeman's auction and bought Victorian, but Cathers remembers that Arts and Crafts pieces in a nearby store caught his eye.

A few years later, Beth was an antiques dealer in Teaneck, where they were living, and David was advertising manager for a publishing house in New York. Their son, Dylan, was born into a home full of Art Deco furniture and pottery, the kinds of things that Beth sold and they loved.

However, that all changed in the early seventies, when David saw an ad in Antiques for the 1972 Princeton University exhibition catalog for *The Arts and Crafts Movement in America, 1876-1916.* He had just missed the recently closed show. David and Beth had lots of books on Art Nouveau, and loved it, but he ordered the Robert Judson Clark catalog, pored over it voraciously, and found himself agog at Stickley. David unequivocally states that this was the moment "that did it for me." Shortly after, they acquired their first Gustav Stickley piece, a common server and nothing extraordinary but very beautiful.

Being David Cathers, he had to meet the author of the catalog. He found Robert Judson Clark's phone number and called him up. Clark invited him to visit, and what David saw was a Princeton apartment crammed with Stickleys, Rohlfs, and Grueby tiles. It was stunning! David knew nothing, but was deeply impressed by the generosity and charm of the man. Clark became his mentor, teaching him how to research and how to find Stickley family members, long before computers and the Internet were available, and he showed him where to find art journals. Perhaps most importantly, Clark taught him how to study.

But David figured out, on his own, the value of perusing furniture trade journals. Fueled by a passion to take in all he could about the Arts and Crafts movement, he regularly went to the New York Public Library at lunchtime and read trade journals. In the seventies, it was still possible to access the library collection without a lot of the red tape that exists today. It was truly a gold mine, yet the material was often dull and tedious. David persisted.

Dylan Cathers and friend with
Gustav Stickley plate rack, c. 1975

l: Signing Gustav Stickley at Dalton's in Syracuse

below: Book signing at Craftsman Farms, used by permission of The Craftsman Farms Foundation, Inc., Parsippany, New Jersey

Meanwhile, David realized his own interest was only in the furniture of Gustav Stickley, although he did buy some pieces from Robert Judson Clark that were originally from the home Rohlfs built for himself in Buffalo, New York. He also had the good fortune to buy some pieces Clark had that were originally from Craftsman Farms, Gustav Stickley's home in Parsippany, New Jersey.

By the mid-seventies, Beth Cathers was buying for Jordan-Volpe, a gallery in SoHo devoted to the Arts and Crafts, and she and David lived with Stickley furniture. David found all sorts of catalogs on lower Fourth Avenue for a quarter or fifty cents, such as Roycroft catalogs and library discards, and there were also easily found ephemera, even before the sale of Louise Stickley's estate. David carefully digested the information and was constantly turning over and studying all of the marks and joinery of the furniture in their house. He wondered why some Gus Stickley was light and delicate, sometimes with a floral touch, and others pieces were heavy and chunky.

The Cathers went for long drives every weekend, searching for Stickley, which David claims was difficult to find in the Northeast, and they were often derided when they admitted what they were after. They did find a bulky, open-space Stickley buffet, arousing the jealousy of other collectors. Another great find was a Gus director's table, which no one had ever seen, but the real coup was the Gus music cabinet that showed up at a New Hampshire country auction, and the three dealers there heatedly debated what it was, one of them insisting that "it's not Stickley." They also bought an occasional piece from Don Magner, who had an enormous inventory, tremendous knowledge, and was dealing Arts and Crafts long before anyone else even knew the term.

As there was very little published information available to Arts and Crafts collectors in the late 1970s, David Cathers jumped on the opportunity to create a tool that would be widely useful to collectors. He had acquired a 1910 catalog, "*Craftsman Furniture Made by Gustav Stickley,*" and a 1914 catalog, "*The Work of L. & J.G. Stickley,*" documents Louise Stickley would have owned. As a collector, David realized the value of the information in these pieces. Working for a publishing house, the idea to reprint these catalogs was in the realm of the familiar for him. He wrote and illustrated with photographs, an informative five pages as an introduction and arranged with Dover Publications, in 1979, to produce *Stickley Craftsman Furniture Catalogs: Unabridged Reprints of Two Mission Furniture Catalogs, "Craftsman Furniture Made by Gustav Stickley" and "The Work of L. & J.G. Stickley."* It gave collectors a handle, something to work from, features to look for, and opened the floodgates for other catalogs to be reprinted as they were found. This simple publication elevated Arts and Crafts collecting, but this was just the beginning for David Cathers.

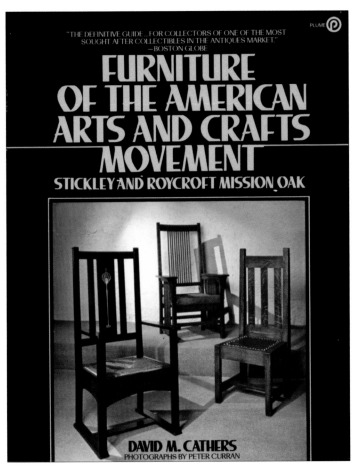

above: The seminal book on the subject, 1981, courtesy of Turn of the Century Editions;

u.r.: David Cathers at Craftsman Farms, used by permission of The Craftsman Farms Foundation, Inc., Parsippany, New Jersey

In 1981, employing in-depth research and careful use of words, David offered to the public, in *Furniture of the American Arts and Crafts Movement: Stickley and Roycroft Mission Oak,* the first close examination of the furniture of Gustav Stickley, L. & J.G. Stickley, and Roycroft—the history, influences on the development of design, the labels, stamps, and decals that were used by different companies in different years, and the advertising of the period. The volume is heavily illustrated with photographs of the craftsmen, the furniture, hardware, labels and decals, advertisements, and miscellaneous details and drawings. Although technically published in the same year, Cathers' important book was available eight months earlier than the equally important *Collected Works of Gustav Stickley* by Stephen Gray (New York Times 1981).

As advertising manager for a large publishing house, David knew how to sell books. Although he didn't do much marketing for this book, it was cleverly sent to and favorably reviewed by Jack Perry Brown of the Cleveland Museum of Art Library for *Library Journal* (April 1981, 786), the standard

journal used by librarians throughout the country to guide their book selection. The first printing was slow to take off, but seven thousand hardcover copies eventually sold, making it a best-seller for nonfiction by industry standards (Copeland 2011). People were hungry for information and pictures of this furniture. David opened wide the doors, stimulating excitement and further exploration.

The writing of *Furniture of the American Arts and Crafts Movement* was actually completed in 1979, but the publication was held up by the photographs. Through either brilliance or serendipity, Furniture was published almost simultaneously with another of David Cathers' writing projects, the catalog to the Jordan-Volpe 1981 exhibition, *Genius in the Shadows: The Furniture Designs of Harvey Ellis*, about the celebrated and short-lived architect who put an impressively light but inimitable touch to the furniture designs of Gustav Stickley.

In her review of the Jordan-Volpe exhibition, Rita Reif, art critic for the *New York Times*, nicely segued through Beth's role at Jordan-Volpe (responsibility for the furniture) to a short review of *Furniture of the American Arts and Crafts Movement:*

> Mr. Cathers, whose wife, Beth Cathers, is responsible for furniture at the gallery (they are Stickley collectors and he wrote the catalog for the show), has distinguished himself with what is a highly literate and scholarly account of the evolution of the movement in America. Documented here are both the philosophy and the technical developments, with a detailed analysis of the most important pieces produced by Stickley, Elbert Hubbard of Roycrofts and others. (Reif 1981)

Reif continued her review of *Furniture* with a brief discussion of David Cathers' treatment of Harvey Ellis and his furniture, which brings her review back, full circle, to the *Genius in the Shadows* (Reif 1981).

David Cathers was an executive in the highly competitive world of publishing. His schedule would not accommodate what he truly wanted to pursue, what would bring satisfaction to him as a writer. It took many years but, in 1995, he resigned from publishing (Nelson 1995) to put his energies into his passion—writing, writing, and writing about Gustav Stickley, his life, his thoughts, his philosophy, his designs, his business, and anything at all having to do with Gustav Stickley.

Four years later, in 1999, *Stickley Style: Arts and Crafts Homes in the Craftsman Tradition*, lavish with photographs and a beautiful and large book, excited the Arts and Crafts community and established David Cathers as more than a writer to the microcosm of Arts and Crafts fans. The striking cover featured a close-up of a Harvey Ellis inlaid armchair, from the seat up, creating a geometric look based on the

lines of the chair and heightened by the sharp contrast of a white background. David had produced a gorgeous book with a broad appeal.

Another four years after that in 2003, the author outdid himself, publishing what many consider his magnum opus, Gustav Stickley, another oversized tome. This monograph offered new, solid, and essential information on the ambitious designer whose sad denouement followed a meteoric rise to fame.

Over the years, David's hand has often been seen in catalog essays, such as in the provocative "The Play of Light and Shade: Gustav Stickley's Early Craftsman Furniture" in the exhibition catalog, At Home with Gustav Stickley: Arts & Crafts from the Stephen Gray Collection (Wadsworth Atheneum, 2008); and in the first essay, "The Moment," in the 2010 Dallas exhibition catalog, Gustav Stickley and the American Arts & Crafts Movement.

David has been a contributing editor to many books, and since 2001, he has written eighteen articles for American Bungalow, many of them on collecting and collections, highlighting individuals such as Elaine Diloff, Ed and Kathy Friedman, and Robert Kaplan. Today, David Cathers lives with his wife, Susan, in a house inspired, as much as possible with twenty-first century building codes and a limited

budget, by Bailie Scott's 'The House With Purple Shutters.' But some interior details, in particular the fireplace and batten doors with sliding wood latches, are derived from 'The Homestead,' a Voysey house completed in 1906 in Frinton-on-Sea. David and Susan live next to a bird sanctuary in upstate New York, surrounded by Arts and Crafts and the beauty of nature.

### References

American Bungalow Website. http://www.ambungalow.com.

New York Times. "Arts and Crafts Furniture Sources." New York Times online. December 10, 1981. http://www.nytimes.com/1981/12/10/garden/arts-and-crafts-furniture-sources.html?scp=1&sq=%22furniture+of+the+american+arts+and+crafts+movement%22+cathers&st=nyt.

Cathers, David. 2003. Gustav Stickley. New York: Phaidon Press.

Cathers, David. In interview with authors at Craftsman Farms. Parsippany, New Jersey. October 16, 2011.

Cathers, David. In interview with authors in Old Chatham, New York. April 21, 2012.

Cathers, David M., ed. 1979. Stickley Craftsman Furniture catalogs: Unabridged Reprints of Two Mission Furniture Catalogs, "Craftsman Furniture Made by Gustav Stickley" and "The Work of L. & J.G. Stickley." New York: Dover Publications, Inc.

o.p.: David and Susan in their upstate New York home;

above: David with plate rack acquired in 1975;

r: Stickley family silver service

Cathers, David. 1999. *Stickley Style: Arts and Crafts Homes in the Craftsman Tradition.* New York: Simon and Schuster.

Cathers, David. 2010. "The Moment"—Gustav Stickley From 1898 to 1900. In *Gustav Stickley and the American Arts & Crafts Movement.* Edited by Kevin W. Tucker, 19-29. Dallas Museum of Art. Exhibition Catalog. New Haven: Published in association with Yale University Press.

Cathers, David. 2008. The Play of Light and Shade: Gustav Stickley's Early Craftsman Furniture. In *At Home with Gustav Stickley: Arts & Crafts from the Stephen Gray Collection.* Edited by Linda H. Roth, 35-46. Wadsworth Atheneum Museum of Art. Exhibition Catalog. Hanover: University Press of New England.

Copeland, Peter. In interview with authors in Eau Claire, Wisconsin. September 14, 2011.

Efreth's Alley Website. http://www.elfrethsalley.org/history. August 16, 2012.

Nelson, Alix. "The Media Business: Advertising—Addenda." *New York Times* online. January 19, 1995.

Perry, Jack Brown. *Library Journal,* April 1, 1981, p. 786 by Jack Perry Brown of the Cleveland Museum of Art Library.

Reif, Rita. "The Subtle Artistry of the Mission Furniture of Harvey Ellis." *New York Times* online. April 12, 1981. http://www.nytimes.com/1981/04/12/arts/antiques-the-subtle-artistry-of-the-mission-furniture-of-harvey-ellis.html

Skidmore, Owings & Merrill, LLP Website. August 16, 2012. http://www.som.com/content.cfm/lever_house.

# 8. Stephen Gray

*As publisher of Turn of the Century Editions, Stephen Gray generously offered essential information to all those seeking to learn more about Gustav Stickley and the American Arts and Crafts movement at a time when there was little published about the subject. Stephen Gray's passion for early Gustav Stickley provided the impetus to many collectors who viewed him as their beloved mentor. Beyond that, he was, indeed, a teacher to an entire generation of collectors. After a long, courageous battle, Stephen Gray passed away on October 27, 2012.*

When we visited Stephen at his Avon, Connecticut home in the summer of 2011, he savored our pleasure at discovering and examining his Gustav Stickley pieces. Their home décor, a mix of Stickley and modern, is a successful combination. The light filtering in from the back glass wall is lovely and the forest very present.

After viewing many rooms with a handful of Gustav Stickley treasures in each, we entered the final room, the guest room, the one room that is entirely Arts and Crafts, entirely Gus. Stephen sat down, and we lingered, absorbing the atmosphere. He spoke of the peacefulness evoked by the room but seemed introspective and melancholy.

Laura Harris arrived after our lengthy visit with Stephen, ushering in new energy. She is a docent at the Wadsworth Atheneum, and she and Stephen are active in the museum and interested in reviving Hartford as a cultural center. Laura supports Stephen in his selection of Arts and Crafts pieces that he will be donating to the Atheneum.

Stephen Gray's Arts and Crafts journey began with the purchase of a new home and his search for an interior décor that would suitably complement it. In 1976, he bought a late eighteenth-century Hudson valley farmhouse that featured wide floorboards, a wooden ceiling, and solid structural beams. The Arts and Crafts period emerged fairly quickly as a good choice of interior décor. Stephen, who had studied architecture and American studies at Syracuse University, became enamored of Charles Limbert, L. & J.G. Stickley, and Gustav Stickley. He was also drawn to the pottery of the period, especially Grueby, but chose to collect Teco because it was more affordable.

l: Stephen and Bogey, 2008;

above: Stephen Gray's kitchen;

over, l: Gustav Stickley sideboard #971, oak, 36" x 54" x 23" and plate rack #903, oak, 20" x 46", from *At Home* exhibition;

over, r: Gustav Stickley table #411, oak, 30" x 30", c. 1901, Gustav Stickley, Oil Lamp #294, c. 1905, next to a Gustav Stickley settle from *At Home* exhibition

To collect is to learn, and Stephen visually and mentally absorbed the broad spectrum of Arts and Crafts—from pottery to prints to metalwork to furniture—by frequenting auctions, flea markets, and antique shops. When a dealer explained the *joiners compass* and other details, Stephen found Gustav Stickley irresistible, and he found Stickley's architectural quality, the simple and straightforward design, and the beauty and richness of the quarter-sawn oak compelling. But it wasn't until he was thoroughly introduced to the furniture by Bill Porter, a rabid collector from the Detroit area, that he became hopelessly "hooked on Stickley" (Harris June 2012).

There were not many dealers selling Gustav Stickley at that time. In 1979, Stephen heard of Jerry Cohen, a young Arts and Crafts dealer in California, who had a large inventory of high-quality pieces at reasonable prices. Typical of his thoroughness and passion for collecting, and knowing that collaboration and relationships are essential to successful collecting, Stephen flew from New York to see him (Cohen 2012).

After looking at enough Arts and Crafts examples, Stephen observed that Gustav Stickley's peers were producing works that were heavily influenced by Gustav Stickley designs, so early Gus soon became the focus of Stephen's collection, one that he would spend his lifetime honing. He began studying the ephemera of the period, such as furniture and trade catalogs, pamphlets, and retail plates. So little had been researched from the Arts and Crafts period that Stephen found little information through art museums and historical societies. Instead, "fellow collectors and a few far-sighted antique dealers were actually the most helpful in this quest to learn about and locate the best examples of the style" (Gray 2008, 11). Stephen's tireless pursuit of knowledge about Gus Stickley, his furniture, and the details of its construction enriched him as a collector and strengthened the body of information he would soon offer the community of individuals who were also getting hooked on Stickley.

At the same time he was discovering the Arts and Crafts, Stephen was working in real estate publishing, but in the late seventies the market was dwindling as interest rates

Edwards writes that "this collection of Stickley's writings and catalogs should serve not only to preserve a clear perception of his work but also to continue, as he intended, to be a guide to the arts and craftsman's utopian concept of art as a stimulus to life" (Gray 1981, 7). The book consists of writings and line drawings of the furniture from various publications such as *The Craftsman, Chips from the Craftsman Workshops*, and *Things Wrought*, along with the photographs of retail plates and catalogs. In most cases, dimensions and the original prices of individual pieces of furniture and hand-wrought metal are given. Drawer pulls and escutcheons, hinges and hinge plates, andirons, serving trays, chandeliers, and lamps are also shown; wood finishing methods and fuming with ammonia are also described.

In the conclusion to *Collected Works*, Stephen presciently writes

> As the revival of interest in the American Arts and Crafts movement gains momentum, its acceptance as an important period in decorative arts history will develop. Consequently, the furniture of Gustav Stickley will find its way into the marketplace in greater numbers as more people learn and appreciate its timelessness. . . . Catalogs such as this should help simplify the task of sorting through the many thousands of pieces that still exist in the possession of collectors and dealers and as heirlooms. (Gray 1981, 165)

Auction houses, dealers, and collectors now had a reference work of primary sources to authenticate the works of Gustav Stickley. This was the first of eighteen reprinted catalogs Stephen assiduously put together and published through his Turn of the Century Editions. He "spent a lot of time putting books together intelligently so people could use them" (Gray 2011). These publications energized the Arts and Crafts revival. People everywhere were combing through antique shops, flea markets, and attics, and finding pieces in such unexpected places as beauty parlors, restaurants, roadside inns, and summer resorts, and bringing them into the larger marketplace. Once they became familiar with the aesthetic, people were finding Arts and Crafts furniture and decorative arts everywhere.

were skyrocketing. He wanted to publish books on Gustav Stickley, and he had the idea of putting together books of Stickley's original retail plates and catalogs.

Bruce Johnson, founder of the Arts and Crafts Conference, points out that Stephen Gray:

> recognized the need to share his discoveries with a larger public. When he came upon one of the original catalogs issued between 1901 and 1915 by Gustav Stickley, he set upon his task of finding and publishing other such catalogs. . . . he had begun reprinting catalogs by Gustav Stickley, L. & J.G. Stickley, Charles Limbert and the Roycrofters. (*Arts and Crafts Collector*, March 9, 2011)

In 1981, Stephen Gray published his first book, *Collected Works of Gustav Stickley*. In the introduction, Robert L.

Bruce Johnson describes the importance of Stephen's publications on his website, Arts and Crafts Collector:

> The value of these reprint catalogs to Arts and Crafts collectors cannot be exaggerated. Long before the launching of Style 1900 and American Bungalow magazines, long before Arts and Crafts books began to cover coffee tables, long before the first Arts and Crafts conferences, these small reprints provided collectors with the vital information needed to identify and distinguish the work of the major Arts and Crafts designers and manufacturers from the plethora of imitations which soon followed. (March 9, 2011)

The influence of British Arts and Crafts designers such as Charles Rennie MacIntosh, C.F.A. Voysey, and Baillie Scott was evident, but Stephen Gray maintains it was Arthur Wesley Dow, the renowned American teacher and artist, who "articulated an aesthetic that became the basis for the American Arts and Crafts movement in all aspects of applied and fine art and ultimately emerged as the visual definition of this category" (Gray 2008, 16). Dow's classic 1899 book, *Composition*, strongly influenced the development of Stephen's "unparalleled eye" (Friedman 2011). With a focus on early Gustav Stickley, Stephen began to create rooms in his country house to unify the interior, grouping together furniture and accessories to create the balance and harmony Dow espoused (Gray 2008, 17), and which would become the basis of the 2008 exhibition, *At Home with Gustav Stickley: Arts and Crafts* from the Stephen Gray Collection.

By the mid-1980s, Stephen knew what was important and what was not. When he was the underbidder at auction, he would sometimes be offered a similar piece afterwards. Things came his way because of who he was—an approachable person, a publisher of important reference materials, and someone with a growing reputation for his encyclopedic knowledge, expertise, and experience.

Stephen felt that establishing a mentor is a vital element of collecting. Over the years, Stephen mentored other collectors, stressing the importance of collect-

ing with a focus and setting a goal for the collection. His generous spirit made him a natural teacher, accessible and freely sharing knowledge with others. Stephen Gray met Ed and Kathy Friedman in 1982 and soon became their lifelong friend and mentor. "Steve would come into our house and tell us what to weed out to hone and refine our collection." (Cathers 2004)

Stories abound of Stephen's passion for the Arts and Crafts and his drive to teach and share. Robert Kaplan, a collector and dealer, remembers being an underbidder at auction on a piece of Teco pottery in 1990. He'd left the auction a few minutes earlier and was walking down the street when he "heard a horn honking and a guy yelling out the window, 'You're really interested in Teco, kid?'" (Kaplan 2012). It was Stephen Gray. He, characteristically, proceeded to share his knowledge about Teco with Robert, and it was the beginning of a long friendship (Kaplan 2012).

Stephen lived his commitment to furthering the knowledge and awareness of the Arts and Crafts. He was actively involved over the years at Craftsman Farms, the home Gustav Stickley built for himself and his family in Parsippany, New Jersey. In 1995, Stephen Gray and Donald Davidoff jointly curated the Craftsman Farms exhibition, *Innovation and Derivation: The Contribution of L. & J.G. Stickley to the Arts and Crafts Movement*, and coauthored the catalog (Craftsman Farms).

Gathering information for his books was not necessarily easy or inexpensive. The year after *Innovation and Derivation*, an auction in Amherst, Massachusetts, offered a Jarvie Shop of Chicago catalog, circa 1904–09. It was the only extant catalog of its kind, and Stephen wanted the information in it for another reference book he was creating. John Bryan of Chicago, one of the biggest Arts and Crafts collectors in the country, knowing Stephen's intentions, suggested that he would buy it but, before actually taking possession of it, would let Stephen use it as needed. With this as a backdrop, Stephen planned on leaving the auction with the historic catalog in hand (*Maine Antiques Digest May 1996*).

o.p.: Stephen Gray with Teco pot;

o.p, l.r.: Stephen Gray in office of Treadway-Toomey auctions; Stephen Gray's catalog reprints, Turn of the Century Editions

However, another collector, Jordan Lubitz, was also determined to buy the catalog. Before the bidding started, the two collectors confronted each other, verbally expressing their determination to outbid the other. The bidding started slowly and went up by five-hundred and thousand-dollar increments until Stephen's final bid. The loose-leaf catalog brought nearly as much ($30,250 with buyer's premium) as the record-setting pair of Jarvie brass candlesticks at Skinner's in 1988, which went for $31,900 (*Maine Antiques Digest May 1996*). It is fortunate for the Arts and Crafts world that Stephen took home the Jarvie catalog because Turn of the Century Editions was able to reprint it in 1997, offering once again a significant amount of primary source information to the insatiable Arts and Crafts market (Turn of the Century Press 2012).

In 1998, after more than three years of work, Stephen offered an amazing gift to the Arts and Crafts world with the release of the complete run of *The Craftsman*, Gustav Stickley's monthly magazine, published from October 1901 until December 1916, on CD-ROM, including all text, images, and advertisements, and featuring a first-time-ever index to the magazine and original essays by Beverly K. Brandt, David Cathers, Marilyn Fish, Stephen Gray, and Shax Riegler (William Morris Society 2001). This presented almost 26,989 pages of Gustav Stickley primary source material (Adobe 2012).

Three years of working with a digital studio in New York City to produce such a massive undertaking led to a very expensive set of CD-ROMs, selling to individuals for $995 and to libraries and organizations for $1,495 (Adobe 2012).

Notwithstanding the cost, the door to such information had been thrown wide open, and learning and interest in Stickley and the Arts and Crafts movement skyrocketed.

Jill Thomas-Clark, Arts and Crafts scholar and author, remembers when *The Craftsman* was first available on CD-ROM.

> *When Stephen did the first CD of The Craftsman, it was very expensive. It was the first digitized Craftsman. I still have it, and I still use it. It was well done and it was printable. I give Stephen a great deal of credit for that, and we were one of the first people who bought it. You could search by words.*

> *The CD has ads, and it was high-res at the time. I remember it took him years to develop, and it was quite important for scholars and others. You can get it now for $35 on the Internet. But Stephen did it, and it was a big deal. (Thomas-Clark 2012)*

For some years, Stephen Gray and his now ex-wife, Nancy McClelland, who was then head of Twentieth-Century Decorative Arts at Christie's New York, together were a force in the Arts and Crafts world—lifting scholarship, influencing the development of the most serious collections, and emphasizing the importance of the early works of Gustav Stickley. Ed Friedman remarked that more than anyone else, "Steve and Nancy injected connoisseurship into the Arts and Crafts" (Friedman 2011).

Stephen Gray believed "the American Arts and Crafts movement represents an original expression of American thought in furniture and laid the groundwork for the aesthetics of the Bauhaus school and the Modern movement" (Gray 1995, 16). "The commitment to understand more about Gustav Stickley's philosophy, ideas and innovation in modern design eventually became my life's work" (Gray 2008, 11–12). This is evidenced by the exceptional quality of his collection, his mentoring, his advising, and his publication of invaluable reference materials.

By 2003, Stephen felt the time was right to finally sell his labor of love, Turn of the Century Editions, to Peter and Janet Copeland. He sold it to them because he knew they were people who would maintain the original concept and, subsequently, was very pleased that his instincts had been correct. In addition to his Turn of the Century Editions, Stephen also "shared his extensive knowledge . . . through other publications, serving as a contributor to influential books, an advisor to noted authors, and as a consultant to major Arts and Crafts collectors and collections" (Johnson 2008).

Stephen also shared his collection through a major exhibition. In 2008, the Wadsworth Atheneum in Hartford, Connecticut, exhibited *At Home With Gustav Stickley: Arts and Crafts From the Collection of Stephen Gray*. Rooms from his country house that began his Arts and Crafts journey in 1976 were the inspiration for the presentation of Stephen's furniture in *At Home With Gustav Stickley*: rooms were filled

with exquisite examples of early Gustav Stickley furniture, metalware, and lighting; Teco, Newcomb College, and Marblehead pottery; Gustave Baumann, Bertha Lum, and Arthur Wesley Dow color woodcut prints; Dirk Van Erp lighting; and other examples of the finest decorative arts from the period. It was a magnificent display of visual harmony. Stephen "contributed about twenty objects to the Wadsworth Atheneum after the exhibition. He has bequeathed about fifty more works including lighting, woodblock prints, pottery, metalwork, and furniture" (Harris June 1, 2012). Rooms in the Atheneum are carefully and thoughtfully being developed for displaying the pieces donated by Stephen. This major gift enhances the Atheneum's American Arts and Crafts collection (Englund 2012) as it includes many pieces, but also because the pieces are rare and beautiful examples of early Gustav Stickley.

Like Arthur Wesley Dow, Stephen Gray was a teacher. His propensity for sharing was evidenced by his publications, exhibitions, and mentoring. "Over the past several years, he has been sharing his extensive personal library and knowledge with the curators of the Atheneum. In the future, he hopes to share with the public his carefully selected group of objects that will tell the Arts and Crafts story for generations" (Harris June 1, 2012).

At the 24th annual Grove Park Inn Arts and Crafts Conference in February, 2011, Stephen Gray was honored by Bruce Johnson with the coveted Arts and Crafts Lifetime Achievement Award. In Johnson's follow-up article in his Arts and Crafts Collector website, he noted that

> *Stephen Gray was among a handful of individuals who in the 1970s recognized the importance of the Arts and Crafts movement in America. At that time the furniture of Gustav Stickley, the pottery of Grueby, Teco, and Marblehead, and the metalware of Robert Jarvie, the Roycrofters and the Kalo Shops had long been overlooked and under-appreciated. (Johnson March 9, 2011)*

Johnson went on to say that by sharing valuable and otherwise inaccessible information through his publications, Stephen was creating more competition as well as a larger market for pieces he himself wanted to collect.

*Instead, he shared his research with the general public through his publishing company, Turn of the Century Editions, and later, by loaning examples from his collection to major Arts & Crafts exhibitions. Ultimately many of these pieces were donated by Stephen to public institutions where they continue his goal of educating Arts and Crafts collectors. (Johnson March 9, 2011)*

The accomplishments of Stephen Gray are almost overwhelming. They have profoundly determined the development and duration of the American Arts and Crafts revival.

## References

Adobe Spotlights. "Preserving the Craftsman in PDF Format." October 3, 2012. http://www.adobe.com/print/spotlights/craftsman/index.html.

Cathers, David. 2004. "With a Little Help from Their Friends." *American Bungalow* 43 (Fall). http://www.americanbungalow.com/category/magazine/magazine-articles/issue-43.

———. 2008. The Play of Light and Shade: Gustav Stickley's Early Craftsman Furniture. In *At Home with Gustav Stickley: Arts & Crafts from the Stephen Gray Collection.* Edited by Linda H. Roth, 35-46. Wadsworth Atheneum Museum of Art. Exhibition Catalog. Hanover: University Press of New England.

Cohen, Jerry. In phone interview with authors. May 20, 2012.

Edwards, Robert, and Stephen Gray, eds. 1981. *Collected Works of Gustav Stickley.* New York: Turn of the Century Editions.

Englund, Alyce. In interview with authors at the Wadsworth Atheneum. Hartford, Connecticut. July 19, 2012.

Friedman, Ed and Kathy. In discussion with authors. Pittsburgh, Pennsylvania. September 12, 2011.

Friedman, Ed. In phone interview with Judith Budwig. April 2, 2012.

Gray, Stephen. 1995. This Exhibition: A Preview. In *Innovation and Derivation: The Contribution of L. & J.G. Stickley to the Arts and Crafts Movement.* Edited by Donald Davidoff and Stephen Gray, 15-19. The Craftsman Farms Foundation. Exhibition Catalog.

———. 2008. Introduction. In *At Home with Gustav Stickley: Arts and Crafts from the Stephen Gray Collection.* Edited by Linda H. Roth, 11-17. Wadsworth Atheneum Museum of Art. Exhibition Catalog.

———. In conversation with authors. Avon, Connecticut. July 15, 2011.

Harris, Laura. In e-mail with authors. May 21, 2012.

———. In e-mail with authors. June 1, 2012.

Hewett, David. "The Inside Story Behind the $30,250 Record-breaking Arts and Crafts Catalog, or, The Bidder with the Commission versus the Bidder with a Mission." *Maine Antiques Digest,* online, May 1996. http://maineantiquedigest.com/articles_archive/articles/jarv0596.htm.

Johnson, Bruce. "Stephen Gray To Receive A&C Lifetime Achievement Award." *Arts and Crafts Collector* (artsandcraftscollector.com). January 26, 2011. http://www.artsandcraftscollector.com/in_the_news/stephen_gray_to_receive_a_c_lifetime_achievement_award.

———. "Stephen Gray Honored at Arts & Crafts Conference." *Arts and Crafts Collector* (artsandcraftscollector.com). March 9, 2011. http://artsandcraftscollector.com/in_the_news/stephen_gray_honored_at_arts_crafts_conference.

Kaplan, Robert. In interview with authors. Maplewood, New Jersey. March 4, 2012.

Thomas-Clark, Jill. In interview with authors. Elmira, New York. March 31, 2012.

Turn of the Century Press website. http://www.turnofthecenturyeditions.com.

William Morris Society website. Updated January 4, 2001. Retrieved October 3, 2012. http://www.morrissociety.org/publications/newsletters/newsltr-jan98.html.

o.p.: Stephen Gray receiving Arts and Crafts Lifetime Achievement Award in 2011 at the Grove Park Inn

l: Stephen Gray and Laura Harris

The Wadsworth Atheneum in Hartford

Vase #261
c. 1903
Teco by the Gates Potteries, B.G. Benedict

Vase #141
c. 1902
Teco by the Gates Potteries, Fritz Wilhelm Albert

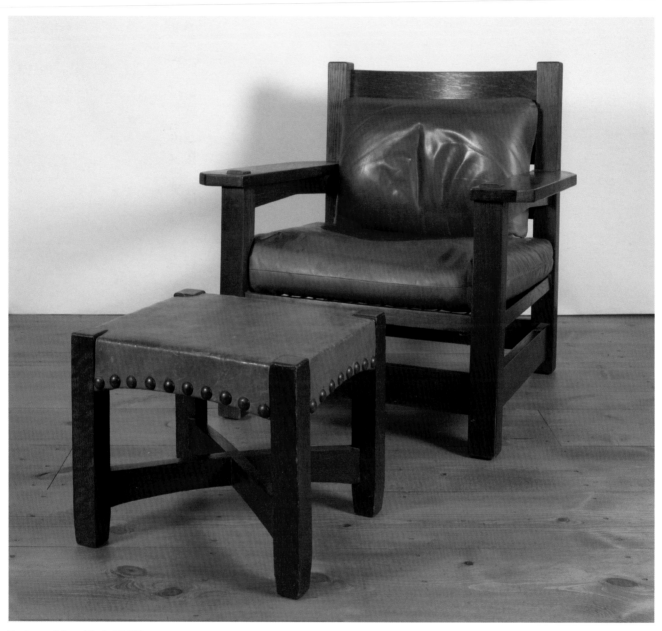

Eastwood Arm Chair #2638
c. 1903

and Seat #725 (footstool)
c. 1901
Gustav Stickley

Cedar Lined Chest (Bridal Chest)
c. 1902
Gustav Stickley

Reclining Chair #2340 (Bow Arm Morris Chair)
c. 1901
Gustav Stickley

Woodblock, *Marsh Creek*
c. 1905
Arthur Wesley Dow

Tile, Ipswich Salt Marshes, c. 1905,
decorated by Arthur Baggs,
after woodblock by Arthur Wesley Dow

o.p., Arm Chair (with inlay)
c. 1903
Harvey Ellis for Gustav Stickley

Base detail
o.p., Bookcase #510
c. 1901
design by Henry Wilkinson
for Gustav Stickley

top: Beth Cathers and Nick Dembrosky at Cathers & Dembrosky with Gustav Stickley bridal chest in foreground at 1000 Madison Avenue in New York;

bottom: Nick and Beth with Dirk Van Erp lamp;

o.p.: Beth examining Jarvie chamberstick

# 9. Beth Cathers – Robert Kaplan

*Beth Cathers was not just one of the earliest Arts and Crafts dealers but one of the most important. Because of her expert eye, engaging personality, and tough-minded business sense, she played a pivotal role in the unfolding revival. A connoisseur with a full understanding of the history and influence of the Arts and Crafts period, she deals in the rarified world of the very finest examples of Arts and Crafts material.*

In the mid-seventies, Beth Cathers supplied Vance Jordan and Tod Volpe with caches of Arts and Crafts furniture in preparation for a gallery they were opening in SoHo. Tod Volpe very smartly brought her in as their furniture consultant in 1976, the year they opened Jordan-Volpe Gallery. She had the knowledge, the resources, the business sense, and the determination to make the gallery a success.

An expert at finding outstanding pieces of Gustav Stickley and other Arts and Crafts, Beth was responsible for the furniture. She bid at auction on behalf of the gallery and bought from a variety of other sources. The timing was right. The market boomed, and by the 1980s the appreciation for the Arts and Crafts was enormous. The gallery sold to a broad base that included major collectors like Sydney Lewis and Max Palevsky, both of whom bought extensively from Jordan-Volpe.

Vance and Tod were feeling their way as they went and were learning in the process, but by 1980, a recession had arts markets slowing. The overhead of the gallery was substantial. And additionally, Jordan-Volpe pulled out all the stops for the Martin Brothers show in November 1981, the last big

show they did. It was spectacular but left them financially exposed. David Rago has vivid memories of the exhibition:

> *The Martin Brothers show was unbelievable. Jordan-Volpe was one long space, maybe 100 feet wide and 200 feet deep. Inside the gallery was a place that was two-thirds the length of it. There was a wall with arched windows around the outside, and Venetian windows with Martin Brothers figures, and when you walked back in, there was a forest of trees and moss ... and running water ... and bird sounds piped in. The Martin Brothers figures were sitting in the moss. (Rago 2011)*

Her time at the high-profile Jordan-Volpe served Beth well in developing her future. She was recognized as one of the experts on the furniture of the Arts and Crafts period and had a particularly extensive knowledge of Gustav Stickley. She also had excellent connections and contact points around the country that were strengthened during her ten years at Jordan-Volpe. She knew who would have pieces and where to find them.

Nick and Beth at auction preview

o.p., Robert Kaplan with wife and twin sons; Robert Kaplan next to his Jean-Michel Basquiat painting and Charles Rohlfs chair

## *Cathers & Dembrosky*

Demand for the Arts and Crafts was increasing rapidly. John Bryan, a major buyer, began developing the Crab Tree Farm collection in 1985 and many museums established Arts and Crafts collections for the first time.

Jordan-Volpe Gallery had created a publicity campaign for the Arts and Crafts that generated a tidal wave of interest and passion. Even traditional galleries were attempting to capitalize on the growing popularity of the style, but without the knowledge and understanding of the period, it was an empty gesture of indiscriminate buying.

When Jordan-Volpe closed, Beth worked with private clients while planning a new venue with Nick Dembrosky, her life partner. In May 1988, they opened Cathers & Dembrosky, an Arts and Crafts gallery at 1000 Madison Avenue where they served major clients. In the early nineties, Cathers & Dembrosky moved to 43 East 10th Street in Greenwich Village.

Nick had studied philosophy in graduate school. Through the designs of Frank Lloyd Wright and then the works of Gustav Stickley, he recognized the philosophical elegance of the objects of the Arts and Crafts movement intended for everyday use.

*Involvement with them could take place in a familiar and intimate way. Their meaning, however, is not reducible to mere function. Like constellations which can be used to navigate, the beauty of their presence vastly overflows any function they may have. It is a beauty which leads man back along a path to himself. Involvement with objects of the American Arts and Crafts movement is not a retreat into the fantasy of a nostalgic past. Rather, it retrieves the possibility of allowing man to live close to a primordial sense of beauty. It is by living in an intimate manner with this sort of presence that man can continue to feel himself at home in the twentieth century. (Cathers 1988)*

Every August for ten years, Nick and Beth worked the Branchville, New Jersey carnival, part of the carnival company his family owned. Rural New Jersey was a welcome change from their fast-paced life in the city. Nick bought a plane because he loved flying, and they would fly to auctions in places that were difficult to access or a long drive away. Life with Nick was an adventure. Tragically, he died in May 2000 at the age of 49.

## Robert Kaplan

In the summer of 1985, Robert Kaplan began collecting Arts and Crafts. He became acquainted with Paul Morrissey, an important figure in Andy Warhol's Factory who lived down the street from the Metropolitan Museum of Art and had a collection that included Stickley and Grueby. Morrissey had built his collection at a time when few people were aware of the Arts and Crafts movement or Gustav Stickley. A lender to the 1972 Princeton exhibition, his collection was complete by 1973. He gave Robert *Craftsman* magazines and shared his valuable insights. When Kaplan asked where he could find more resources for learning, Morrissey told him the best places to learn were the study room at the Met and Jordan-Volpe Gallery. Robert started visiting an array of dealers and collectors and looked forward to weekends when he could see more Arts and Crafts pieces.

Robert was fortunate to have both Paul Morrissey and collector Stephen Gray as mentors. After Robert was the underbidder on a piece of Teco at auction, Stephen introduced himself. Recognizing Robert's passion for Arts and Crafts, Stephen began sharing his extensive knowledge.

Robert Kaplan and Beth Cathers (Cathers & Kaplan) behind Gustav Stickley director's table with early 1902 Gustav Stickley china cabinet (on left) and early 1902 Gustav Stickley sideboard (on right); rare Gustav Stickley candlesticks on top of sideboard, 20" x 7" square; George Nakashima Conoid dining chair; five hanging Gustav Stickley light fixtures

Like Stephen, Robert collected early Gustav Stickley. A serious-minded collector from the beginning, Robert had a discerning eye and was focused on the importance of condition, explaining that the "furniture is not ornate, so the condition is everything. The subtle detailing in the wood and grain patterns become the decoration."

Kaplan knew many of the Arts and Crafts dealers. He and Beth conducted business together but they were also friends. In the year after Nick died, Beth decided she wanted to continue in business but felt it would be better to have a partner. Robert was at a crossroads in his life. He had been living in Tel Aviv managing professional tennis players and was ready for a change.

## Cathers & Kaplan

In March 2001, Robert and Beth formed a partnership as Arts and Crafts dealers. From the beginning, they shared the same vision. For the first several years they were together, they exhibited at the Grove Park Inn Arts and Crafts Conference antiques show. They had exciting pieces with the highest prices. For many, it was the most anticipated booth. Over the years they found that sales at shows were slowing down, so they decided to shift their focus.

Beth and Robert haven't exhibited in eight years, partly due to the impact of the growing popularity of auctions. With the building of great collections by foundations and museums, rare pieces are not recycling back into the market. Cathers and Kaplan closed their shop but continue to serve clients privately.

bottom

Fern dish
Karl Kipp, East Aurora, New York
Handwrought copper
c.1912   5 3/4"(D) x 3 1/4"(H)

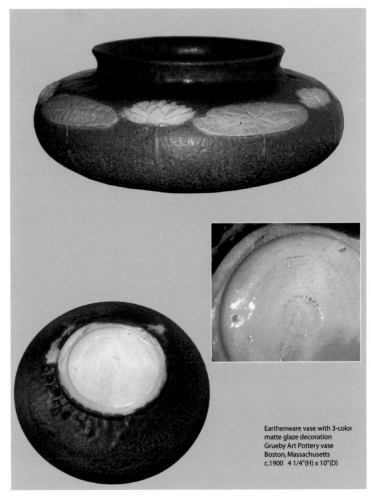

Earthenware vase with 3-color
matte glaze decoration
Grueby Art Pottery vase
Boston, Massachusetts
c.1900   4 1/4"(H) x 10"(D)

### References

Cathers, Beth. In interview with authors. March 4, 2012. Maplewood, New Jersey.

Cathers, Beth and Tod M. Volpe. 1988. *Treasures of the American Arts and Crafts Movement, 1890–1920*. New York: Harry N. Abrams, Inc. Text by Alistair Duncan. Introduction by Leslie Bowman.

Kaplan, Robert. In interview with authors. March 4, 2012. Maplewood, New Jersey.

Rago, David. In interview with authors. July 26, 2011. Lambertville, New Jersey.

Gustav Stickley 1901 lamp table, H. 29½" x D. 30⅛". Similar form in *Chips From the Workshop* catalog, different detailing on the upper legs. Leather top

Dome, panels of Amber; tinted Hammered Glass; 20" square; library table; Oak, Poplar, Leather, Brass tacks: 30³/₈" x 48³/₄" x 30 ⁷/₈"

Corner cabinet
Quarter-cut oak with handwrought iron hardware
Gustav Stickley, Eastwood, New York   c.1902
46 1/2"(W) x 71 1/2"(H) x 24"(D)

Details of corner cabinet

Eastwood Arm Chair #2638
H. 37" x W. 34" x D. 33"
Gustav Stickley, c. 1902

Robert Kaplan and Beth Cathers

Jerry and friends

# 10. Jerry Cohen

*He cuts through the clutter with a simple, "What are you trying to say?" Jerry Cohen is unassuming, very soft-spoken, and extremely likable, never threatening or devious. He is calm and has a calming presence, but he is a tour-de-force businessman, the Warren Buffet of the Arts and Crafts revival. He studies a situation, assesses the likelihood of an outcome, and makes a decision based on rational thought. Yet, he is a very warm person and stays out of cliques and politics. He has been bold in his decisions and in his investments and has been a quiet but unmistakable presence in the commerce and culture of the Arts and Crafts revival.*

In 1974, Jerry Cohen was designing and writing computer systems in San Francisco when he rented a cottage in Berkeley and needed to furnish it. He discovered a local antiques shop and began buying inexpensive Victorian oak furniture. He became friends with the shop owner, who raved about what a great life it was selling antiques and suggested that Jerry open a store next to his so they could sit out on the sidewalk in rocking chairs shooting the breeze and waiting for customers. When Jerry found himself with two weeks of vacation time that spring, he bought an airline ticket to Boston, rented a U-haul truck, and drove to auctions buying claw-foot tables, serpentine dressers, pressed-back chairs, and stacking bookcases. He hauled the stuff cross country to California and stored it in his garage before he realized he would have to rent a storefront to sell all that furniture. Six months later, after running his new antiques shop during the day and writing computer programs at night, he knew he had to give up one or the other and resigned from his computer job.

An enthusiastic east coast dealer introduced Jerry to Arts and Crafts furniture in 1977, pointing out its quality and workmanship, and that it cost a lot less than Victorian furniture of inferior quality. He told Jerry "you're paying me three hundred fifty dollars for claw-foot tables and Larkin sideboards, and I've got these superior pieces made by Stickley for a fraction of their price. You should buy them" (Cohen). Jerry reluctantly did—an L. & J.G. Stickley sideboard with strap hinges for $125 and an L. & J.G. Stickley 54-inch dining table for $135. He drove the Stickley out to Oakland, where the pieces sat forgotten in a corner of his shop until two Berkeley professors came in and made a beeline for them. They gave Jerry a crash course in Stickley and said they would buy every piece he could find. And then—only after all that—they asked for prices, and Jerry found out he could make a lot more selling Arts and Crafts furniture than Victorian.

Jerry wanted to learn more about Stickley, but in the late seventies, there was still very little written on the Arts and Crafts. The only book he had was *The Forgotten Rebel: Gustav Stickley and His Craftsman Mission Furniture*, a book that predated the revival of interest in the Arts and Crafts. This was unfortunate because Jerry passed up an inlaid music cabinet for $1,000, thinking its Stickley signature looked like a "brand new decal someone had applied to trick an unwitting person into buying a fake" (Cohen). Two weeks later he ran across the 1972 Princeton exhibition catalog and read about Harvey Ellis and his inlaid furniture designs. Realizing his mistake, he tried to locate the inlaid cabinet he had passed up, but by then it had already found its way to the collection of David and Beth Cathers.

At that time, Jerry's interest in the Arts and Crafts was strictly mercenary—he says prices were so cheap it was easy to make a good profit. He had yet to fall in love with the style or the philosophy behind it. That changed in 1980 when he purchased a little Dirk Van Erp bean-pot lamp from a local home (for $200) and brought it home. He loved the lamp and placed it on his carved Victorian sideboard, but it didn't have the proper setting. One by one, each of his Victorian pieces left the house and was replaced by a piece of Stickley, so his lamp could be displayed in its proper setting.

Frequent trips to the east coast gave Jerry inventory for his Mission Oak Shop in Oakland. In 1984, Jerry was in a Liverpool, New York, antique shop, when he spotted two leaded-glass floor lamps. He bought both, took them back to his shop in California and sold them through a Marin lighting dealer, Ron Collier, to George Lucas. Lucas was building Skywalker Ranch at the time and purchased the lamps for his library, but they sat in Jerry's shop for three

l.: Connecticut home Jerry remodeled in Arts and Crafts style; l.l.: office; below: dining room

weeks waiting to be picked up. During that time, many customers came into his shop and wanted to purchase them. Jerry asked Roger, the shop owner back in Liverpool, to send him more of these lamps, so Roger leaned on the craftsman to send him more. After a year of Jerry's attempts to get these lamps, an exasperated Roger told Cohen that, for $500, he'd give him the name and phone number of the artisan.

Michael Adams was the struggling artist making these lamps. Most antiques dealers at that time wouldn't go anywhere near modern crafts as there was no market for them. Roger had been paying Michael so little that Michael only made the lamps when he was desperate for the cash flow, and the meager supply never came close to meeting demand.

With name and phone number now in hand, Jerry approached Michael and offered to pay whatever it took to make it worthwhile for him to start making the lamps again. Michael was very pleased. As Jerry put it, "We were two guys looking for each other." Adams' background was in making stained glass, but after a couple of years he tried working in hammered copper. Jerry firmly threw his support behind

Adams and first gave him an original Stickley chandelier to copy, and then his treasured Dirk Van Erp bean-pot lamp.

Although still living in California, Jerry knew Michael and appreciated the excellence of his work. In addition to providing originals for Michael to copy, Jerry boldly invested in the business so that both the size of the studio footprint and the number of employees could be expanded. Recognizing talent and being an astute businessman, Jerry Cohen teamed up with Michael Adams in 1985, to found Aurora Studios, "a high-end artist's studio devoted to the production of hand-crafted hammered copper Arts and Crafts lighting" (artsn-crafts.com). In their partnership, he was relieving Michael and his wife, Dawn Hopkins, of much of the business and marketing end of their company, which would give them more time to devote to their craft and a wonderful opportunity to grow their company. This benefited everyone involved in the Arts and Crafts.

Jerry moved back to the east coast in 1988. He bought an enormous building in downtown Putnam, Connecticut, and moved his Oakland antiques business, The Mission Oak Shop, into one corner of it. He named the new building Antiques Marketplace. Jerry's investment in the building sparked the revitalization of Putnam's historic downtown, which had been written off in the 1960s when shopping trends moved from local Main Streets to new large shopping malls (artsncrafts.com). Jerry's investment provided a needed boost to the local economy. Antiques Marketplace became a desti-

above: kitchen; u.r.: pond; r: living room

nation for many shoppers, whose presence downtown made it feasible to develop the underutilized buildings that surrounded his store.

The outdoor antiques market in Brimfield, Massachusetts was *the* place for antiques dealers to buy in the 1980s and 1990s. There were endless amounts of Arts and Crafts pieces being pulled out of houses, camps, churches, offices, and other places, and a lot of these things would show up for sale at Brimfield for amazingly low prices. During these decades, Brimfield was a major source of inventory for many dealers. It was (and still is) held three times a year and was a weeklong event. Jerry lived less than an hour away in Connecticut, and he would shop Brimfield every single day it was open.

One of the first to shop the outdoor market with this kind of frequency, Jerry would sometimes buy whole truckloads of Arts and Crafts furniture from dealers at Brimfield. After a couple of years, dealers knew him and trusted him. They often would save a prime piece just for him, keeping it under a tarp and away from the public eye. Jerry always knew what he wanted to pay for a piece, and if a dealer gave him the right number, he'd say ok. He wouldn't try to talk the price down.

Jerry would make his rounds, look over the merchandise, and if the price was right, he'd simply and quietly say, "I'll be back later." He would trust a dealer to hold that piece for him, and on the flip side, the dealer knew that Jerry was good for his word. For years, Jerry was the major buyer at Brimfield. He'd have a truck go around at the end of each day, picking up all the pieces he'd bought.

Prices in the Mission Oak Shop were very fair. In addition to rare, pristine pieces, Jerry handled a lot that the average collector might be looking for and could afford. He specialized in items for working professionals and never tried to be the dealer at the top of the pyramid who handled only rare and iconic pieces. He strove to be the country's largest dealer in terms of quantity of pieces handled but never in terms of dollar volume. Because Jerry is so likable and easy to get along with, people wanted to do business with him. They not only bought from him, they would bring him stuff they wanted to sell, and if he could get it at his price, he would buy it from them.

Around 1992, the Arts & Crafts market began to change. Mid-level material, which was Jerry's bread and butter, had never been big on the east coast, where collectors had predominantly vied for only the rarest pieces in the best original finishes. But by 1992, New York City galleries like Peter-Roberts Gallery and Gallery 532 had entered the Stickley market, catering to a new breed of east coast collectors and decorators who were happy to buy mid-level pieces, whether refinished or not, at prices often double or triple what Jerry was asking in rural Connecticut. Jerry sensed his livelihood was in jeopardy. He was no longer the top-paying east coast dealer for mid-level material because the New York dealers were now buying in huge quantities.

By 1994, Jerry realized he needed to change his business plan or face irrelevance. He calculated that his best option to be competitive was to enter the auction business. Jerry started Craftsman Auctions with John Fontaine, a Massachusetts auctioneer, and they spent six months putting together their first auction, which took place in May of 1995. It was the convergence of the right time, the right place, and two very hard-working men. The economy was booming and people had a lot of money to spend. Another element

u.l.: Aurora Studios booth at the contemporary crafts exhibit at Grove Park Inn Arts and Crafts Conference;

l.: Aurora Studios display of copper pots

l.l.: Aurora Studios lighting

l.r.: Jerry Cohen

that worked to their advantage was that they had no "baggage" among the Arts and Crafts auction crowd. No one was saying, "I'm not doing business with these guys." There was no history, and there were no grudges to bear, so they could begin their business with a clean slate.

Fontaine offered the facilities, bookkeeping, auctioneering, and such things. He had previously auctioned Victorian, but never much Arts and Crafts, which brought a different clientele. Jerry was prepared to lay out money, and his part of the business was finding and buying inventory, writing the auction catalogs, and getting the word out about the sales. The network of people he had dealt with and the relationships he had established offered many possibilities. Having never run an auction business, in his naivete, Jerry made decisions that ran up against the collective wisdom of auction houses, like giving people advances against consignments and buying pieces to auction. It worked to their benefit. The auctions offered a friendly environment for consignors and were very successful. With the booming economy, every sale saw prices rise to new and higher levels.

With his background in computer technology, Jerry pioneered and produced digitally, on his Mac, a revolutionary 100 percent full-color auction catalog—new to the auction world. Color in auction catalogs before 1995 was prohibitively expensive due to the cost of film, drum scanning, and making four-color separations. By using Photoshop to

digitally create four-color separations, Jerry was able to reduce the cost of each printed color photo in his catalogs from about $300 to $10. The first Craftsman Auction catalog in 1995 pictured every item individually and in color. Consignors liked that because it made their items look more important, which brought more consignments for each succeeding auction.

Craftsman Auctions merged with Rago Auctions in 2000, with six auctions a year planned: three at John Fontaine's gallery in Pittsfield, Massachusetts and three at Rago Arts and Auction Center in Lambertville, New Jersey (Smith 2000). The plan proved too unwieldy after about eighteen months, and Jerry broke off with David Rago to continue Craftsman Auctions in New Jersey. Now called Rago Early Twentieth Century, the sales continue today as a collaboration between Jerry Cohen, David Rago, and Suzanne Perrault, holding major Arts and Crafts sales three times a year in Lambertville.

Jerry Cohen is a member of *American Bungalow* magazine's advisory board and has written articles for the magazine. Perhaps inspired by his involvement at *American Bungalow*, fifteen years ago he completely renovated his 1960s Woodstock, Connecticut home, converting both its structural interior and exterior to have the look and feel of an authentic 1910 bungalow.

The Mission Oak Shop exhibited annually at the Grove Park Inn Arts and Crafts Conference in Asheville, North Carolina for twenty-two years, through 2009, and Jerry continues to buy and sell furniture, metalwork, art, lighting, and pottery from the Arts and Crafts period for his Mission Oak Shop.

Ever enterprising, Jerry established the *Putnam Traveler* newspaper in 2003. He sits on its board and is a contributing writer (artsncrafts.com). Jerry Cohen is civic-minded and deeply engaged in the community, giving warmly of his time and talent. He is one of the few early dealers still active in the business and has intelligently adapted in ways necessary to compete in these times of online purchasing and social networking. His website, artsncrafts.com, is obviously a labor of love and is a valuable resource for those interested in learning more about Arts and Crafts furniture and decorative arts.

## References

Artsncrafts website. "Arts & Crafts: Gustav Stickley Furniture." http://www.artsncrafts.com/aboutus.htm.

Cohen, Jerry. In interview with authors in Putnam, Connecticut. July 14, 2011.

———. In phone interview with authors. May 20, 2012.

Craftsman Auctions website. http://www.craftsman-auctions.com.

Smith, David. "Craftsman and David Rago Merge." *Antiques and the Arts Weekly*. August 8, 2000.

r: Jerry Cohen's flyer

below: Mission Oak Shop booth at Grove Park Inn

### ■ ■ NOW BUYING ■ ■

## L&JG STICKLEY
## GUSTAV STICKLEY
## LIMBERT
## DIRK VAN ERP

With Outlets on 2 coasts we have a very broad range of buyers
We Buy Middle-Line in good condition and High-Line in any condition for California
We Buy Clean High-End Pieces at Top Dollar for New England Customers
We Buy the broadest range of merchandise of any dealer in the country because
we cater to the most diverse clientele.
Absolutely prompt payment made on all purchases.

**in California**
4228 Park Blvd., Oakland, 94602
(415) 482-1420 or (800) 448-7828
open 11:30 to 6:00 Tues - Sat

**in Connecticutt**
RR2 Box 33, Woodstock, 06281
(203) 928-6630
by appointment, call Jerry Cohen

Pam Ashbahian and Don Miner laying out The Bee

# 11. The Bee

*There was a game David Smith played with Leigh and Leslie Keno as they were growing up in Connecticut. They would pass a reference book around. One would pick out an antique, then the next, and then the third boy, and on it would go until everything was chosen. Then they compared collections. The first time he ever heard the word Grueby was from the Keno boys—"Keep your eyes out for Grueby—it's going to be worth a lot of money someday."*

David Smith with Tique

David Smith first collected early glass. As a kid, he bought a "genie bottle" at an antiques shop—he just had to have it, so he bought the whole basket of glass to get it and took the glass he didn't want to the flea market. One flask sold for $100, a lot of money for a ten-year old. By the time he was twelve, David Smith was a dealer, collector, and photographer. It all boded well for his future, but once he graduated from high school, he became indifferent and only cared about riding his motorcycle. One day his father woke him up just before noon and gruffly told him to get up. He pushed him into the dark room and told him to get busy making prints from the negatives (Smith 2012). Because his family ran *The Bee,* a local weekly newspaper, David learned at a young age to take photographs and develop negatives (Smith 2012).

Reuben Hazen Smith began publishing *The Bee* in Newtown Connecticut in 1881, a small-town newspaper he had purchased when it was in financial trouble. He was intent on building up a readership for the paper and went door-to-door, making friends along the way (Clark 1997, 1). "He was so well liked, that the paper grew and prospered in large part by sheer force of his engaging personality and initiative" (1997, 2). Remarkably, even during the Great Depression, *The Bee* continued to grow and a wing was added to the building in the 1930s. The Smith family continues to this day to create a weekly local paper imbued with the playfulness and personable nature that transfers from one Smith generation to the next (1997, 2).

Weathervane atop "The Newtown Bee" offices

Crowd waiting for May's Antique Market to open at Brimfield

Different Smith family members ran the paper over the decades. Reuben's two brothers, Allison P. and Arthur J. took over in 1892 when Reuben left for northern California, and A.J.'s son, Paul, became editor in 1934. The paper's popularity grew in western Connecticut and reading it became a tradition for many families. Paul, David's grandfather, was a smart businessman and believed in the importance of staying current by updating equipment regularly.

R. Scudder Smith joined the staff of *The Bee* in 1961. For years the paper had hosted regular columns on antiques, and featured small ads placed by antiques galleries and auction houses, but two years after he began at *The Bee*, Scudder's interest in antiques and collecting American folk art showed itself.

> *After establishing contacts with the many antiques shops and galleries in the area, Scudder Smith launched, with his father's forbearance, four pages in The Newtown Bee on June 28, 1963 devoted to antiques. The antiques coverage was quickly embraced by area antiques dealers.*
> *(Clark 1997, 3)*

Word spread quickly among antiques dealers, and they began placing ads in the little paper in response to the increased coverage of antiques. Greater ad sales put greater demands on *The Bee's* letterpress shop. In 1967, the paper upgraded to offset printers, which gave it the capability to print expanded separate sections.

In 1969, *The Bee* issued its first separate antiques section, *Antiques and The Arts Weekly*, devoted entirely to antiques and featuring news, articles, advertising, classifieds, and calendars. "The steady growth of *The Newtown Bee* was quickly overshadowed by the phenomenal success of *Antiques and The Arts Weekly*" (Clark 2002, 3). National circulation grew quickly and many subscribers across the country were familiar with the local events in Newtown (Smith 2002, 8).

Scudder Smith, David's father, became editor and publisher of *The Newtown Bee* in 1973 and, within a few years, decided to issue *Antiques and The Arts Weekly* as a separate publication because increased circulation was largely due to the antiques section (Clark 2002, 3). Because the antiques section was part of *The Newtown Bee* for so many years, many subscribers continued referring to the new antiques paper as *The Bee* (Smith 2002, 8).

David Smith became interested in the Arts and Crafts in the 1970s. He loved the furniture and the pottery, and he enjoyed the cast of characters, from the earthy Don Magner to the elegant Nancy McClelland of Christie's. David enjoyed the whole spectrum of personalities and their maneuvering in the Arts and Crafts landscape.

Low key and unobtrusive, David photographed without a flash and took lots of photos of people at auctions. It was David Smith at *The Bee* who covered Arts and Crafts because he was the one who loved it. It was a passion for him. He covered every important event—conferences, auctions, and museum and gallery exhibitions—to give readers the full picture of what was going on in the Arts and Crafts. He flew to Chicago and Cincinnati, he went to Christie's, Skinner's, and Rago's auctions at the Puck Building. He knew all the SoHo galleries, and everyone knew David from *The Bee.*

One of the major flea markets in the country, and some would argue it is the most important, is the Brimfield Antiques Show in Brimfield, Massachusetts. It is set up in fields along a country highway that cuts right through town. The market consists of different venues, or fields, such as Heart-o-the Mart, Quaker Acres, and May's. Hundreds of antiques dealers are set up within each field. It is a huge and important event, so, of course, David Smith is there covering it for The Bee.

People come from all over the country for the seven-day event, and people in such places as Europe, Israel, Tokyo,

above: Richard May under sign

Greg Kuharic, Barbara Deisroth, and Carolyn Holmes of Sotheby's

Nick Dembrosky and Beth Cathers with Jarvie candlesticks

Singapore, and China arrange charter flights so they can attend the market. A lot of dealers rely on and build their schedules around the Brimfield dates because it is so important. Incredible things have been found there and many have ended up in major auction houses. Nancy McClelland, former head of Christie's 20th century sales, calls Brimfield a goldmine.

David found and presented interesting stories to the reader. Through feature stories, he provided an in-depth look at a collector or a foundation or a particular medium. David's reporting, his photography, his personality, and his passion for the Arts and Crafts kept the revival in high gear throughout the late eighties and early nineties. *The Bee* provided advertising, arts calendars, reviews of auctions and exhibitions, and published major front-page stories about a variety of subjects.

In all of it, the aspect David loved the most was looking at and touching the Arts and Crafts furniture, the pottery, and the metalwork.

> *This stuff was meant to be handled. You absorbed it through enthusiasm. You always looked for the premium pieces, but you would walk right by something, then take a look back and see Michael Carey with it upside down, and Dave Rago peeking at him around a room divider with Treadway hiding in a corner. (Smith 2012)*

The Arts and Crafts revival was at its peak in the late eighties and early nineties and *The Bee* circulation was a barometer of the market. In 2002, *Antiques and The Arts Weekly* averaged over 220 pages weekly, up from 75 pages in 1977.

The revival came about very rapidly and because it became popular so fast, problems developed. Prices rose rapidly after 1987, and there was cutthroat competition in some quarters. David Smith maintains that "other periods that have become popular, like early American, have always developed on an even keel." David saw and heard a cross-sampling of everything that went on in the Arts and Crafts community, from one coast to another. He characterized the Arts and Crafts market as "full of back-stabbings and fist-fights, but luckily there were some good, solid people who pushed it along." Although Smith gives credit to Dave Rago as "having a stronger influence on the market in a positive way than any other one individual," he likes to think "*Antiques and The Arts Weekly* played a large role in the ascent of the Arts and Crafts" (Smith 2012).

*The Bee* was the hub of Arts and Crafts information in the beginning of the revival. Before there was Bruce Johnson or i-phones, news was disseminated through *The Bee*, the fulcrum point of *who*, *what*, *where*, *when*, and *how*. David Smith covered everything and knew everyone. He could tell you that "Marilee was the driving force at Skinner" and that "Rosalie was at the forefront of the whole Arts and Crafts pottery movement running ARK auctions." David was there

Nancy McClelland of
Christie's, 1988

as a keen observer of people and events, and it was from *The Bee* that much of the national media picked up their background information on stories about Brimfield, Christie's, saving the Farms, the His Craft exhibition, the first Grove Park Inn Arts and Crafts conference in 1988, and even up to Rudy Ciccarello and the Two Red Roses Foundation.

In 2006, R. Scudder Smith received the Antiques Dealers Association of America (ADA) Award of Merit, for his leadership in "a marketplace substantially shaped by *Antiques and The Arts Weekly* over the past four decades" (Beach 2006, 68). The vice president of the ADA, Arthur Liverant

> noted the publication's long support of 'the common interests of dealers, collectors, curators, museums, historical societies, auctioneers and show promoters.' Few journals have a more catholic regard for the news: Antiques and The Arts Weekly has long been the one place where nearly every arts organization enjoys a hearing.

> Antiques and The Arts Weekly, solely Scudder's invention, is a daunting accomplishment. The 16½-by-11-inch tabloid is up to an inch thick on a typical week. An average 200 pages, it seasonally spikes to as much as 360 pages. Auction ads account for about one-third of the paper. For years, Scudder put out Antiques and The Arts Weekly with just two assistants, an editor and an advertising manager.
> (Beach 2006, 68)

The market for Arts and Crafts has cooled down since the halcyon days of the nineties, but *The Bee* has not stood still. In 1995, it was one of the first newspapers to go online and commit staff to updating webpages regularly. The paper established its commitment long ago to staying current with technology "so that news and information can be delivered quickly and efficiently to as many readers as possible" (Clark 1997, 12). The idea was to complement the printed paper, not to replace it. The future of print media is uncertain, but the role of *The Bee* in the Arts and Crafts revival is indelible.

### References

Beach, Laura. 2006. R. Scudder Smith: 2006 ADA Award of Merit Winner. *Newtown Bee*. March 31, 2006.

Clark, Curtiss. 1997. The Newtown Bee Has Changed and Grown With the Town That Gave It Life. *Newtown Bee*. June 27, 1997.

———. 2002. Reporting Newtown's Story in Three Centuries. *Newtown Bee*. June 28, 2002.

Smith, David. In interview with authors. July 19, 2012. Newtown, Connecticut.

Smith, R. Scudder. 2002. Antiques and the Arts Weekly—An Antiques Success Story Grows Out of The Bee's Agrarian Tradition. *Newtown Bee*. June 28, 2002.

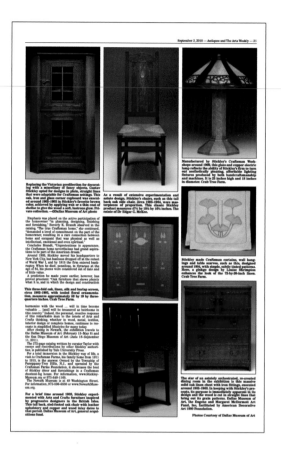

Review of the Dallas Museum exhibition, Gustav Stickley and the American Arts and Crafts Movement

o.p., top: Review of "Tiffany Favrile Pottery and the Quest of Beauty"

o.p., bottom: *The Bee* coverage of "The Jewelry and Metalwork of Marie Zimmermann"

r.: David Smith with camera

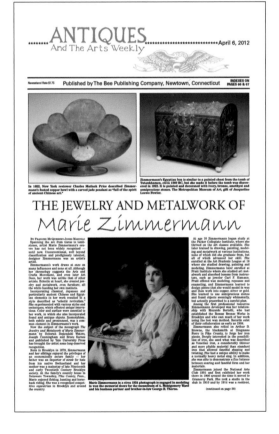

o.p.: David Smith with camera

o.p.: Review of *At Home* With Gustav Stickley at the Wadsworth Atheneum in Hartford, Connecticut

above and right: *Rudy Ciccarello and The Two Red Roses Foundation: Preserving the American Arts and Crafts Movement*

# 12. Spring Street

*Richard Caggiano Antiques, Michael Carey American Arts and Crafts Furnishings, Peter-Roberts Antiques, and Gallery 532 built onto the excitement created by Jordan-Volpe with the opening of their gallery in 1976. The Spring Street area was the cool place on the New York gallery circuit to look for Arts and Crafts.*

Newly acquired Gustav Stickley willow settle (No. 70) for Richard Caggiano's shop

Richard Caggiano setting up his booth at the Grove Park Inn, 1990

## Richard Caggiano Antiques 1977–1987

Richard Caggiano opened his antiques shop on Spring Street in 1977. He started when he was twenty-three years old and sold a variety of antiques. When Michael Carey's shop opened in 1980, it was an inspiration to Richard. His girlfriend worked in a neighborhood coffee shop, so Richard walked by Michael Carey a few times a day and was constantly looking at things in his window. Once in a while he would go in and would be amazed by the simplicity of it. Richard remembers a child's wardrobe and a Gustav Stickley six-leg settle and feeling that these were unbelievably beautiful things. Those images of beauty stayed with him.

One of the places he went to buy inventory was an auction in the Adirondacks. He would buy rickety old dressers and rockers. On one trip, he noticed two pieces that looked like pieces Michael Carey sold. They were an L. & J.G. Stickley drop-arm morris chair and an L. & J.G. daybed with tapered posts. They were solid as rocks. He bought those two things for nothing—$80 for the morris chair and $160 for the daybed. That was it. It was the beginning of the Arts and Crafts for him, and it was the spring of 1981. He never looked back, and he never again bought rickety old stuff.

Richard was the dealers' dealer. Not by choice, but his location was out of the way of gallery hoppers. Although he was on Spring Street, he was on the other side of Broadway, and no one went that far. "I was like a ghost, but I had a great space, and I loved it" (Caggiano 2012).

While Don Magner was in his own Brooklyn shop on weekends, he was a familiar face during the week in the Spring Street galleries, making deals with the dealers. Very opinionated, he used to get irritated at Richard because he had *The Bee*, a weekly trade paper, visible to anyone who came in. Don didn't want the retail public to know what was up for sale at auctions, like Skinner in Massachusetts.

Richard knew his prices were too low and that's why all the dealers—Peter Smorto, Barton Kaplan, Michael Carey—would buy from him. He had no choice because there was so little retail foot traffic coming into his gallery.

The first person to sell Arts and Crafts furniture in Manhattan was Beth Cathers at Jordan-Volpe, then Michael Carey, and then Richard. (But there had always been Don Magner in Brooklyn.) Richard was in his first Spring Street space from 1977 to 1980, then he moved across the street to a much bigger space until 1987 when he opened an antiques shop in the

In 1979, before Richard discovered the Arts and Crafts at his 51 Spring Street shop

Woodstock, New York area, where he is still selling Arts and Crafts today.

In 1988, after he had moved to Woodstock, Richard heard about six tall-back spindle armchairs in Illinois some guy was selling out of his house. Tall-back spindle armchairs were very much in demand and had set records at auction, one going for $9,500. There were three other dealers also interested, so instead of fighting each other, they decided to get together. The odd but not so funny thing is that L. & J.G. Stickley would be reissuing the spindle reproduction chairs within months, so it took the four dealers years to sell the original chairs. The market had reached a point of saturation, so they made money on one or two of them, broke even on one or two, and took losses on a couple.

51 Spring Street, 1984

Michael Carey's gallery at 107 Spring Street, 1987

## Michael Carey American Arts and Crafts Furnishings 1980–1989

Even a year before Michael died, he had big plans, big visions. He always thought big. Nothing was insurmountable to him, ever.

One day in 1979, Michael Carey entered Jordan-Volpe and fell in love. He was familiar with the Arts and Crafts movement but didn't appreciate the furniture until he saw lighting and settings that emphasized the simplicity of form as perfect beauty and elegance.

Carey had moved to New York in 1977 from Texas. By 1980, he opened Michael Carey American Arts and Crafts Furnishings, selling general antiques in a nine-hundred square foot shop on the northwest corner of Spring and Mercer. It was packed full of antiques of many styles and periods, with nothing of any consequence. Most memorable were the narrow trails through the tall stacks of antiques, barely wide enough to squeeze through, but as crowded as it was, it was evident that Carey had a good eye.

The Jordan-Volpe Gallery had profoundly inspired and amazed Michael Carey by their sumptuous, but spare, presentation. His dream now was to specialize in Gustav

Derek Danton at an auction preview, 1989

Michael Carey on Spring Street, 1982

Stickley's work. His new partner, twenty-two-year-old Derek Danton, joined Carey in the gallery in 1980, helping him reduce the inventory and replace it with Arts and Crafts.

Pickers do not have their own retail space and find antiques that they sell to dealers at good prices. Picker-dealer relationships are important. In the early days before Michael Carey had developed relationships with pickers, he and Derek bought a lot of furniture from Don Treadway in Cincinnati, who was already entrenched in Arts and Crafts and maintained a good inventory. In January of 1980, Michael and Derek put every dime they had into Carey's dream. Danton remembers that they flew out to Cincinnati, loaded up a truck, and drove back in a blinding snowstorm—"Oh my god! I thought we were going to go down the side of the mountain, driving a truck full of Arts and Crafts furniture" (Danton 2012).

Slowly, it came together. They painted, built platforms, and did stenciling, but they consciously avoided giving the gallery too much of an Arts and Crafts look. One of the striking aspects of the furniture was that it did not need an Arts and Crafts environment to look good. Michael and Derek pushed the boundaries of presentation by placing the furniture in a very contemporary setting, with statement-screaming modern paintings on clean walls and furniture upholstered with modern fabrics and sumptuous leathers.

The personality of the owner is as important to the success of a gallery as the presentation and the selection of merchandise.

> *Michael was in your face if you wanted something. He was a bit of a Svengali in that respect because he had tremendous charm. And you could be easily seduced by his intensity and his passion. I used to sit back and watch him talk to clients, and he was just*

*amazing with the facial expressions, the intensity—they just ate it up, loved it. His entire body—you could feel it. He was a remarkable salesman of anything—anything at all. (Danton 2012)*

Michael Carey American Arts and Crafts Furnishings exhibited at the trendy Sanford Smith's Modernism show in the early 1980s at the Park Avenue Armory, a good venue for gaining well-to-do customers. Carey did some spectacular things. He was one of the first dealers to actually develop and carry out a concept for a booth. He and Derek covered the walls with fabric, hung lighting sconces, built platforms, and then brought in the furniture. They picked up a lot of business from the shows and continued doing them for years. The whole experience was also very enjoyable for them.

In 1982, they acquired a Texas client whose architect had suggested an Arts and Crafts décor for a ranch she was building in high country. She loved the look, and she and her husband acquired Greene and Greene fixtures by having Michael bid on them at auction.

According to Nancy McClelland, in charge of twentieth-century sales at Christie's in New York,

*"Frank Lloyd Wright and Greene & Greene material has appreciated at a greater rate than the other decorative arts." ... These pieces, designed to be handcrafted for specific commissions, were not simplified for industrial production, and they are extremely limited in number. Greene & Greene material comes from only a handful of houses. (Giovannini 1986)*

Danton describes this period as "working on all cyclinders. With that client, we were able to make an impact on the auction market." Celebrities became interested and many became their clients. Michael Carey was the main dealer to Barbra Streisand, Bruce Willis, Brad Pitt, and Richard Gere. Record auction prices for Arts and Crafts furniture inflated the market and raised the bar on what people expected and were willing to pay.

Window display

However, the dealing of the limited Greene & Greene pieces by galleries and auction houses created a controversy in the art and auction world.

*The high prices have encouraged the owners of some pieces to place them on the market. There have also been controversial instances of homeowners compromising houses by removing parts such as stained-glass windows. Miss McClelland says, however, "We never encourage clients to remove architectural elements from houses. If some house parts have been recently removed, there may be resistance to them at auction." Several beautifully crafted lamps with stained glass and inlaid silver, taken off the Blacker house [Greene & Greene in Pasadena], have been on sale for about six months at Michael Carey American Arts and Crafts, a New York store; prices start at $30,000. Preservationists voiced strong objections to the removal of the pieces, which were integral to the house. (Giovannini 1986)*

Gustav Stickley Eastwood chair; G.S. crib settle; rare Roycroft armchair

After two years of planning and hard work, Michael and Derek opened a second gallery in Austin in 1985. But it was a different concept from their Spring Street gallery. They mixed in even more contemporary pieces with design gems, from Josef Hoffmann through Stickley, on through deco and into mid-century. According to Danton, it was spectacular and unbelievable but, unfortunately, no one in Austin understood it at the time. "It was an incredible gallery, so beautiful, but people just didn't know what to think—'Is this a museum? Do we need to pay to get in?'"

They were moving furniture between New York and Austin every week, and Michael, who had tested positive for HIV, was getting sicker by that time. By 1987, Danton alone was handling the entire business of two galleries. Michael spent all his time in Texas, where he was originally from, and died in 1989. They had planned on moving their gallery to Mercer Street when the Spring Street lease expired.

*It was all on me, and it was a mess. Our lease was up so we had to move out of that space on Spring Street, and the place on Mercer was still under construction.*

*When it did open, the gallery on Mercer was remarkable, a beautiful gallery, a really, really beautiful space—with platforms—just a beautiful space. But Michael died in 1989, before it was finished. The construction on Mercer wasn't happening fast enough. All the inventory was stacked to the ceiling in my loft, so I took a temporary space on Wooster Street for a year or so, and then we opened on Mercer in late 1991. (Danton 2012)*

Danton closed the gallery in Austin in 1990 after Michael died. It was too much work and too much overhead. He had to move the inventory back to New York. Also in that year, Danton opened the Wooster Street shop. "Yeah, it was rough, really rough. We had that gallery going on, and then Tim Gleason who worked for me in Austin moved to New York, and when I opened the Mercer gallery in 1991, he worked for me."

David Rago liked Michael Carey.

*He opened around the corner from Tod [Jordan-Volpe], with furniture. Then Michael became a big deal because he was the real deal—I liked Michael a lot. I did a lot of business with him. I mean, we didn't always get along, but Michael was a straight shooter, a real straight talker. He did his stuff—Michael was a cool guy, and I appreciate him more than ever now. He was a decent guy who was struggling to make a living and could be irascible, but you knew what you were getting with him. (Rago 2011)*

Michael Carey's vision and energy helped detonate the Arts and Crafts in the early- to mid-1980s. Danton, the ever-steady hand, went on to pursue his own successful enterprises, and continues working very hard and enjoying life in his original SoHo loft.

u.l., clockwise: Dirk Van Erp lamp; Grueby vase on L. & J.G. pedestal; Michael at Austin, Texas gallery; Spring Street; rare early chest

Peter Smorto and
Robert Melita

## Peter-Roberts Antiques 1986–2001 (on Spring Street)

Six years after Michael Carey opened his gallery, Peter Smorto and Robert Melita opened Peter-Roberts Antiques, directly across Spring Street from him. Their gallery quickly developed a reputation as one of the important galleries in the fast-paced Arts and Crafts revival.

> People were just discovering the integrity and value of the works of Gustav Stickley, his brothers, and the other Arts and Crafts artists, and Robert, with a discerning eye and gracious manner, helped usher in a new era of discovery for this solid and dependable furniture style. (Smith 2005)

Roycroft collector, David Kornacki, visited the SoHo gallery district in 1992, remarking that

> it was sort of the peak of the Arts and Crafts mania and there were many galleries in SoHo: Gallery 532, Peter-Roberts Gallery, Michael Carey Gallery, and so on. I was amazed by the stuff I saw and thought that someday when I could buy real furniture I would love to get some. I remember being shocked at the sticker prices—I would turn over a Roycroft vase and it cost a $1,000. (Keane 2008)

Peter Smorto describes the ten-year period as a "solid wave" of good fortune, and points out that the Arts and Crafts revival lasted longer than the original movement, but he recalls the halcyon days of selling a Gustav Stickley settle for $15,000, saying that one would bring only $4,000 or $5,000 today (Smorto 2012).

At auction preview, early 1990s

*I think I sold a half dozen Gus 208 settles for $12,000
each. Back in the day, I was putting leather and
everything else on them. By the time you were done,
you had $7,000 in them.*

When their Spring Street lease was up, they had a huge
inventory of Arts and Crafts but the market had shriveled up.
Sales of Arts and Crafts had slowed in 1998 and by 1999
they began rethinking their mix of inventory because they
felt the revival was in its last stages. September 11 added
to their challenges.

In 2001, after fifteen years on Spring Street, Peter-Roberts
Antiques moved to 39 Bond Street. The gallery combined
mid-century furniture, especially George Nakashima, with
their extensive Arts and Crafts collection. Realizing that the
designs from that period were harmonious with the strict
discipline of Stickley, Peter-Roberts Antiques established
themselves as trend setters in the field and went to great
lengths to emphasize the harmony between the styles of the
beginning and the middle of the last century (Smith 2005).

Robert Melita was extremely handsome with penetrating
blue eyes. Sadly, he battled colon cancer for many years
and died at the age of fifty on November 9, 2005 (Smith
2005).

Peter Smorto, president of Peter-Roberts Antiques, still
owns and runs the business today and is one of the most important dealers buying and selling George Nakashima in the
current market.

*I was asked to vet the New York Winter Antiques
Show last year, and I was honored to do so. I vetted
all the Nakashima on display. When I went to the
opening night gala, I didn't recognize most of the
guests. It was a clientele with a more sophisticated
eye and taste level, and I got the impression these
people didn't go to your typical antiques show. They
were used to seeing very high-end material. This is
probably the most prestigious antiques show in
all of America.*

Robert Kaplan, Peter, and Robert

*The material at the winter show is of more importance than most other shows I've attended in the past. That and the quality of the material being offered at the Winter Antiques Show is more important than the price—price is not the main concern here, and this is what makes it the most important antiques show there is. Another thing that sets it apart is you have to be invited to do this show—you cannot go to them to buy a booth. This says everything about the integrity of the Winter Antiques Show. (Smorto 2012)*

Today, when people call Peter-Roberts inquiring about buying and selling Gustav Stickley pieces, he always refers them to Richard Caggiano at Partition Street Antiques (914-388-3607) in Woodstock, New York.

Peter-Roberts is alive and well today, thriving and working out of Long Island (Smorto 2012).

Robert DeFalco and friends in front of fireplace at Grove Park Inn. Robert standing, center, in white shirt

## Gallery 532

Robert DeFalco's Gallery 532 on Wooster Street opened on Amsterdam Avenue as an Arts and Crafts gallery in the 1970s, and it moved to SoHo in the 1980s. It was a 10,000 square foot gallery space with large display windows. It was in a vibrant neighborhood with coffee shops and stores, and around the corner from Michael Carey and Peter-Roberts galleries. Robert DeFalco presented significant exhibitions, such as Kindred Styles: The Arts and Crafts Furniture of Charles P. Limbert (1995) and Martin Brothers: An Exhibition (1995). Robert DeFalco was one of the major dealers in the early 1990s, serving celebrity clients such as Danny DeVito and Penny Marshall. DeFalco is a lighting specialist and is the foremost expert on Handel lamps. He has written two books on the subject, *Handel Lamps: Painted Shades and Glassware,* written with John Hibel (1986); and *Handel Metal Overlays* (1999).

## References

Caggiano, Rich. In phone interview with Jeffrey Preston. September 23, 2012.

Danton, Derek. Interview by Jeffrey Preston in New York, August 13, 2012.

Giovaninni, Joseph. 1986. Antiques. Early Wright Chairs Are Prized. *New York Times*. March 30, 1986. http://www.nytimes.com/1986/03/30/arts/antiques-early-wright-chairs-are-prized.html.

Keane, Maribeth. 2008. An Interview With Roycroft Arts and Crafts Metalwork Collector David Kornacki. CollectorsWeekly.com. October 1, 2008. http://www.collectorsweekly.com/articles/an-interview-with-roycroft-arts-and-crafts-metalwork-collector-david-kornacki.

Rago, David. Interview by authors in Lambertville, NJ, July 26, 2011.

Smith, David. "Robert N. Melita, 50, Of Peter-Roberts Antiques." *Antiques and the Arts Weekly*. November 22, 2005. http://antiquesandthearts.com/Antiques/TradeTalk/2005-11-22__09-33-27.html.

Smorto, Peter. In phone interview with Jeffrey Preston. September 16, 2012.

Richard Caggiano's card from his old Saugerties gallery; he moved Partition Street Antiques to nearby Woodstock, New York.

Richard Caggiano's L. & J.G. Stickley corner cupboard, c. 1907

Michael Carey and Derek Danton's gallery on Spring Street

Flyer for Kindred Styles
exhibition, produced by
Robert DeFalco, Gallery
532, SoHo, 1995

Robert A DeFalco

presents

# KINDRED STYLES

The Arts
and Crafts Furniture
of Charles
P. Limbert

## NEW YORK-CHICAGO

**Exhibition Catalogue Available**

128 Pages & 165 Photos

Text by A. Patricia Bartinique

Commentaries by Bruce Johnson, Robert Edwards, Ralph
Kylloe, Roy Pedersen, Jeffrey Preston, Robert A. DeFalco

A Comprehensive Study with Advertisements, Rare
Examples, Shopmarks, Original Factory Finish Formulas,
Examples of Hardware, Ephemera, Close-up Details.

$28.50 Postpaid 212-219-1327

**In New York: October 20-
November 19, 1995
Reception with Speakers
October 28, 6-9:30 PM at**

**Gallery 532 Soho**
117 Wooster Street
New York, N Y 10012

Limbert lamp and Limbert octagonal library table from
Gallery 532's Limbert exhibition

above: Kitty Turgeon on her porch;

r: woodblock of Kitty Turgeon by
Laura Wilder (www.laurawilder.com)

# 13. The Roycroft Renaissance

*I am an Innkeeper. My role is to greet the guests of this century, to make them comfortable, to hear their stories and tell them ours; to impart the spirit of all things Roycroft ... inspired by tradition, alive with history ... so that our guests may leave our little haven, go back out to the world, and encourage others to make the century old Little Journey to East Aurora, New York.*

*– Martha B. Augat, Innkeeper, The Roycroft Inn*

Two photos of Elbert Hubbard

There are fierce spirits at work in East Aurora, but the heart of Roycroft is the spirit embodied by the Roycroft Inn, delicate yet powerful.

Many people know of Elbert Hubbard and his tragic demise on the sinking Lusitania with his muse, Alice in 1915. His son Bert took the lead at Roycroft but was not the promoter his father had been. He made a genuine effort to keep the Roycroft campus viable, but the Great Depression and war took their toll on the community.

1938 was the year things died on the Roycroft campus (Hamilton). Production stopped and jobs disappeared. Fifty years later the decrepit Roycroft Inn, neglected and abused, had a chance to become something close to what it originally was. It was closed for major renovations for ten years.

above: Entrance to the Roycroft Inn; r: A historic tribute to celebrate the 1995 reopening of a National Historic Landmark

Martha Augat, Innkeeper

The Roycroft campus was placed on the National Register of Historic Places in 1986, due to the persistent efforts and hard work of Kitty Turgeon and Robert Rust. They had applied ten years earlier, but the government office had misplaced their application (Turgeon 2012).

The beautiful Roycroft Inn reopened in 1995, just after Martha Augat became innkeeper. Martha is calm and even tempered, very important qualities in the vortex of East Aurora. She is diligent yet sees the overall scheme of things. Perhaps most importantly, she infuses the atmosphere with positive feelings about her work, the community, and the Roycroft Inn.

The porch (Larkin Room) overlooks the beautiful courtyard gardens of the Roycroft Inn

Boice Lydell in Bungle House; r.: Program insert for Roycroft Campus Arts and Crafts Conference, 1984

Driven by deep passion for the Roycroft culture and descended from two original Roycrofters, Boice Lydell has a grand vision—to have a working museum with interpreters, in the style of Old Sturbridge Village—artisans who would dress and act the part of original Roycrofters. Boice has had large ambitions before. As a teenager, he decided to have the largest Roycroft collection in the world, and he probably does. He began collecting in the 1960s. Not only does he have extensive collections of metalwork, jewelry, books, and ephemera, but he owns several buildings on the Roycroft campus (Lydell 2012).

The idea to hold an Arts and Crafts conference with expert speakers and an antiques show originated with Boice at the Roycroft campus. He presented his idea to David Rago, John Toomey, Don Magner, and Jordan-Volpe, and interested the dealers in being involved in an antiques show. With the help of Kitty Turgeon, Robert Rust, and Linda Hubbard Brady, he held the conferences for three consecutive years, 1984–1986. Because the inn closed for renovations, Bruce Johnson was able to take Boice's idea to the Grove Park Inn in Asheville, North Carolina for its first 1988 Arts and Crafts conference.

Clockwise from u.l.: Program insert for Roycroft Campus Arts and Crafts Conference, 1984; Boice Lydell; Elbert Hubbard; Boice in Bungle House; Detail of Roycroft bookcase copper hinge

Photos from Roycroft Campus Arts and Crafts
Conference, 1984

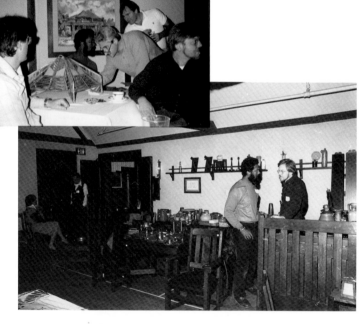

Kitty Turgeon on porch of her home,
Fournier House

Roycroft hanging light fixture, c. 1912

Elbert Hubbard

German students with statue of Elbert Hubbard (Kitty Turgeon in dark dress, front; Linda Hubbard Brady, center front); Roycroft mark

Kitty Turgeon is the spirit of the Roycroft campus. She moved to East Aurora in 1971, and she speaks of Elbert and Alice as though they are family members. She senses them. "I always wonder what Elbert would do, or what Alice would do—I feel Alice very strongly over there. There'd be no Roycroft without her" (Turgeon 2012). Kitty has worn many hats as a Roycrofter. She owned the inn at one point and was innkeeper.

Many people on the Roycroft campus have worked tirelessly to revive it. Buildings have been restored, Kitty and her former husband, Robert Rust, founded the nonprofit Roycrofters-At-Large Association in 1976, which certifies artisans to use the Roycroft name—the "RR" (Hamilton). This label of distinction and excellence promotes the renaissance, or revival, by creating standards and sanctioning contemporary craftsworkers who consistently meet those standards in their work. This is significant in the future success of the Roycroft artisans as a whole. It adds legitimacy to their work.

Many books could be written on the Roycroft Renaissance because so many individuals have invested themselves in the revival of the Roycroft campus and way of life. And the campus is on the ascendancy. Charles F. Hamilton is the historian and has written numerous articles and books on Roycroft. He is one of many who dedicate themselves to a better life through community and the Roycroft ideals as taught by Elbert Hubbard.

Elbert Hubbard; Courtesy of Linda Hubbard Brady

## References

Augat, Martha B. 2005. "The Roycroft Inn 1905–2005: Celebrating a Century of Hospitality." *East Aurora and Beyond: 2005 Visitor's Guide*. East Aurora, New York: The Greater East Aurora Chamber of Commerce, Inc. www.eanycc.com.

Brady, Linda Hubbard. In interview with authors. East Aurora, New York. September 20, 2011.

Hamilton, Charles, Kitty Turgeon, and Robert Rust. Buffalo, New York: "History and Renaissance of the Roycroft Movement" Published by Buffalo & Erie County Historical Society.

Lydell, Boice. In interview with authors. East Aurora, New York. March 17, 2012.

Turgeon, Kitty. In interview with authors. East Aurora, New York. March 18, 2012.

Linda Hubbard Brady, granddaughter of Elbert Hubbard, has been involved for decades in the Roycroft Renaissance. Since childhood, she has devoted herself to helping others and preserving the memory of Elbert Hubbard.

ERECTED JULY 2 1916
TO THE MEMORY OF
ELBERT AND ALICE HUBBARD

ELBERT HUBBARD
BORN JUNE 19 1856
BLOOMINGTON ILLINOIS

ALICE HUBBARD
BORN JUNE 7 1861
WALES CENTER NEW YORK

BOTH WERE LOST IN THE IRISH SEA
WITH THE LUSITANIA MAY 7 1915

THEY LIVED AND DIED FEARLESSLY

Gustav Stickley 1902 sideboard; oak, iron; 80" x 70▯" x 25½"; photo courtesy of Dallas Museum

# 14. Ted Lytwyn – Cara Corbo

*Ted Lytwyn and Cara Corbo collect Arts and Crafts out of pure love for the period. They both have successful careers completely unrelated to the arts and live with pottery and furniture collections that reflect sophistication and focus. Initially Ted and Cara wanted their collections to represent each important artist of the Arts and Crafts movement but as they developed their tastes, they chose instead to focus on a few artists.*

Cara Corbo in 1970

They discovered their first Arts and Crafts furniture at a country auction in 1979 and returned home with an L. & J.G. Stickley settle, a rocker, and a morris chair. Their tastes have since evolved. Cara's passion is for early Gustav Stickley because it is so tactile and sensual. She experiences the smell, the feel, the look of the wood, and the very simple lines as pure pleasure.

Ted collects metalwork and American art pottery. His interest in accessorizing began early when they found a pair of Roycroft hammered-copper bookends and noticed how well they complemented the dark furniture. At the time they began collecting, copper pieces were very affordable. Roycroft was often available at flea markets, and it was usually less than fifty dollars.

Ted likes knowing about the individual coppersmith who handcrafted the piece and for that reason generally prefers Roycroft copper over Stickley. It is unknown which artisans made Stickley metalwork. Ted and Cara go for the best works in their collecting and sometimes sell a few lesser pieces to subsidize the cost of a better one. To Ted and Cara, metal evokes the spirit of the Arts and Crafts more than any medium:

*To us, the metal is the best and basic expression of the Arts and Crafts. A craftsperson with a piece of copper, with a hammer, ideally can create a masterpiece. Copper is [was] inexpensive and available, and the very fact that someone put their energy into it makes it a personal piece of art. (Rago 1998, 72)*

Green Pewabic vase, 1903

1903 photo of Mary Chase Stratton making exact vase pictured at left

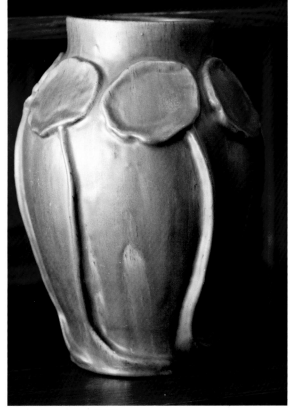

Pewabic vase, c. 1903

Pewabic vase, c. 1903

Ted Lytwyn and Cara Corbo in living room

Photo of Jane Byrd Whitehead and son, Peter, Byrdcliffe Colony; photo by Eva Watson-Schutze, c. 1905

Ted considers metalwork to be masculine because it takes a hammer and strength to create, while pottery is more feminine and requires more sensitivity in handling. He enjoys balancing his collections between the strength of metalwork and the fragility of pottery (Rago 1998, 72).

A piece of pottery initiates a journey for Ted as he responds viscerally to its shape, color, texture, and glaze. He researches everything he can about the potter's history, personality, desires, and accomplishments, and all these discoveries create a context for the piece, making it come alive through the life of the potter, whose spirit permeates the clay and is just under the skin of the glaze.

Ted collects Pewabic and Walley potteries as well as the works of Leon Volkmar and Theophilus Brouwer, Jr. The Pewabic glazes, in particular, enthrall Ted because the potter's fire creates the iridescent qualities and sensual drips yet, at the same time, the potter maintains control.

Roycroft mugs, one signed by Karl Kipp,
copper and German silver with jade,1910

The potter becomes three dimensional for Ted through companion pieces or ephemera such as photographs or letters. Whatever fleshes out the artist appeals to Ted's collecting instinct. For example, above his two-door bookcase displaying his Leon Volkmar pottery hangs the artist's framed bronze medal award from the 1937 Paris International Exhibition (Cathers 1999, 159).

Ted and Cara have had some interesting things happen through their years of collecting. They were constantly looking at books and magazines on the Arts and Crafts, and Gustav Stickley's magazine, *The Craftsman*, was a tremendous resource with detailed and precise illustrations and photos. They saw a fumed oak sideboard with wrought iron hinges by the United Crafts in *The Craftsman* of May 1902, showing Russian copper vessels in the overhead cupboard. They both fell in love with the piece.

In October 1985, Ted was at Rosalie Berberian's ARK Antiques auction. She held auctions in a motel in Connecticut and sold pottery first, then sold pieces of Stickley or other Arts and Crafts furniture. Ted recognized the sideboard immediately, even though it was only the top half of the cupboard. He purchased it at the auction, tied it to the top of his 1980 Volkswagon Jetta—uncovered—and he drove it from Connecticut to their home in New Jersey where they placed it on the floor of their living room as a great display piece for their pottery collection. They used it that way for five years.

About ten years later, in the mid-90s, Ted got a call from a dealer who had heard that he and Cara owned the top of this piece. He and a partner had bought the bottom of one of these pieces at an auction held out of a barn in Maine. They wanted to buy the top from Ted because they wanted to approach Barbra Streisand with the piece and sell it to her.

There was no way Ted was going to sell the top. He expressed his desire to buy the bottom, and they went back and forth like that for months. They wanted to come and measure the piece so they could have a top made and Ted said, "Certainly, go ahead. But first of all, I doubt anyone could make that—the joinery is so complicated—and even if you could find someone that could make that top, try finding a buyer for a half-remade sideboard. The dealer went to Ted's and faked measuring it—still hoping to get the piece from Ted.

The dealers offered to partner with Ted on the piece. He was offered a good amount money for it. He kept telling them he was not selling it. He wanted the bottom half, and finally they understood. The two pieces were joined on December 12, 1990.

Years later Ted found out that it was a prominent auction person who had let the dealers know that the top piece had been sold at Rosalie's auction. The dealers had gone to Rosalie and asked her to go through her records to find out

Pewabic vase, silver drip over black, 1918

Ted, in front of their sideboard, looking at photograph of their sideboard in Dallas Museum Gustav Stickley exhibition catalog of 2010

1901 Gustav Stickley sideboard with Lytwyn-Corbo collection of Pewabic pottery and Roycroft/Karl Kipp metalware

Karl Kipp copper trademark plaque, which was hanging in his workshop

Early 1902 Gustav Stickley library table with arched cross-stretchers, Cara Corbo's favorite, with Pewabic pottery

who purchased it. She found the records in her attic and let them know it was Ted who had bought the top. That is how Ted was contacted, and he ended up with one complete rare and beautiful piece. When the pieces were joined, there were marks on the wood indicating, without a doubt, that this particular top originally went with this particular bottom.

Another satisfying story is about Ted's Karl Kipp collection. He saw a plaque from the Kipp workshop pictured in *The Bee* with a little ad that it was going to be sold. Ted was involved in phone bidding on the piece and at some point he gave up and stopped bidding. He deeply regretted it. It haunted him for years. He had one of the better collections in existence, and this would have topped the collection off. It was a very rare piece.

Years later, Ted was visiting Geoffrey Diner in his Washington, DC gallery, and there in his office on top of a bookcase was a little piece of round copper protruding, and it was the

Karl Kipp plaque. He mentioned it to Jeffrey and was told he'd been trying to sell it for a couple of years. The piece now resides with other fine pieces of Kipp's work in Millburn, New Jersey, and Ted learned something important about building an outstanding collection. Go for the best and seize the opportunity to buy a fine piece when it's there.

Ted Lytwyn and Cara Corbo are serious and important collectors. They pursue what they want relentlessly. In addition to their collecting, they have been very involved over the years with Craftsman Farms, serving on the board and assisting in a variety of ways. From its inception, they have supported the Farms through their membership and their generous gifts of furniture and decorative arts. Equally important has been their expertise, clear thinking, and unselfish consideration of the Farms' best interests. Ted and Cara radiate a joy for the Arts and Crafts and further the mission of Craftsman Farms by their quiet actions.

above and r.: Volkmar pottery collection

Bronze medal awarded to Leon Volkmar in the 1937 International Exposition in Paris for tall vase on right in upper right photo

*Ted in living room*

### References

Cathers, David and Alexander Vertikoff. 1999. *Stickley Style: Arts and Crafts Homes in the Craftsman Tradition*. New York: Simon & Schuster.

Corbo, Cara, and Ted Lytwyn. In interview with Jeffrey Preston. Milford, New Jersey. November12, 2011.

Kahn, Eve M. 2004. "Past Perfect." *Style 1900*. Summer/Fall 2004. 17(3): 38-43.

Lytwyn, Ted. In interview with Jeffrey Preston. Milford, New Jersey. October 7, 2012.

Margolies, Jane. 2012. "Passionate About Pewabic." *Style 1900*. 25(2): 66-68.

Rago, David. 1998. "Collecting Metal: A Visit to the Home of Ted Lytwyn and his Wife, Cara Corbo." *Style 1900*. 11(2): 72-73.

Cara and Ted in the Caribbean

above: Ed and Kathy in their dining room; r.: Ed and Kathy enjoying their Arts and Crafts style kitchen addition

# 15. Ed and Kathy Friedman

*Ed and Kathy Friedman are warm and engaging and their home reflects the same. They live with their early Gustav Stickley collection in a comfortable relationship, without fussiness or apprehension about using the things they have, and they love to talk about the Arts and Crafts.*

Ed and Kathy Friedman were in Gloucester, Massachusetts in 1975 when they found an old black table in a basement for $40. With the energy of newlyweds, they spent the next week refinishing it, removing the black color. Ed liked building furniture, but they knew little about refinishing and less about Arts and Crafts furniture. It was an early Gustav Stickley table made of chestnut with massive flaring cross stretchers and a faceted vertical dowel, or finial, pinning them at the center. It was their first piece of Arts and Crafts. Kathy remembers feeling "totally hooked. We got the table refinished in a week and got to see how it was put together—it was like eating steak." They were so impressed with its beauty and construction that they wanted more.

After buying that table, Ed and Kathy were on a hunt for Arts and Crafts and any information they could find. Ed went to the library at Columbia University to find *The Craftsman* in the stacks, and they were all stolen. The only thing anyone had were the original references—*The Craftsman*, the catalogs, or the Roycroft publications. This was before Stephen Gray's reprints. Ed had been trading photocopies of the catalogs. "I had a 1905 and someone had a 1902, so you'd trade. You walk around the flea market and pull out your papers."

In January 1977, *New York Magazine* published "Move Over, Deco—Here Comes Mission," highlighting Jordan-Volpe, a New York Arts and Crafts gallery. After seeing the article, Kathy remembers they "became obsessed—I mean, for me, it was like zero to sixty miles an hour in one second."

Auctions became their weekend entertainment, running all over the Hudson Valley. They were two people feeding off each other's obsession. The timing was good because it was early on and they were able to acquire a lot of furniture and other things.

They learned important things about collecting from Elaine Dillof, whose collection of early Gustav Stickley impressed them. Don Magner, the earliest Arts and Crafts dealer, became a close friend and freely shared his vast knowledge and offered guidance.

Kathy was studying at Columbia University dental school and Ed was a textbook editor for Random House (Cathers 2004). In the course of looking for their own collection, Ed started buying additional things to sell. For the first time in his life, he felt he was capitalizing on his knowledge. He started going to Brimfield, where he sold David Rago his first piece of Stickley furniture.

If not the most important aspect, the finish is at least as important as anything else about a piece of furniture to the Friedmans. To Ed, the finish is a tactile thing and not visual. To know the finish, he has to touch it. As they touched the finishes and learned the furniture of early Gustav Stickley, they realized that, as beautiful and as interesting as the gallery was, almost every single piece of furniture for sale in Jordan-Volpe was refinished. They had become discriminating collectors.

In 1978, Ed and Kathy moved to Millbrook in Duchess County, New York, an hour north of the city. Kathy was working her first job after dental school, and Ed was busy buying and selling Arts and Crafts.

The Friedmans moved to Pittsburgh in 1980. Kathy practiced dentistry and Ed studied medicine. They bought and restored an Arts and Crafts house in the charming neighborhood of Squirrel Hill.

It was at the Roycroft Inn in 1981 that the Friedmans and Stephen Gray met (Cathers 2004). They became close and engaged in long conversations with him about Gustav Stickley, original finishes, the philosophy behind the Arts and Crafts movement, and anything else that could possibly come up in conversation relative to the early twentieth century movement. They discussed and turned over every aspect and dissected shreds of information. They loved every minute of it. Stephen taught Ed and Kathy a great deal about collecting. He mentored them as collectors and insisted they focus and eliminate anything that did not further the early Gustav Stick-

ley collection they were creating. He often guided them in their selections and sometimes sold them pieces from his own collection. Their collection is exquisite, and they give him a lot of credit for it.

The Friedmans were very close to Stephen, and their children grew up skiing with him. Kathy jokes that when they would stay with him, "Steve was a great $1,000 a night hotel," because by the time she woke up, Ed had bought a piece of pottery or something from Stephen for thousands of dollars.

There were many years when Ed and Kathy would regularly call their friends in the business. They were extremely close with Stephen Gray. Ed would phone him to ask what was going on, and he would tell Ed all about the latest auction preview. Sometimes Ed called Robert Kaplan, another friend. These relationships, and the catalogs, kept the Friedmans connected to the Arts and Crafts world from Pittsburgh.

It was a long drive to New York, but they attended many of Christie's auctions, making every effort to get there. Sometimes Ed flew into the city. When David Rago moved his auction to Lambertville, New Jersey in 1996, the drive there was two hours shorter than the drive into Manhattan.

There were lots of things to find in Pittsburgh. They found a Stickley double-door bookcase the same day Ed was to take an important exam. "You could tell what my priorities were. [laughter] I think you could say that physiology exam

above: Ed displaying Gustav Stickley No. 376 oil lamp with No. 668 shade

o.p.: The Friedmans in conversation

was a resounding failure. [laughter and more laughter] But I had a double-door Gus case." It was early enough in the revival that when Ed saw something at an antiques shop, he could go back a month later and it would still be there.

In the 1990s, the price for good early pieces by Stickley were out of reach for the Friedmans, so they looked for another "underserved" market. They always liked the hunt, the adventure, and the learning. In the hunt for the object, the idea of getting something of value, when no one else cares about it, is very appealing. They discovered an untapped resource—early twentieth-century paintings by Pittsburgh painters. Against the admonishments of Stephen Gray, they began looking for the best paintings. Stephen warned them that paintings would be too expensive and they didn't know enough about paintings. They have paintings by Gorson, Hyette, and Walter, which were reasonably priced and quite beautiful. The Friedmans also began buying more lamps and metalwork in the 1990s, and bought from Cathers and Dembrosky. Robert Kaplan, who is very knowledgeable, has been a good friend to Ed and Kathy over the years and has offered sound collecting advice.

Kathy refinishing first piece of Gustav Stickley

One thing Ed and Kathy learned early as collectors was to go for the best piece, even if it meant feeling some financial pain. The Friedmans were always in debt to the collection, but feel they were in the right place at the right time. In a different time, they wouldn't have been able to do it. They attribute the success of their collection to the combination of luck and persistence on their part. As mature collectors with an exquisite early Gus collection, they buy very little now but enjoy the experience of just being at auction.

Kathy now has her own practice, which their daughter, also a dentist, has recently joined. Ed teaches psychiatry at the University of Pittsburgh School of Medicine in addition to having a private practice. They continue attending the Grove Park Inn Arts and Crafts Conference each year.

**References**

Cathers, David. 2004. "With a Little Help from Their Friends." *American Bungalow* 43 (Fall). http://www.americanbungalow. com/category/magazine/magazine-articles/issue-43.

Friedman, Ed. In phone interview with Judith Budwig. April 2, 2012.

Friedman, Ed and Kathy. In interview with authors. July 14, 2012.

Refinished table

*Living Room by The United Crafts*

Table in April 1902 *The Craftsman* magazine

Four-part tile panel with peacock, 20³/₄" square, signed "Frederick H. Rhead, U.C. 1910" sold at Rago Auction's Early 20th Century sale, October 2012. ("U.C." is University City, Missouri). The estimate was $35,000–$45,000. It sold for $637,500, a record price for any American Arts and Crafts object

# 16. David Rago and Suzanne Perrault

*His father was an artist, and one of his grandparents worked at a pottery factory in Trenton, New Jersey, but David Rago knew nothing about art pottery until his parents began collecting it when he was sixteen. He started selling it in the summer of 1972 as a teenager at the flea market in Lambertville. Today, David Rago and Suzanne Perrault, his stunning wife, are among the foremost experts on American art pottery and hold auctions in an old hosiery factory in Lambertville, New Jersey, reminiscent of the Crystal Palace of the 1851 Great Exposition in London.*

Suzanne Perrault and David Rago, photo courtesy Benoit Cortet

Upon his first trip in 1975 to the famous Massachusetts flea market in Brimfield, Rago "thought I had died and gone to heaven" (Rago 2011). He met a lot of dealers at Brimfield. "It was an amazing time to be in the business, 'cause you could find stuff—but it wasn't worth anything" (Rago 2011). The Arts and Crafts revival had begun a few years earlier, so there was a fledgling market, yet pieces were still affordable—he could buy a pot for five dollars and sell it for ten. During his third year at Brimfield, he found 174 pieces of pottery in three days. On his way back to New Jersey, Rago would usually stop in New Haven to visit his good friend, Rosalie Berberian, spending hours in conversation with her. In addition to the lively conversation, she usually bought some of the pieces he had just found.

Although Bob Ellison, Martin Eidelberg, and some others taught Rago a lot in his early years, and they were very close, Rosalie Berberian, a collector, scholar, and dealer, was perhaps his most important mentor because she "defined an ethical pattern for me in the mid-seventies that I live by today" (Rago 2011). Her influence was particularly powerful because she supported him and always shared his joy in success, rather than feeling threatened.

David Rago learned from his mistakes. He laughingly remembers an article he wrote a very long time ago on Grueby for *Antique Trader*. "I think I thought I was a museum curator,

Painting by David Rago's father, Dominic Rago, 1992

below, David Rago at Collectors' Spectrum, his auction in the Meadowlands, c. 1983; l.l.: David Rago selling pottery in the 1970s; bottom: David Rago up against the wall at the Puck Building

and I got such grief for it—people were asking who I thought I was" (Rago 2011). Rosalie advised him to "just write like Dave—you're not a museum curator" (Rago 2011).

George Ohr, the eccentric Biloxi potter, was not unknown to Rago at that time, but he didn't understand or appreciate his works, and it was difficult to sell Ohr pieces because a market did not exist in the early 1970s. Ohr pots did come Rago's way from time to time, and Berberian had some outstanding pieces that Rago became more familiar with every time he visited her. Over time, Rago developed a profound appreciation and love of George Ohr's aesthetic.

As his appreciation for Ohr grew, Rago started buying his pots from a dealer at the Lambertville flea market, and in 1975 he paid three thousand dollars to buy twenty pieces of Ohr from her. This was a substantial amount of money at that time, especially for him, because it was his life savings. To his horror, he discovered that while the pieces were genuine, they had no value because not a single one had an original Ohr glaze. He lost everything. It took him five years before he could bring himself to buy another.

To develop a reputation as a pottery dealer in the Northeast and build a clientele, Rago became active in antiques and pottery shows and aware of the importance of publicity. In May 1979, the *New York Times* featured him, an exhibitor, in an article on an antiques show in Atlantic City. In the article, David Rago gave a very brief history of American art pottery, which he maintained was inspired by the Philadelphia Centennial Exposition in 1876 (Darrow 1979). Thus he gained legitimacy by being written about and showing his knowledge of both the history and the production of American art pottery to a large and important readership.

An article in the *New York Times* in 1980 covered a pottery show in Secaucus, New Jersey. This article mentioned eight different pottery dealers, six covered in a total of three short paragraphs. One established Princeton dealer received nine paragraphs, while David Rago—his wares, and direct quotes by him about George Ohr and Saturday Evening Girls—also spanned nine paragraphs (Darrow 1980). David was engaging, knowledgeable, and, even in his mid-twenties, gaining valuable publicity in one of the nation's foremost newspapers.

While Rago was developing a reputation as a smart, discerning, and resourceful pottery dealer, his talents did not escape the notice of Tod Volpe. In 1981, Rago became *the* pottery supplier to the very influential and upscale Jordan-Volpe Gallery, which had opened in SoHo in 1976 and specialized in American Arts and Crafts. Rago had an expert eye and the experience of one much older, and he could find beautiful pieces in the midst of the ordinary and banal. For two-and-a-half years he supplied the gallery with pots, much of them from the hands of gifted potters who were virtually unknown to the market at the time (Volpe 2011).

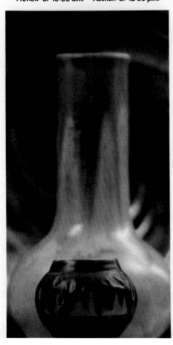

**David Rago - Collector's Spectrum**

Saturday, December 8, 1984 · Meadowlands Hilton Hotel, Meadowlands, New Jersey
Preview at 10:00 a.m. · Auction at 12:00 p.m.

DAVID RAGO—COLLECTOR'S SPECTRUM
PUCK BUILDING, NEW YORK, NEW YORK

SUNDAY, MAY 31, 1987

PREVIEW: 8:00 A.M.    SALE: 10:30 A.M.

But Rago wanted to move on to something more meaningful, so he and Jordan-Volpe parted ways in November of 1983. The constant exhibitions, publications, and other activities of the Jordan-Volpe Gallery had provided an important business model for Rago. He noted that the benefits of educating the client base resulted in the business looking better, more publicity, and increased sales—good for business all around. He remembered these lessons in his future endeavors.

Rather than becoming an independent dealer again, Rago, characteristically, moved to the next step of putting together an auction (Rago 2011). It happened quickly. His first auctions were held jointly with Boice Lydell, a respected Roycroft expert, and took place in 1984 at the Meadowlands Hilton in New Jersey (Lydell 2012), and then moved to the East Side Marriott. But it was at the Puck Building that Rago's auctions came of age. The Puck auctions introduced many people to the Arts and Crafts movement in the mid- to late-eighties, and offered some people their first platform both to learn about the objects being sold and to meet others with similar interests. David Smith, managing editor of *Antiques and the Arts Weekly* ("The Bee"), said that his "favorite times were when Dave was running auctions in the Puck Building. It was really cool" (Smith 2012). And Art Accardi, well-known graphic designer and artist, said he didn't meet anybody until he "started going to auctions in 1985 at the Puck building" (Accardi 2011). The importance of bringing people together cannot be overstated. It was a highly accessible Arts and Crafts auction in the heart of Manhattan.

With his warehouse located in Trenton, holding these auctions in New York was very costly and a true test of endurance. The day before the auction, Rago and his crew would load up two 24-foot trucks and two vans. Early the next morning they would drive into the city to set up for the preview and then the auction; next they cataloged everything left—pieces sold to absentee and phone bidders and bidders who couldn't take their purchases with them, and lots that didn't sell. Then they repacked the truck, drove back to Trenton, and unloaded everything back into their warehouse—all this in one very long day (Perrault 2011).

u.l. and u.r.: Auction catalog covers

below: Rago shooting photos for next auction

David Rago being interviewed for the NBC evening news.

That Rago did this for eleven years is testament to his ambition, determination, and perseverance. Rago's final "Arts and Crafts in New York" auction was in December 1995 (Rago 1995).

After these eleven years of the Trenton-New York trek, Rago took the gamble of moving his auction out of New York and into an old factory he had bought on Main Street in Lambertville, establishing David Rago Auctions, Inc., in 1995. Suzanne Perrault acknowledged that they had wanted to buy a building sooner, but they feared nobody would come, especially from New York City. But they did come—and from all over (Perrault 2011). Rago's auctions were becoming bigger and more sophisticated, paralleling the growing popularity of all things Arts and Crafts. Rago's first two sales, June 1 and June 8, 1996, brought in over one million dollars, and after the second sale, Rago claimed it was his best ever (Solis-Cohen 1996).

Having a base meant something more than just physical space. It also meant being perceived in a new way by collectors, consignors, and the press. Their auction now had a home, and that changed everything. This old hosiery factory, nicknamed the Crystal Palace, needed work. The windows were all broken, and the building was so enormous, they couldn't fill it. But all of a sudden they were "respected as adults and taken more seriously. It was one of those quantum leaps" (Rago 2011). People turned out in greater numbers from all over. A lot of people who wouldn't go into New York City would go to Lambertville.

In the midst of his New York City auction years, Rago had also been creating a new publication that was first issued in October 1986 as an eight-page black-and-white newsletter with photos. Rago directly credits his production of the *Arts and Crafts Quarterly* to Bruce Johnson's stated belief that if you don't give back, there won't be anything left to take (Rago 2011). As the Arts and Crafts revival was on the upswing by 1988, the *Arts and Crafts Quarterly* expanded its format to become a 40-page publication with a cover in color. It was the first glossy magazine devoted strictly to the revival of the American Arts and Crafts (Johnson 2012).

# III ARTS & CRAFTS QUARTERLY III

VOLUME I, ISSUE I, OCTOBER 1986

## THE LAST RIDE

Jean-François Vilain

The last decade of the century in America witnessed a revival of the art of bookmaking, the direct result of the influence of William Morris.[1] His ideals, embodied in the books from his Kelmscott Press, ignited a new generation of enthusiastic and idealistic printers, both in England and in America. These young men were inspired to make books with a soul in which paper, typeface, decorations, printing and binding combined to create a harmonious whole. Profit was not the principal motive: Reverence for the book as art object as well as repository and messenger of ideas was the major concern. The bookmaking revolution began in Boston (Copeland and Day), Portland, ME, (Mosher) and Chicago (Stone and Kimball), (Way and Williams) at about the same time and its message was carried by the *American Printer*, the major organ of the book industry. Private Presses arose across the country, installed in basements, in attics and in barns. Most were run by men longer on ideals than on business savvy and few ever made a profit. The Roycroft Press was an exception; founded in 1895 and established in East Aurora, NY, by Elbert Hubbard, it was a vital component of the renaissance of the art of the book in

America. Although its output degenerated after Hubbard's death in 1915, many books are beautifully designed and assure the press of a place in the history of the book. One of the most acclaimed of these books, Robert Browning's *The Last Ride* was published in 1900.

Hubbard was influenced by medieval craftsmen and by William Morris: He visited Kelmscott in 1895 and dates his interest in fine printing from that visit, though it is not at all clear that he actually met Morris.[2] A successful, retired businessman, he set out to publish well-crafted books that would sell well, attracting talented artists and craftspeople. Under his mercurial direction, the Roycroft community eventually numbered in the hundreds and expanded into other crafts: metalwork, leatherwork and furniture. The Press was, however, the core of the community since one of its major functions was the

monthly publication of three different magazines (the *Little Journeys, The Philistine* and *The Fra*) subscribed to by thousands of readers.[3] These magazines carried paid advertisements (most written by Hubbard) that sustained the community's financial security. Their design and typography reflect the various influences at work in the post-morrisian renaissance. The magazines also carried advertisements for the Roycroft books and therefore, fostered an awareness of the art of the book among people who had never heard of William Morris.

The Roycroft artists are well-known to those interested in the Arts and Crafts Period: Dard Hunter, a polymath whose designs are emblematic of the movement;[4] William W. Denslow, who went on to illustrate the Oz books;[5] Louis Kinder, one of the great book-binders to work in America;[6] Frank B. Rae, who later worked at the Blue Sky Press in Chicago and eventually founded his own company, the Alwil Press;[7] Jerome Conner, sculptor and designer, George Schneider, who did the frontispiece etchings for the Little Journeys and Samuel Warner, designer of *The Last Ride*.

Warner was a solid and prolific journeyman who created many book designs for Roycroft betw[...]

above: David Rago's first issue of the Arts and Crafts Quarterly, 1986; two other quarterlies showing evolution of magazine

David Rago with monumental Grueby vase, early 1990s

The first newly expanded full-length issue of *Arts and Crafts Quarterly* in the spring of 1988, included the well-timed article by Bruce Johnson, "Grove Park Inn—Mountain Masterpiece," recounting the history of the inn with photos. This was issued prior to Johnson's founding the Arts and Crafts Conference in 1988 at the inn in Asheville, North Carolina (Johnson 1988).

In 1986, the same year Rago's *Arts and Crafts Quarterly* began, Suzanne Perrault, a young French Canadian woman with a background in English literature and experience as a model, was training to be a gallerist for Barton Kaplan's New York gallery on Broadway. He was selling Arts and Crafts and rustic furniture, as well as paintings. He taught her about what he was selling—the Stickleys, Limbert, and Ohr. By then, David Rago had developed an interest in George Ohr and would visit the gallery from time to time to see what pots were newly offered.

One year into her job, Perrault arrived at work one day to find the window shades drawn. Barton, who was 39 years old, had died suddenly from arrhythmia. He was to have been married in ten days. The entire Barton family and the gallery staff were in shock. Rago was a help to the gallery during this difficult time. Perrault eventually went to work for his auctions, which were becoming busier and busier.

Rago and Perrault became friends, and he helped her set up a gallery in a small space in Lambertville in 1991. He suggested she pick one thing that really interested her and make that her specialty—she should look at it, learn about it, study it, and write and talk about it. She had an interest in tiles, inspired by the New York subway tiles, and began holding an annual show, gathering a collection of art tiles from various consignors. Perrault would document and photograph them, and produce a printed catalog. She enjoyed

the high drama of the show, with people waiting outside, competing to rush in and put tags on the tiles they wanted.

Perrault's gallery occupied one-half of the Lambertville space, and the other half housed both the publications staff of the *Arts and Crafts Quarterly* and the office staff of Rago auctions. Every inch was accounted for in that close space.

In 1994, *Arts and Crafts Quarterly* changed its name to *Style 1900*, giving the title a streamlined sound with a smack of modern, while distinguishing it from the plethora of books, articles, events, and retail shops using "Arts and Crafts" in the name. In the same year, in addition to running his New York auctions, Rago organized the exhibit, *After the Fire: The Later, Greater George Ohr* at Kurland-Zabar in Manhattan (Reif 1994).

Looking back, Rago believes auctions were very low key thirty years ago, but the nature of them has radically changed (Rago 2011), and Berberian agrees: "The auction today is an event—it's show business, a spectacle, a theatrical occurrence" (Berberian 2012).

o.p.: Rhead tile breaks all Arts and Crafts records, October 2012 auction

above: Suzanne Perrault holding George Ohr vase at Pier Show, New York 2002

u.r.: David and Suzanne with Robert Schultz, designer for Knoll, and his wife

r: With friend, Mira Nakashima

What was once primarily the domain of dealers has become popular with a wider audience, including collectors and specialists of all kinds. Today it's loaded with drama, has lots of branding, and includes slick catalogues filled with high-quality color photographs. Interestingly, Rago insists that "the catalogue is not really for the buyer; it's for the next consignment."

Rago and Perrault, business partners, feature speakers at their Rago Arts auction gallery in Lambertville, hold "Appraisal Mondays," and have been regular appraisers on *Antiques Road Show* since its inception in 1997 (*Antiques Road Show* website). In addition to their body of impressive exhibition catalogues, Rago and Perrault have contributed to the scholarship of American art pottery and American Arts and Crafts, by both hosting and participating in lecture series, writing books on pottery, and actively sharing their knowledge at conferences and other events.

Rago and Perrault have also actively contributed to the Arts and Crafts community, especially at Craftsman Farms, where they were married in 1993 (Bernstein 2009). Three years later, Perrault curated an exhibition at the Farms, *Women's Work: The Role of Women in the Arts and Crafts Movement* (Perrault 2011). Over the years, Rago and Perrault have donated important Gustav Stickley furniture to the Farms. In 2000, David Rago was honored with the prestigious *Als Ik Kan Award*. Most recently, in October 2012, Rago led the live—and lively—auction for the annual gala at Craftsman Farms (Craftsman Farms website).

David Rago and Suzanne Perrault have worked very hard for decades and firmly believe their success should be shared in the broader community. This is evidenced by their generosity and philanthropy, much more far-reaching than the few examples that have been described in these pages. By giving back, David and Suzanne have created opportunities for learning and raised public awareness of the Arts and Crafts movement and the aesthetic of beauty it defines.

Frederick H. Rhead 1910 vase, enamel-decorated with mushrooms, University City, MO; 6½" x 6½", $150,000, June 2012

## References

Accardi, Art. In interview with Jeffrey Preston. Woodstock, New York. July 17, 2011.

Antiques Road Show website: http://www.pbs.org/wgbh/roadshow/appraisers/suzanne-perrault/.

Bernstein, Fred A. 2009. Far From the Gavel, Convenient to Trout. *New York Times*. June 9, 2009. http://www.nytimes.com/2009/06/14/realestate/14habi.html?_r=0.

Craftsman Farms. 2012. Gala to Honor Syracuse University College of Visual and Performing Arts. *Notes from the Farms*. Fall 2012. http://www.stickleymuseum.org/docs/Newsletters/nftf-fall-2012-for-web.pdf.

Darrow, Carolyn. 1979. Big Show in Atlantic City. *New York Times*. May 27, 1979. http://query.nytimes.com/mem/archive/pdf?res=F40810FC3A5413718DDDAE0A94DD405B898BF1D3.

———. 1980 Pottery Show in Secaucus. *New York Times*. December 21, 1980. http://query.nytimes.com/mem/archive/pdf?res=F50711F93F5E12728DDDA80A94DA415B8084F1D3.

Johnson, Bruce. 1988. "Grove Park Inn—Mountain Masterpiece." *Arts and Crafts Quarterly* 2, no. 1 (Winter 1988): 2–3.

Johnson, Bruce. In e-mail with authors. Sept 16, 2012.

Lydell, Boice. In interview with authors in East Aurora, New York. March 13, 2012.

Perrault, Suzanne. In interview with authors in Lambertville, New Jersey. July 26, 2011.

Rago, David. 1995. *David Rago Presents Arts and Crafts in New York*. December 10, 1995. Metropolitan Antiques Pavilion.

———. In interview with authors. Lambertville, New Jersey. July 26, 2011.

Rago Arts and Auction Center website. "David Rago." July 30, 2012. http://www.ragoarts.com/about/specialists/davidrago.

Reif, Rita. 1994. Wrinkled, Even Puckered, But Still Glories of Mississippi Mud. *New York Times*. October 16, 1994. http://www.nytimes.com/1994/10/16/arts/wrinkled-even-puckered-but-still-glories-of-mississippi-mud.html.

Solis-Cohen, Lita. 1996. Rago's First Lambertville Sales Bring $1 Million. *Maine Antiques Digest*. September 1996. http://www.maineantiquedigest.com/articles_archive/articles/barb0200.htm.

Smith, David. In interview with authors. Newtown, Connecticut. July 19, 2012.

*Style 1900* website: http://www.style1900.com/.

Volpe, Tod. In phone interview with authors, August 12, 2012.

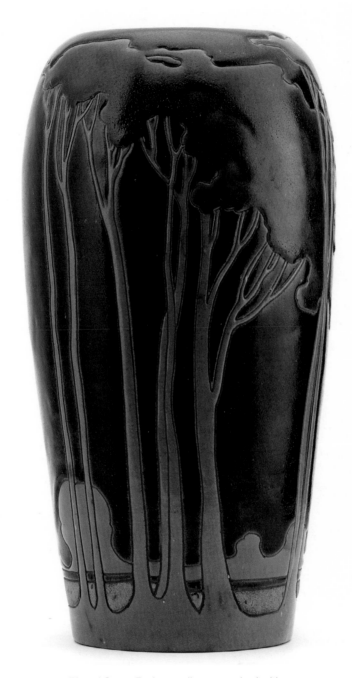

Rhead Santa Barbara tall vase, etched with
a stylized landscape; 11¼" x 6", $516,000,
March 2007

Newcomb College, 1902, 7½" x 9½",
$84,000, September 2006

Arequipa by Rhead, c. 1912, $72,500,
September 2001

Van Briggle, 1904, two-handled tapering vase with mistletoe,
11" x 4½", Yasokichi Asano $90,000, March 2008

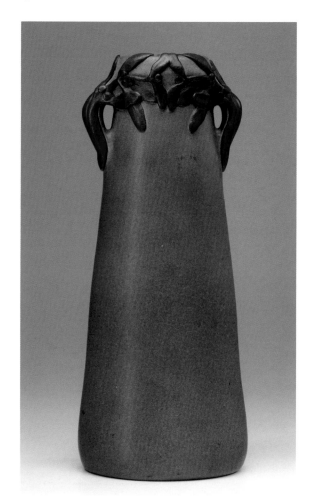

Frances Rocchi, Saturday Evening Girls, Boston, 1909,
3½" x 12¼", $98,875, June 2012

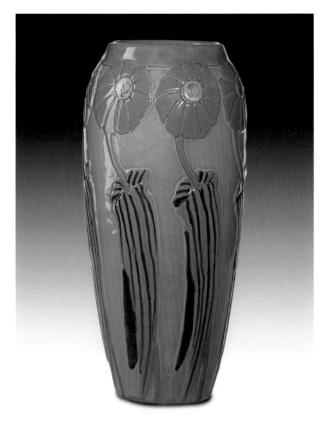

Mary Yancey, Iowa State, 1920s, carved with blue daisies, 9¼" x 5", $45,000, October 2012

Flora Huckfield, North Dakota School of Mines, Apple Blossoms, 9" x 6", $22,500 October 2012

Arthur Hennessey, Marblehead, carved vase with stylized blossoms, 7" x 4", $134,200

George Ohr, tall vase with two ribbon handles,
8½" x 5³/₄, ", $84,000, March 2006

Gustav Stickley four-sided lantern depicting stylized flowers in reds and greens. 13" x 10¼" x 10¼", with chain: 37½", $364,250, September 2004

D'Arcy Gaw for Dirk Van Erp
hammered copper table lamp with
four sockets, 22" x 22", $172,500,
May 2002

Gustav Stickley hammered copper tall candlesticks
20" x 7", $65,000, June 2011

Gustav Stickley, Harvey Ellis-designed,
inlaid writing desk, 29³/₄" x 29½" x 18",
$58,750, May 2004

Charles Rohlfs, 1900 drop-front desk,
55" x 25³/₄" x 20", $193,875,
January 2005

Gustav Stickley custom made massive sideboard with butterfly joints c. 1901, 45¼" x 25" x 100", $72,000, March 2007

Harvey Ellis, c. 1903, mixed media drawing on paper of four men working in a foundry,
19" x 12³/₄", $29,375, May 2005

Finding bids

# 17. Richie Savoia

*No matter the year or decade you see Richie Savoia, you are presented with a genuinely warm and likable person. There was—and is—an Elvis-like persona about Richie, desiring to like and be liked. Easy and relaxed, he is real, accommodating, and simply enjoyable to be with. Auction day at Savoia's was abuzz with the excitement of a packed house. The good, the bad, and the ugly—it was all there, just a two hour drive from New York.*

In 1987, a packed house and younger crowd

You never knew what you might find at Savoia's because along with run-of-the-mill things would be some Arts and Crafts treasures. Richie began holding specialty Arts and Crafts sales in 1982, which included a mix of items, but by 1986 the market demand and the inventory were sufficient that he could hold pure Arts and Crafts sales.

The demand for Arts and Crafts had been growing throughout the 1980s. In August of 1987, a Gustav Stickley high-back spindle armchair was on the block. There was no phone bidding, so everybody was there—Beth Cathers, Don Magner, Dave Rudd, Jerry Cohen, Rich Caggiano, Stephen Gray, Peter Smorto, and Michael Carey. Within forty-five seconds, the bid was above $9,000. Don Magner suddenly jumped up from his seat and shot across the room to the underbidder and whispered something in his ear. The bidding immediately halted.

The chair went for $9,500 and would have gone higher were it not for Don Magner. What he had whispered was, "That chair's in my window for $3,000." Michael Carey was the buyer. The dealer who consigned the chair had inherited a house in Cambridge, Massachusetts, that had an attic full of Gustav Stickley. As it happened, he had just taken the chair to Savoia's the day before the sale. To this day, dealers refer to the sale of that high-back spindle armchair as the beginning of the surrealistic Arts and Crafts market, with soaring prices.

What had been Savoia and Fromm auction was simply Savoia's by 1988. In the heyday of the Arts and Crafts revival, everybody knew everybody, and Richie recognized that the number one dealer, bigger than anyone else, was Michael Carey, who was everywhere and on everything. The number two guy was Stephen Gray, who educated a lot of

Twenty years ago, dealer Norman Weinstein, was telling everyone that the high-back spindle armchair that sold at Richie Savoia's auction in May of 1986 for $9,500, was the beginning of the crazy insane prices for Stickley furniture—"everyone points to that chair and that auction, that's when it all started."

Looking for a signature at a Savoia auction preview

people through his acquisitions and books. Buyers were also sellers, and there was no one else who came close to the activity level of Michael Carey or Stephen Gray. Even the number three dealer was not working at the level of activity as those two (Savoia 2012).

The Arts and Crafts were could be very profitable and many people were doing well during the late eighties and the nineties. Richie remembers a Pennsylvania flea market where he saw a rare mahogany cube chair for $25. He turned around and sold it for $4,000. Another great find was in 1988, when he and a friend went to a house auction in Ohio. During the preview, they found a large copper urn that was sitting on the floor of an enclosed porch. The size of it, the way it was made, and its age indicated it was something important. It seemed very familiar but they just couldn't place who made it or what it was.

They decided on a buying strategy. Richie was going to do the bidding. When the urn finally came up for sale, the bid moved pretty quickly to $750 and Richie hadn't made a move. Richie's friend was getting anxious and nudged him with quick little elbow jabs—so Richie started bidding. Evidently there was an absentee bidder. They were concerned that person knew who the maker was and the value of the piece. Richie kept bidding, the absentee bidder dropped out, at which point a woman in the crowd started bidding. With adrenalin coursing through his body, Richie finally got it for $1,850.

Catching up on news before the auction begins—from left, Suzanne Perrault, Dennis DeVona, John Hibel, and Jim Messineo

When they returned home, they realized immediately that it was a Frank Lloyd Wright copper urn—a very rare piece. The color and patina were magnificent. It didn't take long for the world to find out. Christie's and Skinner called Richie, trying to get him to consign to their auctions. Richie sold it to Michael Carey in his September 1988 sale for $95,000 (plus a 10 percent buyer's premium).

The Internet and e-Bay have changed the market. Richie feels they have destroyed the auction business, partly because fake Chinese stuff on the Internet has brought prices down. It is tough to pull together an Arts and Crafts auction these days because of the difficulty of finding sufficient inventory. Arts and Crafts sales today are held almost exclusively by the specialty auction houses such as Rago, Toomey-Treadway, Sotheby's, and Christie's.

There are very few young people coming into the business, so no one is learning it. Auctions take a tremendous amount of work and Richie doesn't see a lot of young people interested in that kind of intensity. It is essential for younger people entering the business to have older generations to learn from, but the opportunity to work with experienced auction people may be missed because many will be retiring in the next few years.

Richie is all about family and has always been dedicated to his wife and involved in his three children's lives. He is a big but gentle man, people-oriented and sensitive to others. He is the guy you want to do business with because he's honest, nice, personable, and he truly cares for others. Whatever endeavor Richie Savoia takes on, you can be certain it is what he says it is—he is that kind of guy. He moved out of his corrugated metal building in April and has retired. The last auction Savoia held was a charity auction for school kids.

### References

Savoia, Richie. In interview with authors. April 22, 2012. South Cairo, New York.

## Arts and Crafts at Savoia's

Richard Savoia poses with the Frank Lloyd Wright designed urn which was sold to dealer Michael Carey for $95,000, plus ten percent.

Richie Savoia showing the Grueby vases and Frank Lloyd Wright designed urn coming up for his next auction in September, 1988. The urn sold for $95,000 (plus 10 percent) and the Grueby vase hammered down at $16,500 (plus the 10 percent).

People came from New York and Boston, Washington and Chicago, when Richie Savoia held his Arts and Crafts auctions in South Cairo, New York.

Richie executing some of the left bids

Richie Savoia in 2002

Jerry Cohen and Ray Groll, 1987

Richie Savoia in 1988

## SAVOIA'S
### Arts & Crafts Auction
#### September 24, 1988   12:00 Noon

Catalogs $12.00 by mail

Included will be works by firms, artists, and craftsmen such as Frank Lloyd Wright, Gustav Stickley, Tiffany, Limbert, Grueby, Rookwood, L. & J.G. Stickley, Shop of the Crafters, Lifetime, Handel, Roycroft, Fulper, Weller Sicard, Weller Dresden, Roseville Futura, George Ohr, Quaint, Rozane, Hampshire, Newcomb College, etc..

One of several pieces of Grueby to be offered, also included will be an important 29" Grueby vase, one of the largest ever to come to auction.

Shop of the Crafters inlaid desk.

Frank Lloyd Wright copper urn, "probably the finest example ever to come to auction."

Example of Gustav Stickley copper and lighting to be offered.

## Rte. 23, So. Cairo, N.Y. 12482

ARTS & CRAFTS AUCTION
January 13, 1990
12:00 noon

John Toomey and Don Treadway

# 18. Treadway Gallery – John Toomey Gallery

*Today they are among the leading Arts and Crafts auctions in the country. Treadway Gallery is in Cincinnati, Ohio and John Toomey Gallery is in Oak Park, Illinois, where Treadway-Toomey auctions are held. The distance between their galleries provides a greater geographic sweep and more opportunity for consignments to their auction. Toomey and Treadway are passionate about the Arts and Crafts and are experts in the period. A major auction house, they attract buyers and sellers from across the country.*

1902 Gustav Stickley "crib" settle, No. 173, 71" x 34" x 38¼", $18,300, May 2012

Don Treadway unwittingly bought his first Gustav Stickley piece simply for the design of it when he was a freshman in college in 1968. After graduation, he realized he wanted to deal in Arts and Crafts in addition to the art nouveau and Tiffany he had been selling, so he made a serious start in 1973 with $12,500, a lot of money for the time. He knew there was no market for the kind of shop that would interest him, so he took his small inventory and began exhibiting in antique shows. His first show was in Denver.

In the Northeast, there was the legendary New Haven antiques show where Treadway met a lot of the New York collectors, an extremely important opportunity for him. Year after year, he did very well in New Haven. He also participated in Sanford Smith's Modernism Show, which began in November 1986 and was held in the Park Avenue Armory in New York.

Don Treadway was looking for someone to partner with, and a friend had recommended John Toomey. It took Don

John Toomey with daughter, Lucy Toomey, 2012

r.: Don and John taking phone bids

five years to convince him. Treadway-Toomey held its first auction in 1987 and was quite selective from the beginning about what they put into their sales.

Arts and Crafts awareness began in the mid- to late seventies, due in large part to the influential forces of the Jordan-Volpe Gallery and top dealers like Beth Cathers, Michael Carey, and Robert Edwards. The revival revved up in the late eighties, not long after Treadway-Toomey began their partnership and prices escalated steeply. Many serious collectors emerged during that time, and there is still a hard-core group of Arts and Crafts collectors, but it is an aging group.

In 1996 Treadway-Toomey offered the exhibition and sale of the *Kaufmann Collection: The Early Furniture of Gustav Stickley*. The catalog was written by respected collector, scholar, and historian Tom Maher. The Kaufmanns were major collectors and an event as important as this exhibition and sale elevated the Arts and Crafts community. As Maher wrote in the preface to the catalog,

> The inspiration and mentoring from the Kaufmanns and William and Patsy Porter of Birmingham, Michigan provided the education necessary to pursue and collect with thought and discretion. The late 1970s and early 1980s was a time of discovery and confusion for collectors of Arts and Crafts. The opportunity to see and study items in the Kaufmann and Porter collections in their original finish prevented many collecting mistakes. (Maher 1996, 3)

John Toomey believes there is still a market for the Arts and Crafts because there is a hard-core group of collectors, with Rudy Ciccarello as number one. However, not many new faces or young people are coming into the Arts and Crafts because prices are frequently unaffordable. "If the items for sale are really good, there are buyers. If it's boring, there are still buyers, but it's not likely to incite the feeding frenzy that it used to" (Treadway 2012).

In general, customers are looking for either investment pieces or bargains. One enjoyable aspect of live auctions has been lost due to online and phone bidding. The Internet has impersonalized the market, and phone and Internet bidding can monopolize a sale.

In 2012, Treadway-Toomey held the sale, *La Hacienda: The John L. Jerome Collection*. As Thomas K. Maher, writer of the auction catalog pointed out, "From 1972 to 2012, there have been only five important sales of Gustav Stickley furniture owned by the original family or estate," (Maher 2012, 2) and this was the sixth, from a 1902 family estate in Buffalo Park, Colorado. The annotations for each item are well researched, interesting, and often accompanied by a photo insert or a line drawing. The hard-cover catalog is in itself a valuable resource.

The *La Hacienda* sale brought some bids much higher than estimated, such as the Gustav Stickley leather-top library table (lot 19, p. 35) that went for $390,400; and the 1902 Gustav Stickley hall clock that sold for $103,700 (lot 3, p. 15).

Don Treadway, 2012

1902 Gustav Stickley cut-corner tabouret with 10" square Grueby tile; l.: Newcomb, $44,000, December 2000

John Toomey raises an interesting question—is it a real market if it's only two people establishing a price at auction? The question is apropos to today's "market" because it is a frequent auction scenario for prime Arts and Crafts pieces.

What has changed a great deal since the early days of the Treadway-Toomey auctions is that often the buyers are museums and foundations since they may have resources traditional collectors do not. While Gustav Stickley collectors may be boxed out of buying because of the extremely high prices generated at auction, the positive side of it is that as museums and foundations develop their Arts and Crafts collections, they also plan exhibition spaces for providing public display of these pieces so that many people will ultimately have the opportunity and privilege to view great works of the Arts and Crafts period.

### References

Maher, Thomas K. 1996. The Kaufmann Collection: *The Early Furniture of Gustav Stickley*. Exhibition catalog. November 23 to December 21, 1996.

_____. 2012. *La Hacienda: The John L. Jerome Collection*. Auction catalog. May 20, 2012.

Toomey, John. In interview with authors. Oak Park, Illinois. September 14, 2011.

Treadway, Don. In phone interview with authors. August 1, 2012.

Tiffany Studios, $84,000, March 2010

Pewabic, $11,000, March 2012

Roycroft, $18,000,
December 2009

1902 Gustav Stickley china closet,
35½" x 15½" x 64", $35,380, May 2012

Gustav Stickley, footstool No. 728, $20,740, May 2012

1901 Gustav Stickley library table 54½" x 33" x 29", $390,400, May 2012

1902 Gustav Stickley desk, 36" x 20" x 24", $25,620, May 2012

Gustav Stickley, early chest,$132,000,
May 2002

1902 Gustav Stickley morris chair No. 2341, 29½" x 33½" x 37, $17,080, May 2012

Gustav Stickley
1902 chalet desk
24" x 16" x 46", $51,850,
May 2012

Pewabic, $9,760, May 2012

L. & J.G. Stickley, $13,400, May 2012

Charles Rohlfs, $54,000, December 2008

# 19. Skinner Auction

*The Bee covered it as "Auction Action in Bolton, MA." On November 20, 1987, the Arts and Crafts market achieved a new high. The record was broken for a piece of Gustav Stickley furniture at Skinner Auction, surpassing the ebonized crib settle that sold for $66,000 at Phillips in New York the prior June. Michael Carey started the bidding on an original finish inlaid Harvey Ellis secretary. Jim Bakker, Massachusetts dealer, was the winning bidder at $102,300 (including the 10 percent buyer's premium).*

In the early seventies, Stephen Fletcher was stationed at the naval air base in Pensacola, Florida. It was an early twentieth-century train station there that grabbed his attention and pulled him into the world of the Arts and Crafts. The waiting room of the station was filled with mission oak—settles, rocking chairs, and a black-painted early Gustav Stickley trestle table near the ticket window.

It's no wonder that some years later when he started working for Bob Skinner, Stephen put together a substantial personal collection of Arts and Crafts furniture and pottery, enough to buy his first house. Selling his collection wasn't easy—taking things off the walls, lining up pottery and furniture so it looked more like merchandise than things that were part of his life. But the sale was successful.

The following year, Stephen went to Brimfield and easily found Arts and Crafts furniture and at remarkably low prices. His collection was reborn. He remembers an ebonized v-back armchair with an original rush seat he bought for $15. Another find was "a fantastic Grueby vase, very early where the leaves separate from the vase to curl around and join at the top" (Fletcher 2012).

Stephen became a protégé of Bob Skinner and started developing an expertise in American folk art and early American furniture. Fletcher credits Skinner for his status as one of the world's foremost experts. However, Stephen has always had a feeling for the early twentieth-century movement, especially after reading Robert Edwards' *Arts and Crafts in America*. He was fascinated by the catalog, transfixed by the sepia images, and captivated by Edwards' perspective.

Fulper lamp, 1912, $11,000

In the mid-eighties, Skinner became a major auction house, along with Christie's, leading the market in Arts and Crafts sales. Skinner specialist, Marilee Meyer, was also knowledgeable and instrumental in the success of the sales. She was a serious student of the period and genuinely interested and passionate.

In 1986, Jane Prentiss became director of Arts and Crafts at Skinner, a position she held until 1991. She had been a serious Arts and Crafts collector since the early seventies. Stephen Fletcher, Jane Prentiss, and Marilee Meyer were a formidable team that moved Skinner to the forefront of the competitive market. It was an exciting place to be in a time of discovery and awareness.

Marilee Meyer urged patrons to support the 1987 Boston exhibition, *The Art That Is Life*, and attend Bruce Johnson's first Arts and Crafts conference at the Grove Park Inn in 1988. Jane Prentiss advocated education in the various areas of the arts through special events and guest speakers, especially in twentieth-century design and the Arts and Crafts.

Stephen notes that a lot of dealers have fallen by the wayside, and there aren't that many left. A lot of people feel the Arts and Crafts revival is waning, but there is a dedicated group who goes to the Grove Park Inn every year. If an exceptional piece shows up at auction, it does well. The same thing can be said about early American furniture, and Stephen sees it as characteristic of the current market, not just of the Arts and Crafts.

Stephen Fletcher feels that by educating and sharing knowledge, the excitement for another time—for history—comes to life. It is not the acquiring of things, it is an appreciation of beauty that stimulates pleasure and provides a sense of harmony.

### References

Fletcher, Stephen. In phone interview with Jeffrey Preston. November 21, 2012.

Jane Prentiss, Director of Arts and Crafts, 1986–1991

Lamp, Grueby base, 1906, $23,500

Gustav Stickley Divan No. 165, 1901, $27,000

Grueby umbrella stand, $23,000

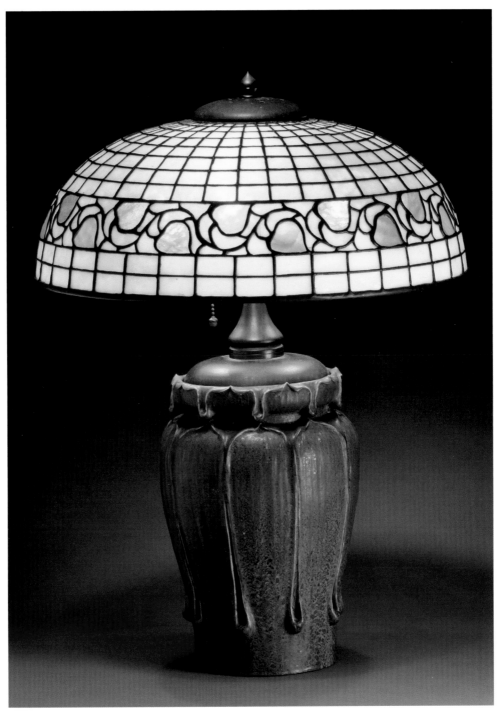

Tiffany shade, Grueby base, 1904, $21,330

Grueby tile, St. George and the Dragon, $7,637

Rohlfs desk, 1901, $17,000

Grueby decorated vase with yellow buds, 1904, $29,625

Saturday Evening Girls bowl with ducks, 1914, $4,700

Gustav Stickley inlaid desk, Harvey Ellis design, 1904, $102,300

Jim Bakker posing with newly acquired Gustav Stickley desk in October 1987

# 20. Nancy McClelland

*Nancy McClelland, head of Christie's department of 20th Century Decorative Arts from 1981 until 2001 had a passion for architecture and the arts that began in her Ohio childhood. It was fueled in her teens by a gift from her father of a copy of Frank Lloyd Wright's autobiography. As a postgraduate, she did the certificate course in art and architecture at London's Courtauld Institute. Returning to New York, she studied the history of ceramics with Carl Dauterman, a curator in the department of European sculpture and decorative arts at The Metropolitan Museum of Art, going on in 1978 to establish the ceramics and twentieth-century sales at Phillips Auctioneers in Manhattan.*

In November 1980, Christie's and Sotheby's held their first Arts and Crafts specialty sales. At the same time the Jordan-Volpe Gallery was bringing attention to the American Arts and Crafts movement with their specialized exhibitions and expert guest speakers. In December, the Philadelphia Atheneum held a day-long symposium on the "Arts and Crafts Movement in America," with speaker Robert Judson Clark, scholar and Professor of Art and Archeology at Princeton University, who had created the seminal 1972 exhibition of the same name at the Princeton Art Museum (Reif 1980). Clark virtually created the narrative for what was to come.

It was within this rekindling of the American Arts and Craft movement that McClelland began working at Christie's in February 1981. Simultaneously she met significant Arts and Crafts collectors, curators, and scholars. Among them, Robert Judson Clark generously shared his great knowledge of international architecture of this period. (McClelland later visited Robert and Nancy Clark in Lafayette, California, and together they undertook tours of west coast craftsman bungalows, Maybeck houses and the Greene & Greene masterpieces in Pasadena and Ojai). Throughout the 1980s, she would sell at auction major objects from the four or five Greene & Greene grand bungalows, most importantly, those from the Blacker House in Pasadena and the Pratt House in Ojai. The 1912 elaborately inlaid mahogany desk (depicting the sinuous California live oak) from the Pratt House brought $235,000 in June1985, a new record for Greene & Greene and Arts and Crafts furniture at that time.

Before the burgeoning scholarship that blossomed in the 1980s, auctioneers had organized 20th century decorative arts sales with the occasional inclusion of Arts and Crafts pieces but with scarce information and virtually no relevant research. Assembling sales for Christie's thus presented specific challenges and required long days. But McClelland enjoyed the pioneering expansion of her knowledge about the field in a pre-Internet era when few books and catalogs existed and in some cases available information was incorrect. In the early 1980s she organized the record-breaking sale of the Frank Lloyd Wright windows and his 'Tree of Life' doors from the Darwin Martin house in Buffalo. (A single

The back wall, from left:
Nick Dembrosky, Beth Cathers,
Tod Volpe, and John Toomey

Standing room only at Christie's; from far left,
Patricia Bartinique, Tom Maher, Marilee Meyer,
Ray Groll, Suzanne Perrault, David Rago, and
Marty Shack

Gustav Stickley's
grandson, Peter
Wiles, consigned
several pieces of
Stickley furniture
to Christie's. The
hammer price was
a world record for
any Arts and Crafts
pieces

Sideboard produced by Gustav Stickley for the interior of his 438 Columbus Avenue house. It sold at Christie's on December 10, 1988 to Barbra Streisand for $363,000.

Highly Important American Arts & Crafts and Architectural Designs and Commissions
Including furniture from Gustav Stickley's house, Syracuse, New York, circa 1903

Saturday, December 10, 1988

CHRISTIE'S
NEW YORK

Christie's auction catalogue for the Gustav Stickley Columbus Avenue sideboard sale

Nancy taking phone bids

'Tree of Life' door brought over $100,000, breaking the auction record for any leaded glass window, including those by Tiffany.) These remarkable things, sold by Christie's for the heirs of the original owner, had been in a Buffalo warehouse for nearly 40 years. Such signature events led to an expansion of important virgin material coming onto the market.

The December 1983 sale of the Chris Elmore estate was one of the highlights for McClelland. He had built a premier Gustav Stickley collection before the American Arts and Crafts were again popular and prices were prohibitive. In planning the sale, McClelland flew to Key West in July and saw the rare and beautiful 1903 Harvey Ellis designed Gustav Stickley inlaid drop-front desk with the cabinets on each side. Chris Elmore had loved the works of Gustav Stickley, believing that one day Stickley would be recognized for his significant contribution to American design (Cathers 2004).

As the number of serious Arts and Crafts collectors increased in the 1980s, steadily rising prices reflected a growing demand. However, prices rose steeply in the late eighties as collectors such as Steven Spielberg and Barbra Streisand made Arts and Crafts fashionable with the film industry set. Some of the celebrities were furnishing large houses or compounds, creating new demand and pressure for something that was produced by small companies for a limited number of years. Adding to the popularity of the style, newspapers and magazines such as Robert Edwards' magazine, *The Tiller*, and *Style 1900* featured numerous articles on the movement and, in the latter instance, how collectors were decorating their homes. With real competition for rare, early Gustav Stickley pieces, auction prices steeply escalated.

Many different talents and skills and a high level of expertise reinforced successful auction sales. It was also essential for McClelland to form productive relationships with potential clients. In the December 1988 Arts and Crafts sale, Christie's sold the Peter Wiles collection of early furniture that Gustav Stickley had designed and produced for his own Columbus Avenue home in Syracuse, New York in 1902. Pre-auction activities included a lecture at Christie's by the designer's larger-than-life grandson, Wiles. He called it "Memories of

Important Frank Lloyd Wright and
American Arts & Crafts Furnishings
including Ceramics

Saturday, December 12, 1987

CHRISTIE'S
NEW YORK

My Grandfather, Gustav Stickley." Gustav had lived with his daughter and her family on Columbus Avenue in Syracuse throughout Peter's childhood and the better part of his adolescence. At this sale, Barbara Streisand bought the massive dining room sideboard for over $300,000, creating a new auction record for Gustav's furniture, which remained unbroken until Christie's sold her collection in 1994. The same auction also featured works by Arts and Crafts figures Frank Lloyd Wright, L. & J.G. Stickley (Gustav's brothers), lighting designer Dirk Van Erp, and potter George Ohr (Christie's 1988).

The following year, in preparation for the December sale, McClelland visited Phyllis and Cyril Farny at Craftsman Farms in Morristown, New Jersey, to review some of the original furniture Gustav Stickley had left when he sold the Farms to the Farny family. Stickley had lived there while owning the great Stickley building in Murray Hill in Manhattan. At this time the garden outlines and many of the original plantings, such as rhododendron, remained. McClelland found particular satisfaction handling pieces rich with history.

As a professional in the auction world, McClelland was living with relentless pressure for success of the next sale. She left Christie's in 2001. At this juncture, Nancy McClelland and Lars Rachen (who in the late 1990s had become head of the New York departmental office and for the last few years ran the international department with McClelland) established an international art advisory service (McClelland + Rachen) dealing in high-end transactions. They focus on helping clients build important art collections, brokering sales and representing clients at auction as both buyers and sellers. She also currently serves as a member of the IRS Arts Advisory Panel.

Nancy McClelland's efforts during this critical period furthered collective knowledge and connoisseurship in the American Arts and Crafts movement.

Illinois Governor Jim Thompson examining Frank Lloyd Wright table lamp with founder of Domino's Pizza, Thomas Monaghan

Governor Thompson successfully purchased all of the lots from the Dana House at what many considered to be bargain prices; $70,000 was the final bid on this architectural rendering of the Dana House by Frank Lloyd Wright.

## References

Cathers, David. 2004. "With a Little Help from Their Friends." *American Bungalow*. 43 (Fall). http://www.americanbungalow.com/category/magazine/magazine-articles/issue-43.

Christie's New York. 1988. *Highly Important American Arts & Crafts and Architectural Designs and Commissions: Including furniture from Gustav Stickley's house, Syracuse, New York, circa 1903.* Saturday, December 10, 1988. Auction catalog.

McClelland, Nancy. In interview with Jeffrey Preston. Stonington, Connecticut. September 9, 2012.

Reif, Rita. 1980. Antiques: Arts and Crafts Designs Capture the Limelight. *New York Times*. November 9, 1980. http://query.ny-times.com/mem/archive/pdf?res=F60A17FC3C5512728DDDA00894D9415B8084F1D3.

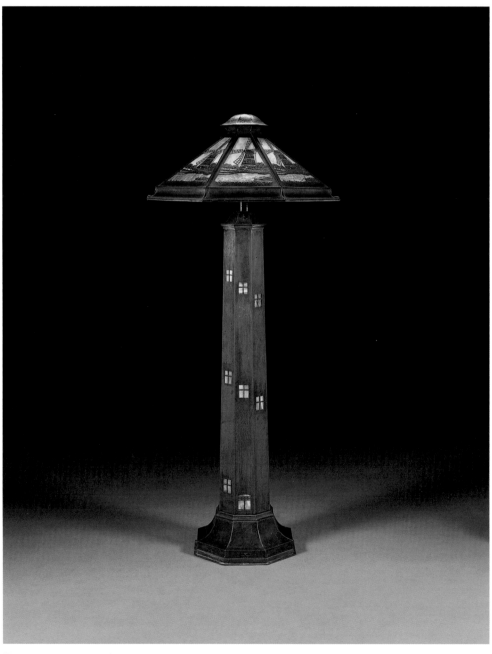

Charles P. Limbert copper and glass "lighthouse" floor lamp, 67¼"h x 32¼" (diameter of shade), $18,400, June 7, 1996

# 21. Christie's

Christie's was the number one auction house during the Arts and Crafts revival throughout Nancy McClelland's tenure. Specialized sales, usually in June and December, with high-quality catalogs often led the way, setting record prices for early Gustav Stickley, Frank Lloyd Wright, Greene and Greene, Elmslie, and Maher pieces. Original finish, condition, rarity, and provenance were important elements in the smaller yet high-end sales. The Christie's name often was used to advantage in the marketplace for attracting both consignors and collectors.

Gustav Stickley 1902 double bookcase cabinet, oak, $101,500, June 7,1996

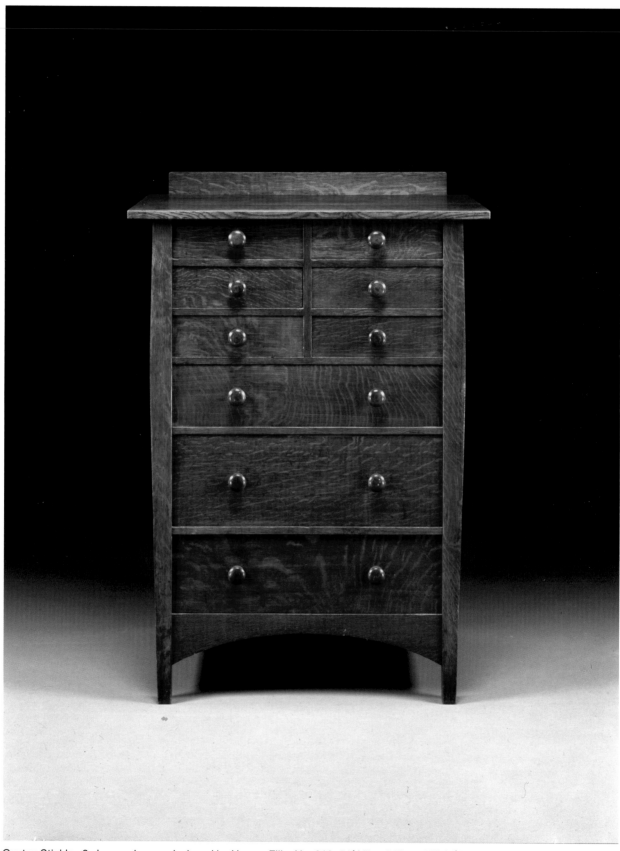

Gustav Stickley 9-drawer dresser designed by Harvey Ellis, No. 913, 51$\frac{1}{8}$"h x 36"w x 20"d, $8,500, June 9, 1995

Frank Lloyd Wright double pedestal lamp (Robie House), 31³/₈"w x 18½" x 23¼"h, $640,000, June 11, 1988

Gustav Stickley director's table, No. 631, c. 1910, 72" x 35" x 30½", $22,000, June 10, 1989

Charles and Henry Greene copper and glass lantern, executed for the Robert Blacker House, Pasadena, California, c. 1907–1909, 33½" x 29" square, $48,000, June 10, 1989

George Washington Maher bronze and leaded glass table lamp, c. 1912, 16¼"h x 21³/₄"w x 11⁷/₈"d, $32,200, Barbra Streisand Collection Part I, March 3, 1994

Limbert window bench, oak, No. 243, 24½"w x 24½"h x 18"d, $7,000, June 10, 1989

Dalton's in Syracuse, New York;  o.p.: David, Debbie, and Kylee Rudd, c. 1990

# 22. David Rudd

*Communities are shaped by history, events, and individuals with vision. Because Syracuse is off the beaten path, Dalton's American Decorative Arts has always been independent and not aligned with a lot of the commercial activity of larger metropolitan areas. This provides ample opportunity for the innovative programs and marketing David Rudd and Debbie Goldwein have created. Enterprising and civic-minded, Dave and Debbie have provided leadership and energy—the weft to the community's warp. Syracuse and the larger Arts and Crafts community are richer for it.*

The Rudd family moved frequently because David's father was in the army, but his parents were interested in antiques and took him to country auctions wherever they lived (Cathers 2004). When Dave was a senior in high school, his father began working at Corning Glass in Syracuse, and they settled down. Although unaware of Arts and Crafts at this point in his life, Rudd was undoubtedly influenced by the Arts and Crafts aesthetic that his subconscious mind absorbed. The L. & J.G. Stickley factory was nearby, and yard sales often included old Arts and Crafts pieces pulled from attics and basements.

Rudd studied design, sculpture, and photography at SUNY Buffalo and then studied two more years at Syracuse University (Cathers 2004). He was intrigued by "the beauty and dimensionality of objects in space" (Rudd 2011). Interestingly, he developed his skills as a woodworker and made a cube chair before he was even conscious of the Arts and Crafts movement.

In the late 1970s, Dave and Debbie were looking for a couch for their first home but hated everything they saw.

They learned about Arts and Crafts and pored over the two books available to them at that time, the 1972 Princeton exhibition catalog, The Arts and Crafts Movement in America, 1876–1916 and Forgotten Rebel by John Crosby Freeman. Their friend and antiques dealer, Mark Eckhoff, taught them even more about Arts and Crafts furniture and sold them an oak settle made by the Phoenix Furniture Company of Grand Rapids, their first piece of Arts and Crafts (Cathers 2004).

That was just a taste. David and Debbie now wanted more Arts and Crafts furniture, so they began the hunt, and by 1981 they were ready to become Arts and Crafts dealers. They rented half a storefront to open Dalton's American Decorative Arts in Syracuse. Within a few years, they were able to buy the building and expand their shop. Theirs is a family business. Dave and Debbie even pulled their daughter, Kylee, out of her third-grade class one day when a rare Gustav Stickley settle from their gallery had sold and was being shipped to the buyer. They wanted to get a photo of her sitting on the settle, knowing she'd never again have the opportunity to sit on one.

Gustav Stickley dinner gong

At the same time their business was expanding, they were becoming more and more involved in the works of Gustav Stickley (Cathers 2004). In addition to finding great stuff in old houses, they bought out lodges and went to many good auctions. In the 1980s, the amount of Arts and Crafts furniture that was available in the Syracuse area seemed endless and was still not terribly well known or appreciated.

Learning more about Gustav Stickley, Dave and Debbie became aware that, at the turn of the twentieth century, Stickley lived in Syracuse and operated his furniture company, Craftsman Workshops, in nearby Eastwood (Cathers 1981). After a horrendous Christmas Eve fire in 1901 (Cathers 2003, 51), Stickley rebuilt the interior with chestnut plank flooring, chestnut wainscoting, and "massive chestnut posts [that] supported heavy oak ceiling beams" (2003, 66). It was a radical new look for interiors. One year later, in December 1902, The Craftsman featured "A Visit to the House of Mr. Stickley," with beautiful and clear drawings of the new interior of the Columbus Avenue house. The colonial revival exterior remained unchanged (2003, 69). Stickley sold the house in 1910 to move his family closer to New York, where his offices were now located (2003, 183). Stickley's daugh-

ter, Barbara Wiles, bought the house back in 1919, and Gustav lived there, some of the time, in a third-floor bedroom where he experimented with wood finishes he hoped to perfect and market (2003, 204).

In the 1990s, the Columbus Avenue house was in danger of being destroyed, so Dave and Debbie Rudd bought it with a partner in 1994, realizing that it was "probably one of the most important twentieth-century interiors in the country. When we first bought it, my partner had ideas of getting the city and state involved and creating some sort of "Williamsburg" type Arts and Crafts colony there" (Woodshop 2012). But the house required more work and money than they could manage and outside funding failed to materialize. Dave had invested a lot in the house, but it required constant repairs and maintenance. They needed to sell it within a year or two, but the city wouldn't buy it, and no one else was interested. Amini Audi, of L. & J.G. Stickley, stepped in and bought it in 1996.

The house is badly deteriorated but tremendous gains were made in 2012 towards restoration of this important piece of American history. ArtDaily.org reported in July, "the Everson Museum of Art and the L. & J.G. Stickley Company announced that discussions have begun to explore the possibility of renovating and restoring the Gustav Stickley House, located at 438 Columbus Avenue in Syracuse, as a historic house and museum operated by the Everson Museum." The executive director of the Everson, Steven Kern, said,

"It is absolutely the Holy Grail of the Arts and Crafts style and aesthetic that swept the country from coast to coast." Kern said he expects the renovation and rehabilitation of the home to take years because it must be done with great deliberation and sensitivity. "You walk into the interior and it leaves you breathless, " Kern said. "There is a lot of work to be done … and the house has certainly suffered, but it is the vessel for this amazing jewel. The flow of space, the woodwork ... the downstairs is absolutely spectacular, even in its current condition."
(Poliquin 2012)

Gustav Stickley book cabinet 1902

Roycroft andirons, designed by W.W. Denslow, 19¾" x 10" x 29", c. 1899; r.: Gustav Stickley hall clock No. 3

On December 28, 2012, The Post-Standard of Syracuse reported that the New York State Department of Parks, Recreation and Historic Preservation recently awarded a half-million dollar grant for the restoration of the interior of the Columbus Avenue home (Moriarty 2012). This is promising in terms of educating the public and raising awareness of Gustav Stickley and the importance of Syracuse in the Arts and Crafts movement.

Growing up with antiques and going to auctions, building furniture, and studying design, photography, and sculpture have all led to Rudd's discerning eye for beauty and its elements. He sees the Arts and Crafts movement as the beginning of modern design, shaking off the excesses of the Victorian era, and that intrigues and attracts him.

Dalton's has taken the lead in Arts and Crafts education since its opening in 1979, by holding special exhibitions and talks. Their first event was an Edward Curtis show in 1982, and they filled their gallery with Stickley furniture for it, a smart way of promoting furniture that people may not be familiar with or appreciate.

They advertised locally in the early days, but they created a website as soon as the Internet was available and broadened their reach. While the Dalton's website (daltons.com) is

well done, a visit to Dalton's explains why people often refer to the gallery as a museum. The large space is not cluttered, and unique items and furniture are beautifully displayed. A settle facing two large desks, where Dave or Debbie might be working, invites visitors to leisurely sit down and have a conversation.

Dalton's has exhibited regularly at the annual Grove Park Inn conference since its second year in 1989. Growing up, Kylee Rudd felt so at home with the annual pilgrimage to the Grove Park Inn that she would run back and forth between the

Gustav Stickley 72" director's table

contemporary crafts exhibit and her parents, critiquing the show for them. As a teenager, she was hired by Bruce Johnson for different small positions during the event, such as a security person holding back the hordes of people pushing to get into the antiques show. Dalton's also had a regular booth at other shows—Philadelphia, Minneapolis, Cleveland, and the Metropolitan Pavillion in New York—but they have pared down their activity over the last ten years.

Continuing to find fresh and exciting Arts and Crafts pieces, David not only plays an important role in maintaining interest in the Arts and Crafts in the Syracuse area through his central location and the beauty of his gallery, but he is one of the leading dealers nationally and travels throughout the country to purchase important pieces and consult with his clients. He writes a regular column in *American Bungalow*, Perspectives on Antiques, a question-answer format on any kind of question having to do with antiques. His column has been educating readers since 2004.

Dave is civic-minded and serves as president of the Arts and Crafts Society of Central New York, which has a focus on education. He also is a member of the board of The Stickley Museum at Craftsman Farms in New Jersey and has been actively involved there for over twenty years, serving in various capacities and influential in major decisions.

Exceptional Arts and Crafts furniture is financially out of reach for most people and there is generally less inventory available as much of it resides with museums and major collectors, but more and more people are mixing new crafts by gifted and diligent artisans and high-quality Arts and Crafts reproductions with their collections of early twentieth-century pieces. Many smart business people are diversifying their inventory to include such wares. Dalton's has been reproducing Onondaga Pottery's 1909 "Tudor Rose" china, originally made in Syracuse, since 1994. New Donegal carpets and custom furniture are also available through Dalton's. The Arts and Crafts revival has changed over time but it is still going strong for David and Debbie. Their influence ensures its vigor on the national level.

## References

Cathers, David. 2004. "Destined to Collect." *American Bungalow* 42: 63–71.

Cathers, David M. 1981. *Furniture of the American Arts and Crafts Movement: Stickley and Roycroft Mission Oak*. New York: New American Library Books.

Cathers, David. 2003. *Gustav Stickley*. New York: Phaidon Press.

Moriarty, Rick. 2012. State Grant Will Help Turn Stickley Home into Arts and Crafts Museum. *The Post Standard*. December 28, 2012. http://www.syracuse.com/news/index.ssf/2012/12/state_grant_will_help_turn_sti.html.

Rudd, David. In interview with authors. Syracuse, New York. September 22, 2011.

Poliquin, Kathleen. *The Post Standard*. Syracuse.com. July 18, 2012. http://www.syracuse.com/news/index.ssf/2012/07/gustav_stickleys_historic_syra.html.

Woodshop News. "Stickley's Home Brought to Life." November 19, 2012. http://www.woodshopnews.com/news/news-desk/502429-stickleys-home-brought-to-life.

Michael Adams at studio, c. 1987-1988; o.p.: Michael Adams and Dawn Hopkins with Gustav Stickley floor lamp, c. 2000

# 23. Michael Adams – Dawn Hopkins
## Aurora Studios

*Tucked away behind a huge, soft fence of evergreens, Michael Adams and Dawn Hopkins live a twenty-first century version of the craftsman life. Their large studio is just steps from their house. The surrounding land is a garden ornamented with rusting, industrial machinery whose sculptural qualities become evident in their setting. Inside their immaculate studio, Michael and Dawn recreate masterpieces of Arts and Crafts lighting and metalwork, often indistinguishable from the original except for the shop marks. They talk of designs that "sing," the Arts and Crafts pieces by the great copper artists of the movement, such as Dirk Van Erp and the metal shop of Gustav Stickley.*

Michael Adams grew up north of Syracuse in the 1950s, in a new house with little architectural character. By contrast, both of his grandparents lived in 1920s homes on the south side of Syracuse. His mother had grown up in a four-square with an Arts and Crafts interior, complete with a stained glass chandelier with four pendants hanging from iron chains. There were also wooden plate rails, built-in bookcases, and a gas fireplace. Michael loved going there and experiencing such a rich architecture, so different from his own suburban home.

The chandelier in his grandparents' home sparked Michael's interest in lighting. Influenced by the memories of the old-fashioned interior, he embarked on the career of a stained glass artisan in the early 1970s. Michael began teaching himself stained glass and traveled to New York City for supplies. On one such trip, he visited his sister who lived with other artists in pop-artist Don Rubbo's studio loft in SoHo. It was a very sixties-seventies environment, emphasizing freedom of expression and creativity. When Rubbo learned of Michael's interest in stained glass, he took him to Lillian Nassau's gallery to see Tiffany lamps and glass on display. Newly inspired, Michael returned to Fayetteville to continue his own work.

After some time and with confidence in his developing skills, Michael took a leap of faith. He contacted the famous Tiffany collector, Egon Neustadt, and told him of his background, his skills, and his passion. Neustadt was impressed and soon engaged Michael to work on various projects with him. Although paid little for the work, Michael felt the hands-on education he received restoring lamps and windows from the era was a rare opportunity, much like an apprenticeship from another time. Michael's working relationship with Neustadt lasted into the late seventies.

Michael was first enchanted by art nouveau but as he began filling his house with inexpensive Arts and Crafts furniture, he became aware of the Arts and Crafts style in the lighting and metalwork he saw in different shops. When he saw his first Dirk Van Erp lamp in the mid-seventies in northern California, he wondered why it did not have stained glass panels in the shade. Little did he know that these very lamps would be an important part of his second career as a coppersmith. The Arts and Crafts began pulling at him.

u.l.: Mike in studio;  u.r.: Mike forming lamp base; l.: Dawn working on mica

With the encouragement and support of David Jenks, an antique lighting collector and dealer in Syracuse, Michael was able to continue his glasswork from a studio in David's basement in the early eighties. This was an important period in Michael's growth and development as an artist. It was a time when he was free to experiment with different techniques and creative ideas, and he designed his first lamp inspired by the Arts and Crafts. It was a wood and stained glass prairie-style design he created, a departure from the Tiffany style stained glass lamps he made, and he sold them on consignment in a local antique shop.

In 1984, Jerry Cohen, owner of the Mission Oak Shop in Oakland, California, discovered two wood and stained glass prairie-style floor lamps in a shop in Liverpool, New York. He was so impressed with the quality of the craftsmanship, he would have bought anything made by the artisan. It took Jerry some time to get the name of the artisan from the shop owner but when he did, Jerry approached Michael with a business idea. They established a partnership, Aurora Studios. Michael established the studio in Oswego, New York, about an hour north of Syracuse. Jerry took care of the business end and financed a significant expansion of the artisans' studio. Aurora Studios produces copies of origi-

nal hand-hammered copper Arts and Crafts masterpieces by Gustav Stickley, Dirk Van Erp, and others (Cohen 2011). For twenty years, Cohen served as distributor for Aurora. It allowed the artist to focus on craftsmanship instead of business dealings. As distributor, Jerry displayed and promoted Adams' work in his Mission Oak Shop and sent pieces to galleries and dealers across the country (Cohen 2011).

Jerry Cohen moved his Mission Oak Shop to Putnam, Connecticut in 1988 and, from the beginning, featured Aurora Studios. Prominently displayed in his shop today is a reproduction Gustav Stickley chandelier created by Michael Adams. Michael had wanted to learn hammered copper, so Jerry began buying original Arts and Crafts lighting for him to copy. The first piece Jerry dropped off was a Gus chandelier that "looked like it came out of Dracula's castle" (Adams). Adams learned the new medium quickly and within a few years could create copper pieces nearly indistinguishable from those of Dirk Van Erp, the most highly skilled of the Arts and Crafts metalworkers (Rago 2011). It was an exciting time for Michael because he could learn another craft that would complement the stained glass fixtures he was already producing.

Clockwise from u.l.: Dawn working on Gustav Stickley reproduction; custom hood; Dawn hammering hood; Dawn hammering detail; Mike working on shade; Dawn working on clockface

l.: Custom hood in production; l.l.: Dawn hammering hood; l.r.: Mike working on hood

Jerry continued buying original Arts and Crafts lighting for Michael to learn from and to copy. Some pieces needed repairing, while other pieces simply offered Michael inspiration. Adams learned the new medium quickly and within a few years could create copper pieces nearly indistinguishable from those of Dirk Van Erp, the most highly skilled of the Arts and Crafts metalworkers (Rago 1989). Jerry proudly states that Michael has never compromised his work. "Michael Adams is the embodiment of the Arts and Crafts craftsman, and he has set the standard for all craftspeople in the Arts and Crafts" (Cohen 2011).

During Michael's formative period in the early eighties, Dawn Hopkins was pursuing her own artistic path. While finishing her BFA in printmaking, she worked summers as a printmaker with her instructor, artist Thomas Seawell. After college, she apprenticed at the Fabric Workshop and Museum in Philadelphia. She met Michael in 1991 and soon after began learning metalwork in his studio. It is impressive that Dawn Hopkins learned the new medium so quickly and is her husband's equal in the consistency and quality of her metalwork. She is lesser known, but their work is nearly indistinguishable, one from the other.

Many consider their level of craftsmanship equal to that of the great coppersmiths of the Arts and Crafts period, and some assert that the craftsmanship of Aurora Studios is better than that of the originals they reproduce. Michael's modest response is that while their work "might be more dimensionally correct, it is difficult to capture the imperfections and spontaneity of the original work. It is a naïve aspect—a Grandma Moses quality—that some early Van Erps possess" (Adams).

It is a true love of design and craft that drives the level of effort and standard of perfection they put into their lamps and metalwork and not a means to earning an income. Very few people, if any, would put their kind of effort into making a lamp. If a piece does not meet their standards, it gets reworked until it does. In addition to the countless hours they devote to the creation of each individual piece, there are many years of exploration built into each fixture.

Mike works on a patina until he is satisfied, which often means many extra hours in the patina room. They believe patina is critical in revealing the workmanship and artistry that make art metalwork complete. He is constantly exploring and researching patinas and continues to develop and fine-tune his own patina methods.

Michael embraced computer technology early and often uses a computer-generated design program to assist in making tooling, specialty rivets, etc. He is conscientious about creating accuracy in a piece, especially when it comes to custom work. "We make a lot of forms—it's ultimately easier" (Adams). They both agree though, there is no substitute for handwork, and they go to great lengths to maintain integrity in their work.

Aurora Studios' reproductions of Dirk Van Erp's trumpet lamp, on left, and milk can lamp, on right

Michael with his work, c. 1988

Aurora Studios booth in the Contemporary Crafts Exhibit at the Grove Park Inn

Mike restoring sailboat

Adams and Hopkins have always been careful to make sure the buyer would never confuse their work with an original, so there are multiple copper-raised "A"s inside their lamps (and in other places) to distinguish the work of Aurora Studios (Rago 1989). The issue of Arts and Crafts reproductions was a sensitive one in the early days of Aurora Studios. David Rago raised the subject with Michael Adams for a 1989 article about him in Arts and Crafts Quarterly, pointing out that people get upset when they spend upwards of $20,000 or $30,000 on a lamp, then turn around and see a reproduction selling for $2,500.

> … Adams replied, "People don't talk to me about this because I'm part of it. I don't hear the negative aspects. But, it's [the reproduction of period material] coming forward with or without me. The L. & J.G. Stickley Company, for one, is in the process of creating a reproduction furniture line which they will offer through over 200 outlets across the country. I can't stop it, and it's silly to say I want to get off. Personally, I can only afford Stickley Brothers furniture, and the reproductions allow me to live with better design. (Rago 1989)

Michael was correct about reproductions "coming forward." A piece by Aurora Studios holds great value in the market, and well-made reproductions are very desirable. As original Arts and Crafts pieces are less available than in years past and very expensive, many Arts and Crafts collectors of today freely mix high-quality reproductions with antiques.

While visiting the Roycroft campus in 1987, Michael heard of the Arts and Crafts show in Asheville, North Carolina from Kitty Turgeon. He knew it was important to participate in the show and have the opportunity to introduce his work to a wider audience. Fortunately, Bruce Johnson provided a room near the antiques show for Michael and Kitty to exhibit in. While the dealers were less than enthusiastic about the arrangement, the attendees seemed interested. Sales were slow until the last day when collector Jordan Lubitz walked into their booth and bought their entire inventory within ten minutes (Cohen 2011). Michael felt this both legitimized his work and supported Jerry's concept that reproductions had a place in the Arts and Crafts market.

Arts and Crafts collectors, dealers, and scholars now recognize reproduction work as very important and rightfully deserving of a place in the body of the revival. Aurora Studios has set a standard for such work that is unassailable, employing the same skills, techniques, and materials that were used to craft the original. The quality of their craft has provided inspiration to other artists and artisans, and their work has provided many homes with lighting and metalwork that not only is indistinguishable from that of the original masters but, in many cases, would have otherwise been unavailable to their client. The work of Michael Adams and Dawn Hopkins has brought respectability to the collecting of reproduction pieces and made it clear that the highest level of craftswork, the level attained by artists such as Dirk Van Erp, is not only possible but expected.

## References

Adams, Michael, and Dawn Hopkins. In interview with authors. Oswego, New York. July 22, 2011.

Cohen, Jerry. In interview with authors. Putnam, Connecticut. July 14, 2011.

Johnson, Bruce. In interview with authors. Mountain Lakes, New Jersey. October 15, 2011.

Rago, David. 1989. "Michael Adams: A Modern Craftsman." *Arts and Crafts Quarterly*. 2(2): 18–19.

Mike sailing his Marlin

Bruce and Leigh Ann Hamon-Johnson

# 24. Bruce Johnson

*The most important event of the year for the Arts and Crafts community is the Grove Park Inn Arts and Crafts Conference, and the single most important individual to the Arts and Crafts revival is Bruce Johnson. He has created an annual event that has become more complex over its twenty-six years and kept the revival flame burning. Bruce doesn't stand still but quickly adapts, as evidenced by the excellent website he has created, ArtsAndCraftsCollector.Com. It is command central for the Arts and Crafts community online.*

Bruce Johnson went to yard sales and flea markets with his grandmother amidst the cornfields of the Midwest. As he got older, his baseball card collection evolved into pressed-back chairs, and sideboards with cheap hardware—things affordable to an English teacher in the early seventies.

In 1977, Johnson left high school teaching to pursue furniture restoration and his dream of becoming a writer. He found a job but was appalled at his employer's refinishing techniques, so he started his own business in Iowa City, Knock on Wood. Always enterprising, Bruce started the weekly "Knock on Wood" column in 1978, which appeared in antique publications around the country. Six years later, he published a book on refinishing, also called *Knock on Wood*.

As a refinisher, Bruce would receive spur-of-the-moment calls from people who were cleaning out attics or wanted to rid themselves of clutter, and they would offer him their antiques. His most vivid memory was the dozen Roycroft dining chairs all lined up in the basement of a family mansion. He was

offered the chairs in exchange for refinishing the family's early American and Victorian antiques. He had no idea what Roycroft was but he was smitten.

Bruce sold the Roycroft chairs in 1978 to Jim Mall, a Chicago dealer, who drove his truck up to Bruce's shop, completely filled with furniture. "He pulled off a sewing rocker and showed me the mark—it was the first time I'd ever seen the Gus Stickley mark." Jim spent an hour showing him what to look for in Arts and Crafts furniture.

Obsessed with the Arts and Crafts, Johnson was passionately researching it and found references to Robert Judson Clark and the Princeton exhibition. He also found a couple of Jordan-Volpe booklets featuring photos of Arts and Crafts settings in the home. In 1981, Bruce bought the Dover reprint of two Stickley catalogs, Gustav Stickley and L. & J.G. Stickley, and David Cather's *Furniture of the American Arts and Crafts Movement*, complete with photographs and shop marks, which became his bible.

Bruce introducing 2011 recipient of the Arts and Crafts Lifetime Achievement Award, Stephen Gray

Once he knew what to look for, Bruce Johnson started scouring Iowa and Illinois and found more Limbert pieces than Roycroft or Stickley. There was only one other Arts and Crafts collector in Iowa City at that time, so Arts and Crafts furniture would often sit unnoticed in a lot of the shops. Nobody knew what it was.

Bruce had to sell pieces to pay for his Gus Stickley habit because his refinishing business did not bring in the needed revenue. Like any beginning collector, Bruce made mistakes, the biggest being an Arts and Crafts style hideaway bed that had appeared in the 1904 Sears-Roebuck catalog. "The thing took about eight men to move because of this massive steel frame, and the wood framework was all done in tiger oak veneer so every time you moved it, you broke off more veneer."

Knock on Wood was sold in 1985, as Bruce headed to Durham, North Carolina, where his former wife, Lydia, was beginning Duke University medical school. Happily, he found a lot of bungalows in Durham and continued the hunt for Arts and Crafts furniture. Not one to stand still, Bruce sent a proposal to Hearst publications with an idea for a new column, "Antiques Across America." Hearst liked it, and it appeared regularly in *Country Living* magazine.

In 1986, Johnson went to an Arts and Crafts conference at the historic Roycroft Inn in East Aurora, New York. It had been conceived and run by Boice Lydell for three years with the help of Kitty Turgeon, Bob Rust, and Linda Hubbard Brady. It featured an antiques show and seminars. This would be the last of the conferences at the Roycroft campus for a few years, however, because the inn would soon be closed for major renovations. Bruce saw an opportunity, and an idea was starting to take shape.

While in East Aurora, Bruce found an essay by Elbert Hubbard about the Grove Park Inn (GPI) in Asheville, North Carolina, both celebrating the building of it and praising the Roycrofters for the furniture they had crafted for it. Bruce had at least an awareness of the inn because he and his family sometimes took weekends in Asheville. In 1987, on assignment for *Country Living*, Bruce walked into the Great Hall at the Grove Park Inn and thought it would be an ideal venue for an Arts and Crafts conference. He took his idea to the management at GPI, and they liked it. Looking back, Bruce remarks that the plan at that time "was so simple by the standards of today—just an antiques show and speakers."

As he was putting together the first conference, Bruce was approached by dealer Jerry Cohen, who insisted he add a contemporary metalsmith, Michael Adams, to the thirty dealers already signed up for booths in the antiques exhibition. Cohen maintained Adams' work was on a par with the original Arts and Crafts artisans. Instead, Bruce created a second exhibition, *contemporary crafts*, that would occur simultaneously with the antiques exhibition. He added a second exhibitor to it, the contemporary Roycroft Shops, represented by Kitty Turgeon and Bob Rust. From the very beginning, Bruce had a clear vision for this conference and did not want people to confuse antiques with contemporary crafts.

Bruce, in his inimitable style, generated excitement for his conference. A central group of Roycroft people, Boice Lydell, Linda Hubbard Brady, Kitty Turgeon, and Bob Rust (the last two representing Roycroft Shops in the contemporary crafts exhibition), supported Bruce's project wholeheartedly, talked it up, and helped to make the first event a success. *The*

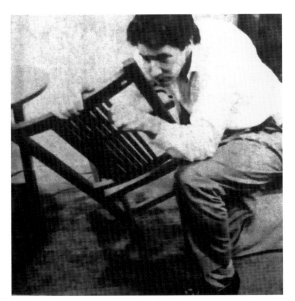

u.l.: Bruce at Skinner auction preview, 1987; u.r.:
Bruce working in office, 2012; l.l.: Bruce with the
family's horses

u.l.: Front of Grove Park Inn; u.r.: 2013 Arts and Crafts Conference poster by Laura Wilder (www.LauraWilder.com); l.r.: Cara Corbo and Ted Lytwyn; o.p.: Views of Grove Park Inn

*Art That Is Life* exhibition, which opened in 1987 in Boston, created another opportunity for Bruce to talk to dealers and influential people like Marilee Boyd Meyer of Skinner auction, who immediately recognized the importance of the upcoming conference.

The owners of the Grove Park Inn had been looking for an identity for years but had looked past the obvious—its Arts and Crafts architecture and history. The exterior of the inn was built of granite rocks that were literally lifted out of the sides of mountains and not excavated. That way each stone would retain its individual shape and character. In addition, the stone workers were instructed not to remove any lichen or moss from a single rock because it enhanced the natural beauty of the stone. Fred L. Seely, who developed the plan for the inn, wildly embraced the Arts and Crafts aesthetic and insisted the stones be placed such that "not a piece of stone should be visible to the eye except it show the time-eaten face given to it by the thousands of years of sun and rain that had beaten upon it" (Johnson 2004, 35). The result was a very stony and highly textured surface. The six-story inn was covered with a mantle of gently undulating red clay tiles.

At the opening of the Grove Park Inn in 1913, Thomas Rankin, Mayor of Asheville, lauded Edwin Grove for this monumental achievement. "Here we see the triumph of architectural skill mingled with a scenic splendor of nature's handiwork, the whole blending in one great harmony never before equaled in the annals of the builders' craft" (2004, 39).

Business thrived and it flagged, styles came and went, and the inn suffered from poor decisions, tough economic times, and a lack of appreciation for its Arts and Crafts essence. Many original features were replaced over time with cheap materials, and original furnishings and lighting were replaced by tasteless pieces in attempts to update the inn (2004, 81).

Charles Sammons bought the inn in 1955. His second wife, Elaine, "encouraged her husband to undertake not simply a remodeling but, more important, a historical restoration designed to preserve the property's heritage" (2004, 93). It was very important to the Sammons to restore the Arts and Crafts character of the original inn, with the immense Great Hall that had been made of stone upon stone, lighted by Roycroft chandeliers hanging from a thirty-foot ceiling, and marked by a massive stone fireplace at each end (2004, 36). Mrs. Sammons "put a stop to the inn's practice of discarding and selling original furnishings handcrafted by the Roycroft Shops and the White Furniture Company" (2004, 94), and she ordered original Arts and Crafts furniture and quality reproductions for the inn.

Mrs. Sammons wanted a historic inn restored to its original charm, while at the same time she wanted to offer guests all the amenities of modern hotels. The Sammons opened a wing in 1984 which, in addition to guest rooms, included a large ballroom and modern kitchen facilities. In addition, renovations to the inn allowed it to be used during the winter months for the first time in many years. Soon after the opening of the Sammons wing, construction began on the massive new Vanderbilt wing (2004, 91).

When Bruce had presented his conference idea to the Grove Park Inn in 1987, he immediately became involved in

From left, Stephen Gray and Bill Porter leading small group discussion

antiques selection for the hotel wings. The Vanderbilt wing opened in the summer of 1988 (2004, 96–97), in time for Bruce Johnson's second Arts and Crafts conference the following February. The Vanderbilt wing, with its lowest floors starting farther down the mountain than the main part of the inn, included exhibition spaces that Arts and Crafts conference attendees are all familiar with. The glass-walled Blue Ridge dining room that overlooks the scenic mountains forms the tenth floor and is the main level of the inn.

The first Grove Park Inn Arts and Crafts Conference in 1988 was scheduled in the month of February because of easy availability of rooms in the winter. In addition, it did not conflict with the only regularly scheduled Arts and Crafts events at the time, the specialty auctions at Skinner and Christie's in May and December. Three hundred people attended the first conference, which was a success, and the group wanted to return the next year. Bruce started planning the next one immediately, locking in the third weekend in February for as many years into the future as could be scheduled.

Bruce Johnson and the GPI management were very compatible, and the inn mainly left Bruce alone to run the conference, select the speakers, and pick the dealers. The management handled food and sleeping arrangements and let Bruce handle the conference as he saw fit. Having a whole year to prepare, Bruce's main challenge was advertising and getting the word out, a more difficult task in pre-Internet and pre-email times. Conference attendees who returned in February of 1989 for the second conference found a larger facility and a bigger crowd. The event was

a marketing opportunity and revenue boost for the Grove Park Inn, especially as the rooms were now occupied in the dead of winter.

The number of antiques show exhibitors grew a little each year, but the number of participating craftspeople burgeoned. Some people suggested holding the conference in a different place each year, but Bruce felt the consistency of the hotel service was important, and he had worked closely with the GPI staff to make sure everything was well organized. Bruce decided to keep the conference at the Grove Park Inn.

While the location stayed the same from one year to the next, the conference itself evolved. Bruce added bus tours, demonstrations, day trips, museum exhibits, and activities in conjunction with the conference. When the seminars got too big for questions and answers, collector Bill Porter suggested holding small group discussions, saying there was a need for interaction. Bruce responded positively to Bill's idea, and small group discussions were immediately popular. Bruce always listened to the ideas of others, and he sometimes acted on them. The number of attendees grew from three hundred in the first year to a thousand by the third.

When the conference began in 1988, prices for Arts and Crafts antiques were beginning to rise above the budget of average collectors and homeowners. This became increasingly problematic for the conference, which "ran the risk of being labeled elitist and unaffordable" (Johnson 2011). By 1990, L. & J.G. Stickley was exhibiting its new

Steven Thomas leading a small-group discussion of collecting woodblock prints

Stephen Gray honored with 2011 Arts and Crafts Lifetime Achievement Award

mission line of furniture in the contemporary crafts show at the Grove Park Inn. Suddenly there were full-page ads in magazines for L. & J.G. Stickley furniture. Arts and Crafts dealers who were exhibiting in the antiques show at the conference felt threatened by the reissue of Arts and Crafts furniture, but

> there was nothing to prevent them from duplicating Gustav Stickley or L. & J.G., right down to the location of the pegs since the Audis had the patents and copyrights. To their credit, the pieces are very well marked and in such a way that no one's going to mistake them for antiques. If you look at the construction, you have to look for details, like modern screws. They were not attempting to make antiques. They were making furniture that looked like antiques—and they did a good job. (Johnson 2011)

The exhibitors expressed their concerns to Johnson at the conference and continued raising the issue throughout the year. "They were very worried about how they were going to compete with furniture manufacturers selling look-alikes down the hall" (Johnson 2011). It was not an easy decision, but Johnson decided the limited exhibition space would showcase only the craftspeople, those whose hands had actually made the furniture or the pottery. The contemporary crafts exhibition would not include furniture manufacturers, such as L. & J.G. Stickley, who had their own large venue twice a year at High Point Market in North Carolina. "When I explained my decision, Alfred and Aminy Audi [owners of L. & J.G. Stickley] were very gracious and understanding. And they continued buying a full-page ad in the conference

above and o.p.: Historic photos of East Entrance, Grove Park Inn

catalog every year without fail, in addition to attending most of our conferences" (Johnson 2011).

There was an ongoing struggle between antiques dealers and contemporary craftspeople, and it was uncertain what the outcome was going to be.

*The controversial issue of Arts and Crafts reproductions was once again raised, as contemporary craftsmen Michael Adams, from Oswego, New York, and V. Michael Ashford, from Olympia, Washington, displayed their merchandise. Many dealers are concerned that the quality of these reproductions is so great that it might harm them in the future; that, were the pieces left to "age" in a barn for a few months, nobody could tell the difference between a newly patinated piece, and its model. (Perrault 1989, 13)*

Absolute clarity for the average collector was always the focus, and Bruce Johnson had established ground rules for the conference from the start. Bruce was adamant that the

antiques and the contemporary crafts be exhibited as two separate shows because some new crafts look so much like original early twentieth-century pieces, they could be confused with antiques. Bruce wanted no confusion.

Bruce also insisted that speakers gear their presentations to the average collector. The Arts and Crafts Research Fund supports scholarship and research, part of the mission of the conference, but scholars must share their work in a way that is accessible to the general Arts and Crafts audience.

*The seminars would give them the information they needed, so they could walk into the antiques show and see the living example of what they had previously only seen on a screen or behind a velvet rope at a museum. Even if they didn't buy it, they could see it. Here they could walk into a room and see a Gustav Stickley settle, and they could look at it, touch it, feel it and see the mark and educate themselves. I think that note hit home with people. (Johnson 2011)*

8. East Entrance, Grove Park Inn, Asheville, N.C.

Exhibition dealers were required to put price tags on every piece. Although some exhibitors were not accustomed to doing this in their galleries at home, Bruce was determined that this was going to be a situation where collectors could come and be able to compare. A young collector would be able to easily learn the difference between a seven thousand dollar Van Erp lamp and a twenty-seven thousand dollar Van Erp because the prices would be clearly marked.

> You have to keep your focus, and it always has to be on the average collector. It has to be. Because if you forget that, you become too highbrow, and then you have the same forty or fifty people in the audience every year. So whether it's bus tours, speakers, or topics, it has to be geared to the proper audience. You have to know who your buyer is. (Johnson 2011)

In Bruce's welcoming letter at the beginning of the catalog to the 12th Annual Grove Park Inn Arts and Crafts Conference 1999, he aptly compared the Arts and Crafts experience to deep sea fishing. "For the first five minutes you think

Great Hall of Grove Park Inn

above: David Rago and Suzanne Perrault; u.r.: Art Accardi;
r.: antiques exhibition

you have him, then you realize you're the one who's been hooked." Bruce developed a national platform through the conference. It was a unique opportunity for collectors to see Arts and Crafts furniture and decorative arts they may never have a chance to see again because of the rareness of the items, and the lectures and small discussion groups stimulated thought and conversation. For anyone interested in the period, it was a compelling weekend and not like anything else. People love talking about their interests, and the Grove Park Inn conference offered attendees a chance to spend days doing just that. The Grove Park Inn, a magnificent Arts and Crafts hotel, was full of people all sharing the same passion, and it was a lot of fun. People became hooked.

The Grove Park Inn Arts and Crafts Conference was one of the essential communication hubs that propelled the revival forward because people were excited about this area and were eager to learn more. Afterwards, they could go home and find Arts and Crafts pieces in thrift stores, flea markets, auctions, and antique shops. A lot of furniture, pottery, metalwork, and other decorative arts were still out there to be found, and most people in the general population didn't know how to recognize it or what the Arts and Crafts meant.

The conference continued growing, and for a lot of people it became a yearly retreat, a reunion, or maybe even a pilgrimage. Even today, some people are die-hard and insist on a room in the original inn, the old section. The rooms have oak drawers built into the walls, high ceilings with original

chandeliers and windows with deep ledges. While not as modern and convenient as the newer wings, the *old section* maintains more of the Arts and Crafts charm in remnants of the original furnishings and architecture.

In the recent economic downturn, some of the dealers who used to exhibit at the conference have left, but new dealers and craftspeople come in every year.

> *Shows are hard work and there's risk involved. To keep it fresh, I think turnover is good. My biggest competition is what I did last year—if I can't compete with that, then people think I'm slipping. Once you lose momentum, it's over. (Johnson 2011)*

One significant way Bruce has kept up the momentum is through his Arts and Crafts collector website. He provides informative articles by different specialists, discussion forums, links to relevant videos, a calendar of events, and the latest Arts and Crafts news. In what is the most

Contemporary crafts exhibitions

compelling section for some, Bruce manages an online marketplace where anyone can post, at no charge, anything Arts and Crafts they want to sell. Bruce also sells advertising on the site and uses it to generate interest and promote the next annual Grove Park Inn conference. It is a work in progress, an excellent site, and becoming more sophisticated by the year. (http://www.artsandcrafts collector.com).

Johnson is realizing his long-held desire to be a writer. In addition to being the official spokesperson for Minwax, Johnson has hosted a collectors' question-and-answer column, "Collectors' Counsel," that he initiated in the late 1990s in what is now Style 1900, formerly Arts and Crafts Quarterly, and he has a website, AskBruceJohnson.Com, that offers advice on furniture refinishing. Johnson has published a number of books on refinishing antiques and has also written on the Grove Park Inn, both in the historical novel genre and in the strict recounting of its history.

The energy and focus of Bruce Johnson are something to behold, and he is perhaps more responsible for the continuation of the Arts and Crafts revival than any other individual. He loves the period and his enthusiasm can be infectious, but that alone would not make for a successful conference. He is a tough and very skilled manager of people and a graceful executor of logistics. The day that one annual conference ends is the day before he begins planning the next.

Bruce has added much to the body of Arts and Crafts scholarship through the conference talks and small group discussions, and through the Arts and Crafts Research Fund that he established, providing financial assistance to individuals researching specific areas of the Arts and Crafts. The entire Arts and Crafts community gratefully acknowledges the importance of what has become Bruce Johnson's lifework.

## References

Johnson, Bruce. 2004. *Built for the Ages: A History of the Grove Park Inn.* Asheville, North Carolina: Grove Park Inn Resort and Spa.

———. In interview with authors. Mountain Lakes, New Jersey. October 15, 2011.

Perrault, Suzanne. 1989. "Grove Park Inn 1989." *Arts and Crafts Quarterly* 2 (4): 13.

Accardi makes his beautiful pottery accessible to people of ordinary means, one of the unfulfilled dreams of Gustav Stickley

# 25. Art Accardi

*Most artists feel ageless because there's always something interesting over the next hill. It's the way you live your life—because you're always making new stuff.*

*— Art Accardi*

His mother was an artist in New York in the 1920s. Living the artist's life was not something he chose.

The arts were flourishing in SoHo in the 1960s and 1970s, and Art Accardi, the artist, jumped in with full-body participation.

> *It was just wonderful. I lived in a loft building, 112 Green Street, that became famous as an artists' collective space on the main floor. Without much financial support, the artists, dancers and musicians all contributed their own resources and time. Some notable art careers were launched in that gallery, Gordon Matta-Clark, Sol LeWitt, and Jean Highstein were favorites, as were the dancers—most notably Trish Brown and the Grand Union dance group. In those days I was a willing body for all kinds of postmodern dance performances, having studied ballet as a child. (Accardi)*

Dance studios in the seventies yielded to art galleries in the eighties in the wake of the groundbreaking Jordan-Volpe Gallery. The galleries sprang up in SoHo and gave Art his first glimpse of the Arts and Crafts revival to come. In the beginning of the eighties, he began buying inexpensive pieces of Roseville and Fulper and joined the American Art Pottery Association (AAPA). Before long, as he became more sophisticated about American art pottery in the early twentieth century Arts and Crafts movement, his tastes began to turn to the more glamorous and expensive pottery from that period. So began a serious collection of Grueby, Rookwood, Newcomb, and his first love, Fulper—but only the best examples he could find.

> *There's something that's always been very appealing to me about the Arts and Crafts period, a romantic feeling I have about it. The wish to recapture the dignity that was lost through industrialization to the craftsman seemed a worthy goal then and it is more so today. (Accardi)*

*BROOKLYN 1960*

Roseville pottery was funky and inexpensive, and Art found an abundance of it in the Midwest, not far from where it was made. Nothing was ever over a hundred dollars, so he loaded up his car. It became kind of a disease, an obsession.

*Yes, I am obsessive. Most collectors are, and the Arts and Crafts pottery collector is obsessive to the point — well, we talked about being purists — people who will not buy a stunning example of any art pottery that is not absolutely mint. You know, I never had that kind of sensibility. I was more into the aesthetic of the piece. I came to this with an artist's sensibility. (Accardi)*

Professionally, Art Accardi was highly successful as a free-lance graphic designer. He worked primarily for large industrial design firms and ad agencies,where he designed literally hundreds of cigarette packages for the British-American Tobacco Company, Philip Morris and Brown and Williamson, liquor packaging for Bacardi, Bolla, Hiram Walker, Guinness, and Glenfiddich. His specialty helped create an appetite for all the approved vices but also soothed the soul with Lipton tea and Barricini chocolates.

Although he had become a collector, he didn't really know anybody in the Arts and Crafts world until 1985, when he started attending David Rago's auctions every few months at the Puck building in Manhattan. Art met other collectors and continued learning about American art pottery. At auction previews, he could hold pieces in his hands and turn them over and inspect them closely, and he could exchange information with and learn from other people. Rago, whose specialty has always been art pottery, was curious about the people attending his auctions and introduced himself to Art Accardi. Because he was evolving as a collector, Accardi was selling as much as he was buying and, in time, offered Rago some pieces to auction. A friendly relationship developed, and Rago taught Art something about how to bid and "how not to have a heart attack when I raised my hand for two thousand dollars. At the time that was scary for me" (Accardi).

Accardi was shocked at the amount of money spent at auctions. After a few years he figured out that to make money it was essential to not only evaluate the items properly but to also spend money. As it turned out, no matter what he did, he could do no wrong because he always turned items over at a profit. Everything he bought turned into gold. Art realized that the market was strengthening because furniture, pottery, and metal dealers got together and worked in conjunction with the auction houses and the magazines to create a market for the Arts and Crafts.

*My experience is in the graphic design world, where cooperation is imperative. Everybody has to help everybody else. It's a team effort that creates a successful package or ad. Not so in the antiques business, where it's all about competition. You have to kick this guy behind his knee, so he falls backwards. Like the first time I met Soandso was a riot. It was at an auction in the middle of nowhere, and I'm looking at a piece of furniture, and he says, "It's cut down." I didn't know what he was talking about. He kept telling me that it was not right, so I believed him. I didn't know what the hell was going on.*

*He looked at me and saw the enemy, so he did a number on me. It's a different world, and not particularly nice—that's one of the lessons that gave me caution in future transactions with my fellow antiques dealers. (Accardi)*

This new dynamic took some getting used to, and Art still found it puzzling. There were competitors who would do very nasty things to each other—archenemies during the day, yet at night they would sit playing poker together, head-to-head. "And I'm saying, I don't get it—they hate each other, talk dirty about each other, then sit down and play cards for an evening, like they're buddy-buddy. I don't get it" (Accardi).

While Accardi did join the nighttime gamblers on the auction floor, he was never a big spender and wouldn't buy a piece just to increase his inventory. His focus was on the aesthetic of each piece and, as a result, he always had an interesting collection of items. He came to realize that his sensibility was admired by a lot of collectors. People would ask him, specifically, what he had in Fulper because they thought he was an expert on that particular pottery.

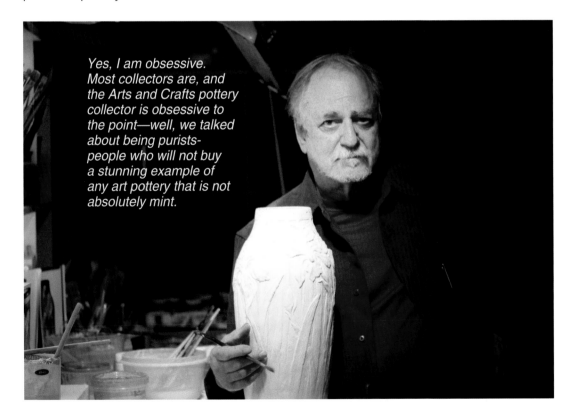

*Yes, I am obsessive. Most collectors are, and the Arts and Crafts pottery collector is obsessive to the point—well, we talked about being purists-people who will not buy a stunning example of any art pottery that is not absolutely mint.*

I always had the arrogance to think that I could very easily recreate what was being made around the turn of the century.

One of a kind and ready to go for the next Arts and Crafts Conference

*It was interesting how it evolved, that part of it. Fulper, in particular, is an aesthetic appreciation because there are some pieces of the same shape, which are crap, but if the glazes are right, they're gems. So I would always buy the pieces that had the great glazes, even if the shape itself wasn't particularly interesting. The glaze could carry it. (Accardi)*

In the mid-1980s, around the same time Accardi started going to auctions, two new galleries opened close to where he lived in SoHo—Peter-Roberts and Michael Carey—so he began frequenting them and they became friendly. Don Magner was the earliest Arts and Crafts dealer, and he was selling pieces through Michael Carey. Art couldn't believe some of the great pottery he got from him. He remembers a Teco piece that was not the typical Teco. It had a fiery glaze, a very unusual piece. He'd seen pieces like that that sold for twenty thousand dollars. It was a museum quality piece and exquisitely beautiful.

Art learned what was out there by buying pieces and studying them. But he also wanted to know about the people who actually made the pots. He was intrigued by the whole philosophy of the Arts and Crafts movement and drawn further into it. It was a revelation to him that there were so many smart people around the turn of the twentieth century, and he found the work and emotional expression of Charles Rennie Mackintosh and his wife, Margaret MacDonald, compelling. He also discovered the richness of thought in the earlier period of the English Arts and Crafts through writings of artists such as William Morris.

On his endless quest to learn more and drink in everything about the Arts and Crafts, Accardi bombarded Peter and Bobby (Peter-Roberts Gallery) with constant questions. But even they were resistant—why bother if he wasn't going to buy anything? But Art was too young and naïve to worry about rejection. Eventually, he started consigning pottery to them and was making a lot of money in the process. Because he was about the only one who consigned to their gallery, they embraced him after a while.

*I was like this kid, and I'd come in and offer them Fulper and all sorts of stuff, and tell them how much I wanted, and they would put outrageous prices on these things and, ironically, they would sell them. They had some famous clients. I had this weird vase—I didn't know what it was—it was a southern piece, and I got it for very little money but it had a great—like a frog skin—glaze on it, and so I wanted big money— my idea of big money—like six hundred dollars, cause I thought it was spectacular. I was so proud when Brad Pitt—he was a big customer of theirs—bought it for two thousand dollars, and he didn't bat an eye about the price. (Accardi)*

Accardi was still freelancing as a graphic designer. Collecting, buying, and selling Arts and Crafts pottery was a hobby, and he was turning things over quickly, buying and selling at an increasingly rapid pace. He started exhibiting at the Grove Park Inn in 1989, the second year of the conference, and doing other shows as well. This was not an unusual progression for collectors. "A lot of the people who are in the business now as dealers were collectors at one time" (Accardi).

The revival has spread like pond ripples out from Accardi because he lives the philosophy of the Arts and Crafts movement, and he passionately creates art.

The young people, the most vital demographic of the revival, who were interested in the Arts and Crafts were buying homes and wanted to decorate them in that style but could not afford to buy high-end original pieces. They were looking for other avenues and could have bought cheap imitations and less expensive things, but they didn't. Those things were not satisfying to them.

However, it wasn't that young people were purists. For the most part, they didn't care about the history behind the pieces. They liked the familiar green in pottery and the heavy oak in furniture, but signatures, labels, and decals were not that important. What was important was the look. Art saw a need and knew the reproduction market was something that hadn't been tapped. He thought the best thing for him to do, as an artist, would be to develop a product for these people.

> I always had the arrogance to think that I could very easily recreate what was being made around the turn of the century, like the Grueby pieces. What did I know? I had no experience, ... but professionally, I was always in that category of can-do, so that was no problem. Unfortunately, it really takes a lifetime to learn, but I got a lot of help, and I was successful right out of the gate, providing products for the young in the Arts and Crafts market. I really did very well with young people. (Accardi)

As he continued studying, collecting, and dealing in the Arts and Crafts, Art gradually scaled down his freelance design business and decided that in retirement he would make pottery. He always assumed there would be a market for his work.

In 1995, Art moved to Woodstock, New York. He left graphic design to make pottery, and he left Manhattan to work in an environment that was less expensive. He had spent over a decade learning about Arts and Crafts pottery and preparing for his transition out of the city. Now he was ready to focus on his own work but there was a lag time before he could start doing reproductions. He did repair work to tide him over until he was in place and his studio was set up.

THIS NEW
ACORN CENTERPIECE DESIGN
IS OFFERED IN AN EDITION OF 30
EACH IS ARTIST SIGNED & NUMBERED, AND,
AS ALWAYS, THROWN AND CARVED BY HAND
SIZE 11" WIDE x 7" TALL  $495 PLUS $35 SHIPPING
(WEST COAST  $45) N.Y. RES. ADD 8 3/4% SALES TAX
CARD OR CHECK IN ADVANCE RESERVES YOUR PIECE
PLEASE INDICATE SUMMER LEAVES (AS SHOWN)
OR FALL LEAVES (YELLOW-ORANGE)
ALLOW 12 TO 14 WEEKS
FOR DELIVERY

THE
ARTS &
CLAY
COMPANY

Peter-Roberts was the first gallery to take his reproductions, and Art was thrilled. It was the only legitimate company that would sell them at the time. However, he felt their decision wasn't so much based on the aesthetic of what he was doing as it was on their need for inventory.

Art Accardi created a niche in pottery comparable to what Michael Adams and Dawn Hopkins had done in metalwork. "Michael Adams is a real practitioner—he makes them exactly how they were made. In a way, my original stuff was also purist, because it was hand thrown, just like the Gruebys. It was very important for my work to be very close to what they were making—originally" (Accardi). Using the highest standards of craftsmanship, Art recreated Arts and Crafts pottery and made it available to those who couldn't afford the original pots.

When Art Accardi first launched his company, the Arts and Clay Company, there was a little bit of resistance from the American Art Pottery Association (AAPA). Art was the first one ever to show up at an AAPA show with reproduction pieces, and he was told he could sell antiques in his booth but not reproductions. This particular show was in Boston, and in those days, they vetted the shows. So Art sold his work out of the back of his car. All the dealers came out to see it, and they all bought his pottery. The biggest buyer was collector Ray Groll, whose support of Accardi from the very beginning has meant a lot to him.

In the beginning, when Art was making reproductions, there were very few contemporary craftspeople at the Grove Park Inn Arts and Crafts Conference. The antiques exhibition was still bigger than the contemporary crafts exhibition. Over the years, Art has observed that a lot of reproduction companies have strayed from original processes or construction methods to make the production less expensive. Maximizing profits can run counter to the Arts and Crafts philosophy if the process or materials are compromised.

The contemporary crafts vendors exhibiting at the Grove Park Inn get better from one year to the next, and there is real talent, but some crafts are being shown that are outside of those made during the Arts and Crafts movement, a point of debate for many. Contemporary crafts in the Arts and Crafts style are a big industry.

In addition to the antiques show and the contemporary crafts show, the Arts and Crafts conference offers many lectures, seminars, and workshops. Art has attended a wide variety of talks. David Rago would occasionally ask him to attend one of his small-group presentations so that Art would help stimulate good questions or contribute something interesting, like the following:

*Well, I have a few secrets. Rago was talking about hidden repairs in pottery, and I taught the class a trick on how to detect really professional repairs. You put the pot in the refrigerator. Pottery conducts, and it absorbs the cold. It'll become as cold as the refrigerator itself, but the repair will stay warmer. So put it in the refrigerator for a few hours, and then feel around, and if there's a warm spot on the pot, you've found a repair. I was repairing pottery, so I knew it was a different medium. The repair is epoxy and has a different coefficient for conducting. I learned it from experience. (Accardi)*

In the course of remodeling his house in Woodstock, Art hired a man to help him and, by coincidence, both the man he hired and his wife were talented potters but unable to make a living. They were making wall pieces and teapots, and such things. The guy flipped over Art's collection of Grueby and Teco. They got together, and Art set up a business arrangement that ultimately benefited each of them. Art spent a lot of money advertising in *Style 1900* and other magazines, and their work flew off the shelves. "That was my strength. I figured I was the merchandiser and the art director, which is what I am" (Accardi).

Art also has helped other talented artists in the Woodstock area by lending his invaluable knowledge and experience, both in marketing and as an artist. Art wants to do his own work now and is surrounded by a team of talented artists and artisans who ascribe to the Arts and Crafts philosophy. Art Accardi embraces the philosophy and includes a little pamphlet describing the history of the Arts and Crafts period when someone buys one of his pots.

Because of Art's graphic design background, he was commissioned to create graphic images and logotypes for Rago's auctions, Beth Cathers' shop, Gallery 532, Robert DeFalco, and he designed books on Fulper pottery and Handel lamps for the Arts and Crafts collector.

The Arts and Crafts revival is unique in the history of art revivals because of both its central philosophy and the industry that has resulted. The revival has spread like pond ripples out from Art because he lives the philosophy of the Arts and Crafts movement, and he passionately creates art. Each pot he crafts is imbued with the essence of the Arts and Crafts movement. Accardi makes his beautiful pottery accessible to people of ordinary means, one of the unfulfilled dreams of Gustav Stickley. Through his artistic drive to make the next pot or realize his next interesting idea, Art Accardi, in a sense, is ageless because the spirituality of his work touches many lives.

### References

Accardi, Art. In interview with Jeffrey Preston. Woodstock, New York. July 17, 2011.

Brooklyn 1955

Large painted tile of harbor scene by Art Accardi

Steven Thomas at work

# 26. Steven Thomas

*Steven Thomas is the premier dealer of woodblocks who lives in Vermont but seems to be everywhere. He is a tireless exhibitor and always shows at the Grove Park Inn in Asheville, the Pier Show in New York, and other major venues. He and his wife, Deborah Bassett, are distinctive, lean and fit with graying hair that seems premature.*

Margaret Jordan Patterson, "Morning Glories," color woodcut, c. 1925

Many collectors and dealers in the Arts and Crafts have written articles and books on the history, furniture, or refinishing. Steven Thomas became a published writer with a book he authored with a veterinarian in the 1980s, *Backyard Livestock: Raising Good, Natural Food for Your Family*. Steven has an air of confidence and gives the appearance of being very good at the things he does; therefore, it is not surprising that this handbook has become the standard reference work for the subject. It has been reprinted several times, the third edition published in 2007. While his area of expertise is unusual—raising your own livestock for the dinner table—it is consistent with the natural lifestyle advocated by Gustav Stickley, one free of the industrial noise of contemporary life.

Steven and Deborah met in 1979. She was an antiques dealer and that intrigued him. The idea of making a living selling art was very appealing to him. Deborah mentored him and encouraged him to find his own niche in the world of antiques and the arts. He gravitated to prints. Steven believes that "knowing what you have is everything, and nobody knew anything about prints." His financial resources were limited, but he bought auction catalogs of prints, studied them assiduously, and learned pricing from them. He also invested in the ten-volume Benezit dictionary of artists and *Who Was Who in American Art*.

The more woodblocks Steven came across, the more he was seduced by them, and that became his specialty. He advertised in trade magazines and his business took off. In 1986, a group of forty Margaret Patterson woodblock prints became available. Steven partnered with Mary Ryan and Jim Bakker in the purchase and, within the year, they presented the first cataloged retrospective of Patterson's work (Thomas 2012).

In 1987 Steven acquired a large number of prints and printing blocks by Provincetown artists that included Agnes Weinrich and Karl Knaths. He curated an exhibit at the Provincetown Art Association and Museum in 1988, *Provincetown Printing Blocks,* the first museum exhibit devoted to printing matrices (Steven Thomas, Inc.).

Steven started exhibiting his prints at the Grove Park Inn Arts and Crafts Conference in1990. He feels that in spite of being an academically oriented group, most people didn't know what woodblocks were. People would timidly peek in, reluctant to enter his booth.

Recognizing the importance of information, Steven regularly offers a small group discussion, "Collecting Block Prints: How to Get Started, What to Look for, What You Can Find."

Gustave Baumann (Amer. 1881-1971) "Winsor Canon," color woodcut, 1921, 10 x 9½"

It has been a good format for teaching people the basics and showing how a woodblock is the perfect reflection of the Arts and Crafts aesthetic. The artist can create a woodblock simply using materials from nature—the wood of a tree, dyes from plants, and fiber from plants for the making of paper. From start to finish, it is the hand of the artist that creates the woodblock.

In the early nineties, David Rago suggested that Steven put some woodblocks into his auction. They became more visible to a broader audience. From year to year, crowds were growing at the Grove Park Inn and so was interest in Steven's prints. The Steven Thomas booth draws the viewer in. The images he displays are evocative of the Arts and Crafts period and are thoughtfully combined on the wall. His booth is often crowded because it is so compelling.

Steven has a large number of Arts and Crafts woodblocks and he exhibits at many shows, including Miami Beach, the Pier Show, and the Baltimore Summer Antiques Shows. However, the Grove Park Inn is the only venue where Steven shows his entire inventory of Arts and Crafts woodblocks. Steven has been promoting woodblocks for over twenty years. Through the articles he has written in *American Bungalow* and *Style 1900*, his special exhibitions, and his booth at art and antiques shows, Steven has elevated awareness of the woodblock print as fine art.

George Senseney (Amer. 1874-1943) [River Landscape with Crescent Moon], color etching & aquatint, c. 1917, 16" x 10". Signed in pencil. Senseney was the first artist in this country to print etchings in color. He was the founder and director of the Holyoke (MA) League of Arts & Crafts

### References

Steven Thomas, Inc. website. http://www.woodblock-prints.com/index.html.

Thomas, Steven. In interview with authors. February 13, 2012. Asheville, North Carolina.

Margaret J. Patterson (Amer. 1867-1950) "Main Street, Nantucket," color woodcut, c. 1920, 7¼" x 10½"

Emma Kaan (American 1860–1949) "Waterway," woodcut with hand coloring, c. 1904, 9¼" x 14"

# ARTS AND CRAFTS

# FURNITURE

# DESIGN

The
Grand Rapids
Contribution

1895 - 1915

Grand Rapids Art Museum
March 13 to May 17
1987

**Don Marek**

# 27. Don Marek

*Tall and relaxed, he's even-tempered and tells a good story. Don Marek owns Heartwood, an antiques shop in downtown Grand Rapids, and he also owns a couple of buildings across the street from his shop that he restored. He appreciates the rich history of the area and has used his talents to make a difference in the community, helping to bring back the city he loves, the once vibrant center of furniture manufacturing, particularly fertile during the Arts and Crafts period.*

As students in 1974, Don Marek and his girlfriend went to a lot of auctions as research for her master's thesis, "the auction as verbal art form," for the Department of Folklore at the University of Indiana. Don noticed things went for far less at auction in the region south of Bloomington than they did north of Bloomington and became interested in the commerce of furniture. He did refinishing as a hobby, and when he moved back home to Grand Rapids, he started a furniture refinishing business. He went to auctions and estate sales looking for furniture to refinish and started noticing and liking Arts and Crafts pieces.

Having always lived in the central part of the country, Don wanted to experience life in the Pacific Northwest while he was still young, so he took his refinishing skills to Seattle in 1975. There was an abundance of European furniture but a shortage of American antiques, and the lack of older culture and the constant rain drove him back to Grand Rapids in 1977.

A good gallery space in downtown Grand Rapids was very affordable in 1977 at one hundred fifty dollars a month including utilities, so Don opened Heartwood and soon discovered why it was so cheap. The neighborhood was rife with drugs and full of run-down houses, and social tensions ran high as a lot of people were on welfare or unemployed. Cynicism was rampant.

When Don Marek's landlord offered the building to him for $29,900, two years later, he decided to make an investment in Grand Rapids. The building had four one-bedroom apartments and some first-floor shops, mostly occupied by long-term tenants. Thirty-five years later, Heartwood is still in that space.

Initially, Heartwood included a small number of Arts and Crafts pieces, but the balance tipped when Don started going to Brimfield, the Massachusetts flea market, in the

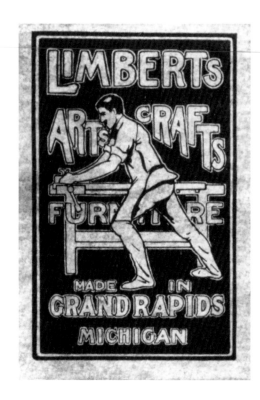

Grand Rapids Bookcase
& Chair Co.
HASTINGS, MICH.
Chair No. 126

Signatures of some of the furniture makers in Grand Rapids that Don has researched. He is the expert in furniture of the Grand Rapids, Michigan area

early eighties. Gradually, Heartwood became mostly Arts and Crafts. Don exhibited at Boice Lydell's annual Roycroft conferences in East Aurora, New York from 1984 through 1986. He saw everything as an education—Brimfield, antiques shows, and talking with other dealers like Boice Lydell, Dave Rudd, David Rago, and collector, Bill Porter.

In 1987, Don curated the exhibition, *Arts and Crafts Furniture Design: The Grand Rapids Contribution 1895-1915*, at the Grand Rapids Art Museum, "to demonstrate the diversity of progressive furniture design in the Grand Rapids area during the American Arts and Crafts period" (Marek 1987, 15). In the exhibition catalog, Marek related a chronology of furniture manufacturing in Grand Rapids and introduced furniture companies to the Arts and Crafts community. Around half of the seventy-two objects shown in the catalog were by Charles P. Limbert and the rest were by Stickley Brothers, the Phoenix Furniture Company and various lesser known companies. There had been very few Arts and Crafts exhibitions since Robert Judson Clark's 1972 Princeton show, and people came from across the country to see his exhibition. While it was not a Limbert exhibit, it showed more Limbert than any previous exhibition, and the catalog, to this day, remains a solid reference work on Limbert and on furniture companies of the area.

Furniture experts and scholars recognize Don as one of the foremost Limbert scholars. In response to an inquiry about drop-front desks, Dave Rudd, one of the leading Arts and Crafts dealers in the country, quotes the Marek exhibition catalog in his American Bungalow column:

*I found this image in The Grand Rapids Contribution, written by Don Marek for an exhibit at the Grand Rapids Art Museum in 1987. Don says of this desk, "The interplay of gentle tapers, arches and cutouts gives this Limbert drop front a strong architectonic quality." I would have to agree. (Rudd 2011)*

Marek's Grand Rapids scholarship didn't stop with the furniture makers. In 1999, he also published *Grand Rapids Art Metalwork: 1902-1918,* which includes coppersmiths and shops of the area, illustrated with more than two hundred photos of lighting, desk sets, jewelry, jardiniers, and other works. Don has further contributed to the body of Arts and Crafts scholarship with the many articles he has written for various magazines, such as *Style 1900*.

The list of antiques dealers who set up at the very first Grove Park Inn Arts and Crafts Conference in 1988 includes Don Marek, who has not missed a single conference, in spite of a harrowing and almost fatal ride home from Asheville in 2007.

*We had gotten off to a good start and were in the mountains of Kentucky by 10 at night. We were in a good mood, the weather was great, and everything was fine. All of a sudden the right wheels of the truck started slipping off the edge of the road, and I yelled, "Mitch, what are you doing? We're going off the road." And he mumbled something like, "I gotta get off, I gotta get off." I yelled, "You can't. There's no exit here, what are you doing?"*

Heartwood, Don's gallery, on
Cherry Street in downtown Grand Rapids

Limbert center table No. 164, oak, 30½" x 33" x 33"

Limbert drop front desk No. 712, oak, 54" x 38" x 13"

*The road curved sharply to the left up ahead and there was a guardrail straight in front of us. I tried to grab the wheel and just then, Mitch blacked out—completely blacked out. I couldn't keep us on the road—his whole body was draped over the steering wheel—and I had a split second to make a choice. It was either hitting the guardrail in the middle of the truck or doing what I did—yanking down on the steering wheel as hard as I could, which sent us off to the right.*

*So we flew off into space, into a ravine a seventy feet deep—at seventy miles an hour. We missed the guardrail, which would have split the truck in two. I just thought, "This is it. We're going to die, there's no way we're going to survive this." We were sailing above the treetops, traveling at least a city block through the air, and as we dropped, we started getting slapped by the tops of the trees, bapping against the bottom of the truck.*

*By all rights, we should never have survived, and the only reason we did was the way we landed. First, we hit a fairly large tree on the right front corner of the truck, which ripped off the right-front fender and the mirror and broke the windshield, and it slowed us down quite a bit and made us spin ninety degrees to the left. Then we hit a much larger tree—just behind Mitch's head. We hit that tree going sideways, so it absorbed most of our forward momentum. It stopped the truck—see, what would have happened had we*

then they hooked onto the rear bumper of the truck, and started slowly winching it up that steep hill. I could hear all the contents crashing, tumbling, and falling inside the truck. When they got to the top, they had to get it over the guardrail, so the second wrecker hooked onto the front of the truck. It was a pretty graceful dance they did, the two wreckers picking up both ends of the truck at the same time and lifting it over the guardrail and setting it down on the right lane of the highway.

The EMT guys were shocked we could walk away from that. It was one of the weirdest things they'd ever seen. We found out Mitch hadn't eaten since breakfast, he'd skipped lunch and dinner, and his blood sugar must have dropped very quickly.

The amazing thing to me is that I had a lot of fragile things in the load, like pottery and glassware and stained glass lampshades, and none of it broke. There were pieces of furniture that were destroyed. There were some screws in the furniture that were three inches long that were bent into an "s" shape, from the force when everything went off to the left, but everything fragile survived. It just amazed me. Considering how it happened, I was just shocked I didn't lose more than I did. Like my life—I really didn't expect to survive when we went off into space cause we were so high up and the ravine was so deep. It had to have been close to a quarter of a mile that we flew through the air, going full speed, like being shot from a gun.
It was really a miracle.

hit the tree in the center of the truck, all the load of heavy furniture would have come forward and crushed us up against the tree, and we would have been killed. But all the furniture moved right, and it bulged out the right side of the box. That's the only reason we survived.

That second tree actually split the box of the truck open, and then we plunged down into the ravine and kept falling until a grove of small saplings cushioned our landing. There was moisture in the bottom of the ravine because of a little stream of water, and there were all these little saplings growing really thickly. We plunged into those, and they all bent over the top of a chain-link fence and created this soft cushion that we went forward into. That absorbed the last of our momentum.

When the truck stopped, I was totally stunned that we were alive and not injured. Mitch was still out. I got out of the truck, not sure what had happened to him. I could barely get my door open enough to squeeze out of the truck, and I'm wandering around in the ravine, trying to figure out how to get to a phone or something. I went back to the truck to check on Mitch, and he was starting to come around. He had his cell phone, so we called 9-1-1.

I didn't know how the heck they were going to get that truck up, we were so far down and wedged in the trees. They brought out two large wreckers and chainsaws and started cutting trees to clear a path,

Don is an extremely calm man. He squared his shoulders and drove to Asheville the following February to participate in the antiques exhibition, never missing a year.

In 2010, on Bruce Johnson's ArtsAndCraftsCollector.com, a reader sent Bruce a photograph of an unmarked brooch in hopes of determining the maker of the piece, pointing out that a similar piece had been shown in an ARK Antiques ad (Rosalie Berberian's company) in an old Grove Park Inn conference catalog. Don Marek, an avid reader of Johnson's website, generously contacted Bruce Johnson to share his expertise on Grand Rapids metalwork. He identified the name, Forest Craft Guild, and gave background information—it had been founded in 1905 in Grand Rapids by Forest Mann, who had studied under Arthur Wesley Dow at the Pratt Institute (Chicago Silver website 2012). The following is from Bruce Johnson's ArtsAndCraftsCollector.com:

> Collecting Forest Craft Guild work has been made more challenging by their inconsistent use of shopmarks. Mann himself often appears to have had little inclination to sign even his own work. A few pieces have the block lettering "Forest Craft Guild," others just the initials "FCG," but as Don Marek reports, "Only a few of the Forest Craft Guild pieces were marked."

o.p. and r.: Heartwood; below:
Don at Christmas; l.r.: Limbert
window bench No. 243, oak,
24" x 24" x 18"

*Fortunately for us, however, Don Marek has included photographs of scores of pieces known to have been produced by Forest Mann and the craftsmen and craftswomen at Forest Craft Guild in his book Grand Rapids Art Metalwork.*

*I should note, though, that this hardback book was privately printed and published by Don Marek, so only a limited number of copies remain. The level of scholarship, detail and accuracy evident in it guarantees that it will soon become a collector's item in and of itself. (Johnson 2010)*

Don Marek is a pillar of the Arts and Crafts community. A careful and thoughtful researcher, he's equally careful with words. Indeed, his writing has helped establish him as one of the scholars who has advanced the revival by his knowledge and his willingness to share it. And his gift for relating events and stories in such an engaging manner enriches the tapestry of the Arts and Crafts revival.

### References

Bartinique, A. Patricia, and Peter A. Copeland. 2012. *The Tobey Furniture Company, Chicago, Illinois: A Brief History*. Eau Claire, Wisconsin: Turn of the Century Editions/The Parchment Press.

Cathers, David. 2003. *Gustav Stickley*. New York: Phaidon Press.

Chicago Silver: Handwrought Metalwork from the American Arts & Crafts Movement. http://chicagosilver.com/fcg.htm.

Johnson, Bruce. "Forest Craft Guild Remains Elusive, But Rewarding." *Arts and Crafts Collector*. May 25, 2010. http://artsandcraftscollector.com/collectors_guide/

forest_craft_guild_remains_elusive_but_rewarding.

Marek, Don. 1987. *Arts and Crafts Furniture Design: The Grand Rapids Contribution 1895-1915*. Grand Rapids Art Museum.

Rudd, David. Perspectives on Antiques. *American Bungalow*. 72 (Winter 2011). http://www.americanbungalow.com/category/magazine/magazine-articles/david-rudd.

View of the central court of Crab Tree Farm

# 28. Crab Tree Farm

*One can get lost in the early twentieth century at Crab Tree Farm. The low white stucco buildings nearly touch as they horseshoe around a large green. White cupolas atop the steep red roofs echo a large central clock tower marking the main building and beyond the buildings are fields, orchards, and a Japanese pond partially obscured by tall grasses.*

Front facade of Ellis House, designed by architect Harvey Ellis (1852–1904)

Inspired by the natural beauty of the location and the 1910 architecture, John Bryan began developing an extensive American Arts and Crafts collection of furniture and decorative arts when he purchased Crab Tree Farm in 1985. The buildings designed by Solon Spencer Beman, noted Chicago architect, offer 20,000 square feet of space. Bryan renovated the interior spaces and created settings largely following those presented by Gustav Stickley in his monthly magazine, *The Craftsman*. The furniture displayed at Crab Tree Farm is mainly the work of Gustav Stickley, and a few of the pieces are original to *Craftsman Farms*, but other collections that complement the Stickley furniture include the decorative arts of his American, British, and European contemporaries.

Located thirty miles north of Chicago on the edge of Lake Michigan, Crab Tree Farm is a working farm with sheep,

horses, cattle, turkeys, and dogs, but it equally supports and promotes craftsmanship through state of the art workspaces and residencies for "woodworkers, ceramics artists, metalworkers, and sculptors" (CTF brochure). It is a living testament to the American Arts and Crafts movement and philosophy, and a dynamic resource, open by invitation to those seeking to know more about the period.

John Bryan is a man of many interests and collections, but traveling almost monthly to Europe for thirty years as CEO of Sara Lee Corporation, he had neither the time nor the patience to sit through "sales," as he calls auctions. He's been to very few, although many years ago he spent two days at an auction of English furniture and got nothing but bought the pieces two days later from the dealers who had outbid him.

The principal room in the Lodge, with its original trusses exposed

Although Bryan had neither the time nor the inclination, he did buy at auction through a variety of dealers, such as Beth Cathers and Michael Fitzsimmons. He never limited himself to a particular one and received good advice from an array of expert dealers over the years, including Don Magner, Dave Rudd, and John Toomey. Bryan claims to be an amateur at most things and relies on skilled people to inform his decisions. Out of the many dealers he knew and worked with, Bryan thought Paul Fiore stood out as an innovative and pioneering dealer. Through him, he met Michael Carey and Tim Gleason, who often served as one of Bryan's dealers after Carey's death in 1989. Bryan remarks that today there are a lot of wealthy people involved in private sales. The market has changed and more and more transactions are taking place that way.

A complete house designed by Harvey Ellis was built on the grounds of Crab Tree Farm in 1993 on the site of the original farmhouse, which fire destroyed in 1972. The plans for the house were based on the Ellis article, "How to Build a Bungalow," in *The Craftsman* (December 1903, 253–260), and "no other actual home based on the drawings has been identified" (CTF brochure). Harvey Ellis was a gifted architect hired by Gustav Stickley to design furniture, but he died

prematurely, only eight months after joining Stickley (Cathers 2003, 81). The interior of the bungalow, Ellis House, is true to the descriptions in *The Craftsman* article and is furnished throughout with furniture designed by Harvey Ellis.

John Bryan generously lends pieces to major exhibitions and works closely with a variety of museums on exhibitions, for example, the Block Museum of Art at Northwestern University and the de Young Museum in San Francisco. The Dallas Museum's 2008 *Gustav Stickley and the American Arts & Crafts Movement* exhibited many pieces on loan from Crab Tree Farm.

In addition, Crab Tree Farm has published books that fill gaps in the scholarship of the period, such as *Arts and Crafts Rugs for Craftsman Interiors* by David Cathers and Linda Parry, and two exhibition catalogues, *Design in the Age of Darwin: From William Morris to Frank Lloyd Wright* and *The Arts & Crafts Movement in the UK and the USA* (Crab Tree Farm website).

Craftsman Farms in Parsippany, New Jersey, honored John Bryan with the Als Ik Kan award, the highest they bestow, citing Bryan's years of leadership in arts philanthropy and his contributions to scholarship through Crab Tree Farm

Crab Tree Farm grounds above and to the right

View of the central court of Crab Tree Farm from Sheridan Road

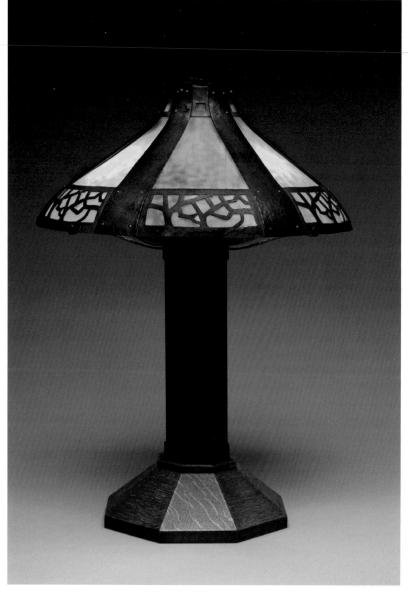

Gustav Stickley jardinière; l.: Gustav Stickley electric lamp No. 625

publications. "In the earliest years of the Craftsman Farms Foundation, he understood the significance of saving and restoring Craftsman Farms for the benefit of the public. Mr. Bryan has supported the Foundation with his knowledge, vision and generosity from the very beginning" (Craftsman Farms 2010).

Crab Tree Farm works with the city of Chicago and the broader Chicago area to meet some of its needs and elevate life through art. At the time of the authors' visit, carved benches were being produced in the woodworking shop for The Crown Sky Garden inside the Ann & Robert H. Lurie Children's Hospital of Chicago. The benches were invisibly wired to allow activation of colored light and sound, enchanting children and enhancing the natural form and grain of the wood. Crown Sky, which opened in the spring of 2012, is an interactive garden for children and is featured in a short video on the hospital's website, http://www.luriechildrens.org/en-us/about-us/building-lurie-childrens/Pages/crown-sky-garden.aspx.

The Crab Tree Farm website (http://www.crab-treefarm.org) is calm and clean. It quietly shows the beauty of the surroundings, the buildings, and, to an extent, the collection. What is particularly striking is the total absence of people in the photographs and the minimum of names mentioned in the information (Gleason 2011), almost reminiscent of a Dow composition. In the entire website, John Bryan's name is mentioned once, only as the fourth name in the farm's succession of owners, rightly taking his place in the history of the dairy farm. Bryan is a private and generous man, and Crab Tree Farm is an important museum of the American Arts and Crafts. It provides a foundation for serious scholarship of the period.

The Crab Tree Farm brochure quotes Gustav Stickley expressing the desire to demonstrate through his magazine, *The Craftsman*, "how to create an environment where simple needs are met in a simple, direct way; in pointing out how a home [should be a place] where lives may be lived out in peace and happiness . . . and where good work may be done because of the silent influences of space, freedom and sincerity." Crab Tree Farm is a beautiful manifestation of *The Craftsman* lifestyle and philosophy lived out in the twenty-first century and a magnificent cultural gift that has enriched many lives and will continue to uplift and strengthen the scholarship of the Arts and Crafts period.

Roycroft table lamp

## References

Bryan, John. In interview with authors. Lake Bluff, Illinois. September 16, 2011.

Cathers, David. 2003. *Gustav Stickley*. New York: Phaidon Press.

Crab Tree Farm brochure. http://www.crabtreefarm.org/sites/default/files/documents/

CTF_BrochureWeb.pdf.

Crab Tree Farm website. http://www.crabtreefarm.org.

Craftsman Farms. "Philanthropist John H. Bryan to Receive Als Ik Kan Award." Notes From the Farms, Summer 2010. Retrieved from Craftsman Farms website, September 3, 2012. http://www.stickley-museum.org/docs/Newsletters/nftf-summer-2010-3.pdf.

Dukoff, Kenny. In interview with authors. Asheville, North Carolina. February 17, 2012.

Gleason, Tom. In interview with authors. Lake Bluff, Illinois. September 16, 2011.

Lurie Children's Hospital website. Crown Sky Garden. http://www.luriechildrens.org/en-us/about-us/building-lurie-childrens/Pages/crown-sky-garden.aspx. Accessed November 14, 2012.

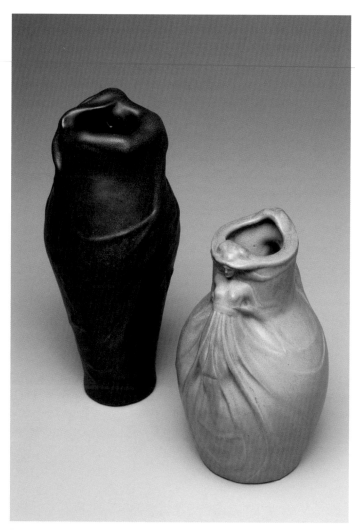

Two Van Briggle Lorelei vases; r.: Teco pottery vase

Grueby pottery vase

Marblehead decorated vase

Gus Stickley adjustable-back chair No. 2342

Gustav Stickley dining table No. 631 (director's table)

Harvey Ellis inlaid desk for Gustav Stickley, c. 1903

Robert Jarvie candelabra

Gustav Stickley mantle clock

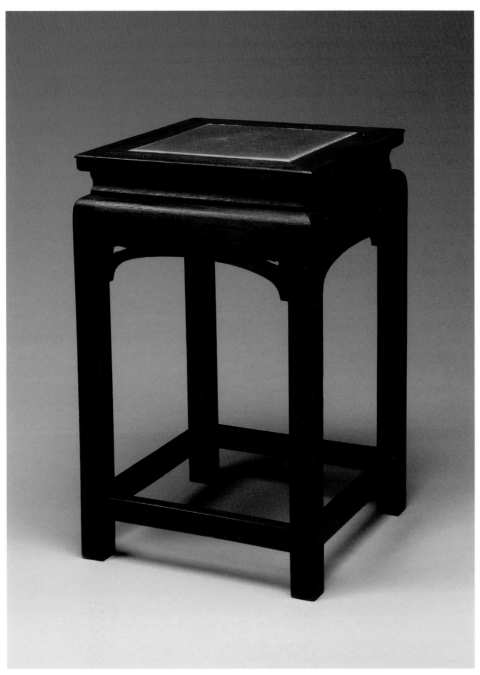

Yeddo plant stand with Grueby tile

Gustav Stickley serving table

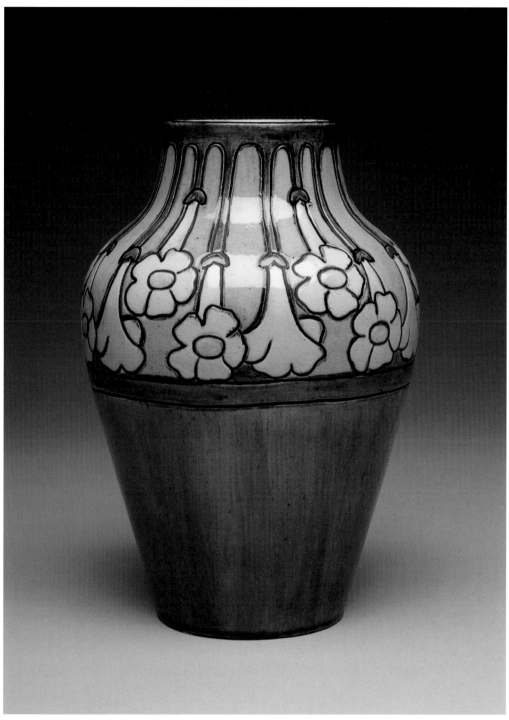

Newcomb College vase

Stone steps to log house, photo by Jeffrey Preston

# 29. Craftsman Farms

*Craftsman Farms represented Gustav Stickley's dream of a peaceful and harmonious life with his family, fostered by simple beauty, honest work, and nature. It was to be a residential community held together by the craftsman ethic of "als ik kan," with a communal farm that created abundant food. He also planned for a boys' school on the grounds.*

Executive director, Heather Stivison, photo by Doug Stivison

When Craftsman Farms was sold by the Farny family in 1986, its existence as a piece of American history came under grave threat because a New York developer, Foreston Development, had bought the property. The January 1987 issue of *Arts and Crafts Quarterly* included an article by Muriel Berson, an activist spearheading efforts to save Craftsman Farms, pleading for people to express their opposition. She described the development plans by the new owner of the property.

> *Fifty-five townhouses are proposed on the "perimeter" of the property which backs up on a residential development ... They will have two stories each with stone and wood outside construction in the "Stickley" style. The developers have said to the homeowners contiguous to the property that all the Stickley houses would be maintained and restored back to the Stickley tradition. However, some of the houses would be incorporated in the total design for the fifty-five units! We feel any physical change to the structures or property would be a loss of this valuable example of integrated design. (Bergman 1987, 5)*

Jack C. Heller, head of the development project, said that he did not care for the work of Gustav Stickley but he was interested in the project because of the prestige it would bring. He has "retained the architect Robert A.M. Stern to replicate the shingle and stone style of Stickley's house in the new residences, which will cost about $400,000" (DePalma 1987).

The organization, Save Our Stickley (SOS), was formed to create a plan and defend the historic site. In Muriel Berson's words, the "powered cast of characters for the developer" (Berson 1987) ensured an uphill fight for the preservationists. Indeed, to her point, any opposition the respected and accomplished Ulysses G. Dietz, Curator of Decorative Arts at the Newark Museum, might have had to the developer's plan was tempered by the impressive reputation of Robert A.M. Stern, the architect being retained for the project, as expressed by Dietz in a letter to the editor of the New York Times.

Murial Berson, Nancy Strathearrn, and Vivian Zoe; r.: The Gustav Stickley Museum from the Southeast

*As a decorative arts curator, an historic preservationist, and just an architecture buff, I lean rather more to the side that would like to see the remaining 26 acres undeveloped, especially with the careless and destructive development that is ruining rural New Jersey today. However, I think Mr. Heller's choice of Robert A. M. Stern shows his sincere desire to produce a project that will, in fact, be sensitive to Stickley's own ideals. (Dietz 1987)*

Berson continued leading the fight for preservation of Stickley's utopian compound and updating readers of *Arts and Crafts Quarterly*.

*Those of us who have seen the site plans are not sure that the developer will come off as he hopes. The main log house is planned to remain untouched and used for a community center. However, the cottages are proposed to be incorporated into larger and more glamorous housing ("in the Stickley style") and in turn will become unrecognizable as Stickley-designed buildings. (Berson 1987, 6)*

Progress was made in the complicated fight against the developers. The Parsippany Zoning Board of Adjustment voted against the proposed development in December of 1988, and Craftsman Farms Foundation was incorporated one month later, in January 1989, so that the property could "be supervised and maintained as an historic site" (Belson 1989, 30). On July 12, 1989, formal condemnation papers on the current owner were filed, and The Craftsman Farms Foundation joined in a contract agreement with the Township of Parsippany "to manage and administer the property" (Ellis 1990, 36). Ultimately, "the Township acquired the property by right of eminent domain from the descendants of Major George Farny" (Bartinique 1992, 120).

Many Gustav Stickley devotees were ecstatic that after a six-year fight against the ruin of the historic site by developers, Parsippany-Troy Hills acquired Craftsman Farms in September 1989. The joyous opening weekend of Craftsman Farms was on April 28, 1990. There was much preparatory work, and furniture was lent or donated by many generous people, including David Rago, Jerry Cohen, Aminy and Alfred Audi, to name but a few (Ellis Winter 1990, 24-26). The chairwoman of

l.: Log house

l.l.: Historic photo of young girl sitting near stone steps

l.r.: View of log house from Northwest, 2012

Bottom: Entrance to porch of log house

the newly formed Craftsman Farms Foundation was longtime Farms advocate, Elaine Hirschl Ellis (Greene 1990).

As a graduate student in the late 1950s, Robert Judson Clark wanted to understand the local Berkeley architecture. Combing through the stacks of the University of California library, he discovered *The Craftsman* by Gustav Stickley. He was riveted and wanted the complete sixteen-year run of the magazine, so he began looking through Bay area bookstores. "The Craftsman's Home" (Stickley October 1908, 78–93) was his favorite of the architectural articles (Clark 1999, iv-v). Stickley described in detail the construction of the house at Craftsman Farms and his feelings behind it.

> *I never before realized how much pleasure was to be found in the building of a dwelling that [so] completely expressed one's own taste and individuality as the painting of a picture or the writing of a book. In fact, I can think of no creative work that is so absorbingly delightful as this creation of a home to live in for the rest of one's life. I have always felt that this must be so and have said and written*

*it many times, but now the realization of the truth of it comes home to me with a force that is entirely new, for this is the first house I have ever built for my own use, from the ground up to the last detail of the completed structure. (Stickley October 1908, 79)*

In 1968, Robert Judson Clark finally had the chance to visit Gustav Stickley's Craftsman Farms. He met Phyllis and Cyril Farny at their home, which their family had bought from the bankrupt Gustav Stickley in 1917. Clark stayed in touch with the Farnys and, in 1973, helped organize a reunion of people who had been associated with the property in any way, since 1910. Three Stickley daughters and other family members met at Craftsman Farms with the Farnys and a few others. Clark remembered this as the high point in his relationship with Phyllis and Cyril (Clark 1999, vi).

Ten years later, Elaine Hirschl Ellis created a Craftsman Farms event, "Gustav Stickley Day," in September of 1983, featuring tours of Craftsman Farms. This was the first time Phyllis and Cyril Farny had ever opened their house to the public. Other events of the day included lectures at the Morris Museum of Arts and Sciences by Stickley experts, Robert Judson Clark of Princeton University, Richard Guy Wilson of University of Virginia, and David Cathers, author of *Furniture of the American Arts and Crafts Movement*. In

addition, there were original *Craftsman* magazines and photographs on display at the Morris County Courthouse. The public was also invited to take their small Arts and Crafts objects, or photos of larger pieces, to the Morristown Public Library for free appraisal by Arts and Crafts dealer, Beth Cathers, of Jordan-Volpe Gallery (Malarcher 1983). Just a few years after "Stickley Day," Phyllis and Cyril sold most of the original Stickley furniture and decorative arts in preparation for their move to Colorado (Fish 1999, 55), and they sold Craftsman Farms, as mentioned earlier, in 1986.

With the saving of Gustav Stickley's home, The Craftsman Farms Foundation was established in January 1989 "to interpret, restore, and preserve Craftsman Farms and the artifacts and ideals associated with Gustav Stickley and the Arts and Crafts movement and to demonstrate the continuing relevance of Gustav Stickley and the Arts and Crafts movement" (Craftsman Farms website 2012). The establishment in 1990 of the Center for the Study of the American Arts and Crafts Movement set the groundwork for the events that were to follow.

The first major exhibition at Craftsman Farms was the 1992 *Gustav Stickley: His Craft*, which was also the "only museum exhibition to date to focus in depth on Gustav Stickley's work," according to the foreword by David W.

o.p.: Gustav Stickley with his grandchild at Craftsman Farms, 1912; clockwise from u.l.: Dining room with sideboard; Gustav Stickley; Gustav Stickley's wife, Eda, and daughter; Bottom: Daughter, Hazel Stickley

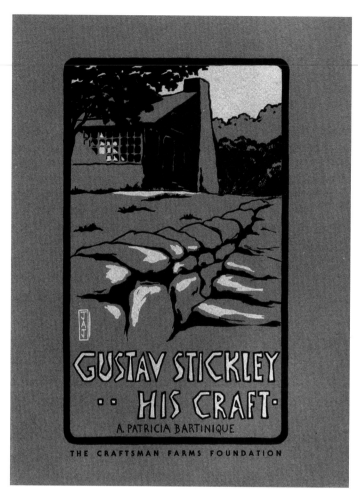

Clockwise from u.l.:

1992 exhibition, Gustav Stickley: His Craft, cover and poster woodblock designed and executed by Judith Ann Jordan. Guest curated by A. Patricia Bartinique;

Gustav Stickley armchair No. 2576;

Armchair No. 331;

Library table No. 410; Detail

Lowden in the exhibition catalog (Bartinique 1992). In her *New York Times* review of the exhibition, Rita Reif quoted A. Patricia Bartinique:

> *"We wanted the exhibition to present the best of Stickley, with as broad a spectrum as possible of the designs he produced," said A. Patricia Bartinique, the guest curator and a professor of English at Essex County College in Newark. "There's been no attempt to show the rooms as they were when the Stickleys lived here. We have none of their furniture from this house on view, but we hope we soon may. Eventually, in fact, we intend to furnish it the way Stickley did." (1992).*

Clockwise from u.l.: Lantern above entrance door to log house; Electric lantern No. 203; Music cabinet with inlay; Exhibition open to public; Patricia Bartinique receiving gift from David Lowden, president of the board, 1992

The exhibition showed one hundred fifty items, all by Gustav Stickley and lent by thirty-five collectors. Bill and Patsy Porter provided a long-term loan of a leather-topped hexagonal table for the 1992 exhibition. Exactly twenty years later, in August of 2012, the table was returned to the Porter's new Michigan house, which features several Gustav Stickley period rooms. The beautiful hexagonal table graced Craftsman Farms and was joined over time by the company of other Gus Stickley pieces, many of which were original to the house. With the *New York Times* review of *Gustav Stick-* *ley: His Craft*, Craftsman Farms received its first national attention as a museum. The importance of this exhibition to Craftsman Farms cannot be overstated. In the words of Ted Lytwyn, "*His Craft* put the Farms on the map" (2011).

A second major exhibition at the Farms, in 1995, *Innovation and Derivation: The Contribution of L. & J.G. Stickley to the Arts and Crafts Movement*, put a scholarly focus on

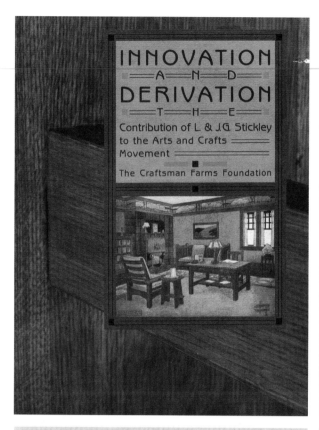

the works of L. & J.G. Stickley. The exhibition catalog included a foreword by noted Arts and Crafts scholar Beverly K. Brandt as well as essays by the curators, Donald Davidoff and Stephen Gray (Davidoff and Gray 1996).

o.p., u.l.: 1995 exhibition, Innovation and Derivation: The Contribution of L. & J. G. Stickley to the Arts and Crafts Movement; u.r.: L. & J. G. Stickley reclining chair No. 410; l.r.: Library table No. 518; l.l.: China cabinet No. 605

*We hope to demonstrate through this exhibition that Leopold and J. George sought to redefine their brother Gustav's work and to extend it to areas he vaguely considered but did not explore. Furthermore, the innovative Handcraft furniture of L. & J.G. Stickley, as well as the earlier, more derivative Onondaga Shop pieces that inform their later work, may provide a more thorough understanding of the specific contributions of the firm to Gustav's legacy in particular and the Arts and Crafts movement in general. (Gray 1995, 16)*

u.l.: L. & J. G. Stickley high-back cube chair No. 408; u.r.: Book table No. 516; l.r.: Exhibition in place

In 1996, Craftsman Farms was the first New Jersey site ever to receive a National Preservation Honor award from the National Trust for Historic Preservation, and it was noted in a *New York Times* article that included a brief history of the Farms (DeMasters 1996).

Shortly after the Historic Preservation award, Tommy McPherson moved to Craftsman Farms as the new executive director. He brought with him an expertise in Arthur Wesley Dow and a scholarly approach to the Arts and Crafts. In addition to the necessary grant writing and maintenance of the physical plant, he worked in conjunction with David Rago to offer a series of symposiums and crafts fairs over his six-year tenure (McPherson 2012).

There was a lot of controversy surrounding the Farms' reacquisition of two Gus Stickley corner cabinets in 1999. McPherson, with a steely determination to acquire them, had proactively raised money in advance to ensure the Farms' purchase of the cabinets at the Christie's November 29 Streisand sale and alienated Barbra Streisand in the process (Streisand 1999). McPherson was one of the first directors of house museums to use such aggressive fund-raising methods to recapture furnishings original to the house, as noted in an article in the *New York Times* (Hamilton 1999).

above: Nancy Strathearn; u.r. and l.r.: Nancy, above, and Ray and Ula Stubblebine at Farms event

*Arrangements with larger, more prestigious institutions, like long-term loans or the promise of gifts, present themselves less frequently to small house museums. "It can take generations to get it right," Morrison Heckscher, a curator of American decorative art at the Metropolitan Museum of Art, said of fruitful relationships with collectors. "It's not something that can be rushed."*

*But the specter of public sale can produce impatience, if not panic. Tommy McPherson, executive director of Craftsman Farms Foundation, is prepared to take a quicker offensive, and risk professional disapprobation, as the foundation is doing with the Streisand sale. "It would be more unfortunate for the foundation not to attempt to return them and simply wait for another generation of collectors to return them," he said. (Hamilton 1999)*

Craftsman Farms paid $142,500 at the November 1999 auction to reclaim the Gustav Stickley cabinets original to the site (*New York Times* 1999). Many other pieces were returned to the house through purchase or donations, but the

Streisand sale purchase received the most publicity. Tommy McPherson left Craftsman Farms in 2005 to become Director of the Mobile Museum of Art, in Alabama (McPherson 2012).

Interviewing for the open executive director position, Heather Stivison found the people she met at Craftsman Farms to be knowledgeable and engaging, but the defining moment for her was when she entered the log house. She walked in and inhaled. "I could not believe what it was like to be here, how beautiful it was, how meaningful I found it." It was very early spring, in March, and she fell in love with the building. Working as Deputy Director of the impressive Montclair Art Museum in Montclair, New Jersey, Heather Stivison was looking for a change.

Her daughter told her she was glowing when she returned from the interview. Heather said the place was amazing, and they talked for hours about the potential of Craftsman Farms. The Farms became Heather's passion. She thought of the challenges, satisfaction, and new experiences the position would bring. She also was ready for a position with greater scope, and this had it.

u.l.: Conservation to roof; u.r. and below: Rooflines in 2012

Heather Stivison began as Executive Director of Craftsman Farms on May 1, 2007. The first thing she did was to go through the records, and she realized there had been twelve people that had been administrators or interims. That was a lot of turnover, but Heather knew that is part of the evolution of an organization initiated by volunteers trying to save a site. "I'm not vain enough or stupid enough to think that my planning and vision for the Farms is going to be the ultimate end for the Farms in perpetuity. I may end up as just a stepping stone along the way—that's the reality." The richness of the opportunity and the potential were obvious to Heather, and the ideas she could explore excited her.

Heather has a background in fundraising and development, she was president of the State Association of Museums, and she worked in a variety of positions at the Montclair Art Museum. Currently, she is the president of the Mid-Atlantic Association of Museums, a regional organization which covers New Jersey, New York, Pennsylvania, Delaware, Maryland, and Washington, D.C. She also serves on the board of directors of the statewide lobbying group, the Advocates for New Jersey History.

Something Heather noticed in her first week of work was that there were many Craftsman Farms members from far-flung places like Maine, California, and Florida, but there were very few from the immediate area. Having a core constituency that can attend and benefit from events and activities is essential. These members were not people who were going to do that, so Heather took on her first challenge.

After reading documents, Heather also realized that the Craftsman Farms property is owned by the Township of Parsippany, and the Farms leases it from them. She read the operating agreement which states that Craftsman Farms must benefit the community, but the reality was that there were no programs in place to meet that responsibility. The museum was doing wonderful things for a particular audience but not for anyone else. That needed to be addressed right away.

The first event Heather established was Family Day, in 2007. Craftsman Farms was obligated to serve the community, and Heather was exceptionally nervous about how it would be received, but she felt the Farms had to be known in the community. Craftsman Farms had to introduce the history and this type of site to kids.

u.l., u.r., l.l.: Refinishing workshop by Bruce Johnson; l.r.: David Rago discusses Fulper pottery; o.p.: details of log house

activities children were doing when the Stickley family lived at the Farms. They do sack races and tin cans—those are things kids don't have today—and the staff gets them to imagine what life was like for their great-grandparents. The kids come with parents, they come with grandparents, and sometimes with aunts and uncles. Heather can barely contain her excitement as she recalls the recent event. There were seven hundred people, many of them sitting on the lawn with their families eating box lunches, all spread out but not on top of each other, and all having a lovely day. "The family thing is so amazing. You hear them talking as they leave, and the kids are full of what they just did, but they've also had their parents' undivided attention. They begin to talk about things they wouldn't be talking about otherwise, and their thumbs are not busy playing a video game. They're not staring at the TV or a computer screen, and neither are their parents." Heather holds the strong conviction that children are the future. She insists that is not a trite and worn-out statement but the key to the success of Craftsman Farms.

Very hands-on, Heather works the admissions table at all the events because it's important for her to be visible and not just sitting in her office. She wants to be part of it. In addition, she wants to see who the Farms is serving, their reaction, and what they need. She wants to see what they're happy about, what they're unhappy about, and what they want.

Stivison points out that children, especially the younger ones that come to the annual Family Day, have no concept of *then* and *now*, no idea of what life was like in the early twentieth century. So when children participate, they do the same

Before she could plan, Heather had to identify which audiences to serve. Children were the biggest audience

missing—simply not there. When Heather looked at the statistics, she saw that twelve children visited Craftsman Farms in 2007, her first year. From the beginning, Heather has led the staff in discussion about how to engage kids beyond the local group, and the idea for the scout programs emerged from such conversations.

Heather needed time to run the museum, develop programs, and do the other necessary work of a director, and she needed someone who could be responsible for the important work of education. Heather went to the board with the idea of creating a new position, director of education, and the board took a leap of faith, knowing they were going to be in debt for it, but also knowing it would eventually pay off. Vonda Givens was hired in 2008 as the first education director. No one could be more talented or dedicated to the Farms than Vonda, and the benefits of Heather's decision to hire her are obvious. In 2011, over two thousand children visited the Farms, and Stivison is adamant that what they are doing is exactly what they should be doing.

The Farms is pursuing original ideas and reaching more audiences. Heather is pleased with the diversity. Heather's ideas and planning involve long-term projects that take a while to develop, and the board understands that. People coming from different paths are arriving at the same decision—that they want to be involved at Craftsman Farms. There's a range of collectors, scholars, and seniors, and their needs are all different. Heather feels their most important achievement is that they have educated people about Craftsman Farms, and they have done it carefully, one step at a time.

Craftsman Farms started other programs as well, like the Emerging Scholars Symposium. Stivison insists that if the Farms is not offering graduate school scholars a platform, an opportunity, or a challenge, then those young academics may drift into other areas, not realizing the Arts and Crafts is worthy of that level of thought. The Emerging Scholars Symposium is an important platform for the presentation of unpublished scholarly papers. It provides opportunity for Arts and Crafts scholars and can inspire other research, and audiences benefit from hearing original work. Without uplifting emerging scholars, Craftsman Farms cannot be vital because it is the heart of what any museum should be doing, and many museums are currently emphasizing this kind of scholarly support.

The Farms collaborates and partners with other organizations for mutual savings and benefit. The New Jersey Historical Commission is very tight in these times, and it involves a great deal of time to prepare the applications for funding. Heather points out that though Craftsman Farms is a National Historic Landmark, the only operating support they receive from any government entity is a small grant from the New Jersey Historical Commission. Though this grant has increased from $16,000 to $25,000, it still covers less than five percent of the day-to-day expenses of operating the site. With nothing guaranteed, each year they start with zero funding and seek support through grants, memberships, and donations. Funding for restoration and projects is required above and beyond the basic operating costs. Since 2007 the Foundation has been awarded over

$1.3 million in project and restoration grants. Heather states that though she is proud of the restoration that has taken place under her watch, this barely scratches the surface of what is needed to restore all of Craftsman Farms.

Heather maintains the number one goal is to be thorough and effective in all of their projects, in spite of a tight budget. Doing them poorly is absolutely not acceptable, but keeping the bar high on quality is a constant challenge. Heather feels that if you do something badly, you don't get a second chance. What Craftsman Farms produces has to be good.

Heather and Vonda meet regularly and confirm what they'd like to ultimately see. For instance, as they begin to refurbish the buildings on the three-and-a-half acres that are on the other side of Manor Lane, they imagine artists giving demonstrations and actually working on a regular basis. But the complexity and the reality are such that this would not be attempted unless it were sufficiently well planned. This sort of project takes many years of preparation.

In general, exhibitions are planned five years out, seriously planned three years out, and within two years, publicity is already getting out. However, the fashion exhibition, *Styling an American Family: The 1910s at Gustav Stickley's Craftsman Farms* was an exception because it was planned and executed in just under a year from the day the project was conceived. The project met Heather's criteria of a job well done. It opened in September 2012 and offered a careful display of thirty-four period fashions set in eight themed "environmental vignettes styled as moments frozen in time" (Craftsman Farms Summer 2012, 1).

The garments were from Syracuse University, and the show was curated by Jeffrey Mayer of the College of Visual and Performing Arts. Syracuse was selected as the fashion source because of the size of its collection of the period 1910–1915, and "the majority of the pieces were purchased, made or worn in and around the Syracuse, New York area, where the Stickley family members lived prior to their move to Craftsman Farms" (Craftsman Farms Summer 2012, 1). The show was based on an ingenious and creative idea that worked perfectly with the interior setting of the Stickley family home.

Heather Stivison has brought her intelligence, passion, and her museum expertise to Craftsman Farms, but it is her rock-solid vision of the importance of young people that will carry the Farms forward and engender a younger generation who will treasure the history of the Arts and Crafts movement through the dreams of Gustav Stickley. Heather is truly a gift to Craftsman Farms and to the entire Arts and Crafts community.

o.p.: Heather Stivison, executive director

above: Stickley family living room

Living room, south
fireplace of log house

## References

Bartinique, A. Patricia. 1992. *Gustav Stickley*: His Craft. Parsippany, New Jersey: The Craftsman Farms Foundation.

Bergman, Andrew and Muriel Berson. 1987. The Plight of Craftsman Farms. *Arts and Crafts Quarterly* 1 (2): 4-5.

Berson, Muriel. 1987. Latest Information on Stickley's Craftsman Farms. *Arts and Crafts Quarterly* 1 (4): 6-7.

Berson, Muriel. 1989. Update on Craftsman Farms Acquisition: April, 1989. *Arts and Crafts Quarterly* 2 (4): 30-31.

Cathers, David, ed. 1999. *Gustav Stickley's Craftsman Farms: A Pictorial History*. With a Foreword by Robert Judson Clark. Morris Plains, New Jersey: Turn of the Century Editions in association with The Craftsman Farms Press.

Clark, Robert Judson. 1999. "Foreward." In *Gustav Stickley's Craftsman Farms: A Pictorial History*. Edited by David Cathers, iv-viii. With a Foreword by Robert Judson Clark. Morris Plains, New Jersey: Turn of the Century Editions in association with The Craftsman Farms Press.

Craftsman Farms. "Log House to Come Alive With Period Fashions." *Notes from the Farms: The Newsletter of the Craftsman Farm Foundation*. Summer 2012, p 1.

Craftsman Farms website. 2012. Craftsman Farms Foundation, Inc. http://stickleymuseum.org/general-info/the-foundation.html.

Davidoff, Donald and Stephen Gray, eds. 1995. *Innovation and Derivation: The Contribution of L. & J.G. Stickley to the Arts and Crafts Movement*. With a foreword by Beverly K. Brandt. Morris Plains, New Jersey: The Craftsman Farms Foundation. Exhibition Catalog.

DeMasters, Karen. 1996. Preservation Trust Honors Its First New Jersey Site. *New York Times*. November 3, 1996. http://www.nytimes.com/1996/11/03/nyregion/preservation-trust-honors-its-first-new-jersey-site.html.

DePalma, Anthony. 1987. The Battle to Preserve a Jersey Utopia. *New York Times*. March 22, 1987. http://www.nytimes.com/1987/03/22/realestate/the-battle-to-preserve-a-jersey-utopia.html?pagewanted=all&src=pm.

Dietz, Ulysses G. Letter to the editor. *New York Times*. April 19, 1987. http://www.nytimes.com/1987/04/19/realestate/l-craftsman-farm-564087.html.

Ellis, Elaine Hirschl. Winter 1990. News from New Jersey. *Arts and Crafts Quarterly* 3 (1): 36.

Ellis, Elaine Hirschl. Fall 1990. The Opening of Craftsman Farms. *Arts and Crafts Quarterly* 3 (4): 24-28.

Fish, Marilyn. 1999. "Craftsman Farms: 1917-1989." In *Gustav Stickley's Craftsman Farms: A Pictorial History*. Edited by David Cathers, 51-55. With a Foreword by Robert Judson Clark. Morris Plains, New Jersey: Turn of the Century Editions in association with The Craftsman Farms Press.

Gray, Stephen. 1995. "This Exhibition: A Preview." *In Innovation and Derivation: The Contribution of L. & J.G. Stickley to the Arts and Crafts Movement*. Edited by Donald Davidoff and Stephen Gray, 15-19. With a foreword by Beverly K. Brandt. Morris Plains, New Jersey: The Craftsman Farms Foundation. Exhibition Catalog.

Greene, Elaine. 1990. Parsippany Home of Gustav Stickley Opening This Weekend. *New York Times*. April 26, 1990. http://www.nytimes.com/1990/04/26/garden/parsippany-home-of-gustav-stickley-opening-this-weekend.html.

Hamilton, William L. 1999. Design Notebook: House Museums Get Pushy. *New York Times*. November 18, 1999. http://www.nytimes.com/1999/11/18/garden/design-notebook-house-museums-get-pushy.html?pagewanted=all&src=pm.

Lytwyn, Ted. In interview with Jeffrey Preston. Millburn, New Jersey. November 21, 2011.

Malarcher, Patricia. 1983. Honor for Stickley. *New York Times*. September 25, 1983. http://www.nytimes.com/1983/09/25/nyregion/honor-for-stickley.html.

McPherson, Tommy Arthur. Curriculum Vita. 2012.

*New York Times*. 1999. N.Y./Region. Museum Pays $142,500 for Streisand's Cabinets. November 30. http://www.nytimes.com/1999/11/30/nyregion/museum-pays-142500-for-streisand-s-cabinets.html.

Reif, Rita. 1992. Feeling Totally at Home With Furniture by Stickley. *New York Times*. November 29, 1992.

Stickley, Gustav. Als ik kan: A Message From Craftsman Farms. *The Craftsman*. XXI (1): 112–113. October 1911.

Stivison, Heather. In interview with Jeffrey Preston. Parsippany, New Jersey. September 25, 2012.

Streisand, Barbra. 1999. Craftsman Farms Conducts Trumped-Up Press Campaign to Try to Force Barbra Streisand to Donate Stickley Furniture. December 13, 1999. http://www.barbrastreisand.com/us/truth-alert/craftsman-farms-conducts-trumped-press-campaign-try-force-barbra-streisand-donate-stickl.

Looking back: log house in rearview mirror

# 30. A. Patricia Bartinique

*Sitting on her L. and J.G. Stickley settle while her two kittens bat at each other across her lap, Pat Bartinique talks softly to her older cats who are perched on an early Gus postal desk, cautiously eyeing the antics of their new siblings. Collector and scholar, Pat has made a life's work of Arts and Crafts research and sharing it through lectures and articles. She has never missed a Grove Park Inn Arts and Crafts Conference and has been involved in it in numerous ways, some visible, such as developing and leading the book club or being a small-group discussion leader, and much of it behind the scenes. Pat does not seek the limelight, but she deserves recognition for her steady, consistent involvement in important ways over the last twenty-six years.*

In July 1992, Pat Bartinique drove through the hills of north-western New Jersey on her way to Dingman's Ferry, Pennsylvania to see Suzanne Jones, a member of the board of Craftsman Farms Foundation. She had an idea to share.

Craftsman Farms was struggling, going through a difficult period. Bartinique had been at a meeting at the Farms during which there had been discussion of a small exhibition of a few examples of Gustav Stickley chairs, accompanied by a brochure. The underlying idea was that such a presentation would bring much-needed publicity to the Farms. After further thought, she realized a golden opportunity was right there for the Farms. Bartinique's suggestion was a comprehensive exhibition that would open in November. Suzanne liked the idea and called the president of the board, David Lowden. He thought it was a great idea. It would be the first catalogued exhibition of Gustav Stickley's works ever—anywhere. *Gustav Stickley: His Craft—A Daily Vision and a Dream* opened November 15, 1992 and closed the end of January 1993.

There was a narrow window of time, four months, to accomplish all the work involved in a catalogued museum exhibition. Bartinique, as guest curator, wrote the catalog and Judy Jordan created the cover and other artwork for it. Collectors had to agree to lend pieces, the pieces needed to be picked up. Craftsman Farms rented a truck, and Judy Jordan and Jeffrey Preston drove to the Midwest and various places in the Northeast picking up pieces, carefully wrapping and securing them, and driving back to the Farms with them. Bill and Patsy Porter lent their leather-topped hexagonal table. It was returned to them in 2012, after a long-term loan of twenty years, and it was the first piece of their Stickley collection to be moved into their new house.

Meanwhile, Bartinique was researching for her writing of the catalog. Bob Zarrow, Bruce Johnson, Tom Maher, Beth Cathers, Michael FitzSimmons, Ray Stubblebine, Joe Farmarco, Mark Taylor, Judy Jordan, Norm Weinstein, Isak Lindenauer, and Jeffrey Preston, all Arts and Crafts specialists, contributed articles, which were then edited before the

The *New York Times* gave a very positive half-page review in their Sunday Arts section. The following week saw lines of people that stretched a quarter mile waiting to see the exhibition.

design and production of the catalog. The final result is a stellar catalog which is a primary source for researchers. It is now in its third printing.

Gustav Stickley's log house had to be prepared for the first exhibition ever to take place at Craftsman Farms. Every part of the house, with the exception of the kitchen, was used as a display area. One upstairs room featured ephemera such as catalogs, patents, and letters. The sun porch was a major exhibition area, and UV film had to be installed on each of the many windows. Wooden platforms were built, custom-sized to each piece of furniture that would be displayed.

Many people helped make the exhibition a reality. Ray Stubblebine, a Reuters photographer and board member, volunteered to take photos for both the exhibition catalog and of the opening event. Ted Lytwyn, another board member at the time, and his wife, Cara Corbo, helped in countless ways, including the important process of moving the heavy wooden furniture. In the end, one hundred fifty-five pieces of Gustav Stickley's works were displayed.

Rita Reif, art critic for the *New York Times*, wrote a review of the exhibition and *The Bee* (*Antiques and The Arts Weekly*) presented a cover story written by Bartinique. Reif's review was favorable. In her half-page on the exhibition, she said that in the "first comprehensive exhibition of the modernist innovator's works, … the Stickley story comes alive in this house" (1992). The *San Francisco Chronicle* also picked up the story, giving it West Coast exposure. In addition, Noah Adams, of National Public Radio's "All Thing Considered," did a piece on the exhibition. It was also mentioned by Joan Hamburg of WOR, the New York radio station, and PBS created a video of the exhibition, underwritten by the Geraldine Rockefeller Dodge Foundation and distributed by Craftsman Farms.

Large crowds turned out for the show, and Craftsman Farms achieved recognition and legitimacy as a historic museum. After the exhibition closed, a number of pieces from *His Craft* traveled to the Grove Park Inn in Asheville, North Carolina and were exhibited at the sixth annual Arts and Crafts Conference in 1993.

Pat wrote the cover story for *Antiques and The Arts Weekly* about the exhibition at Craftsman Farms.

Robert DeFalco produced the exhibition, Pat was the curator, Judith Jordan did the cover art for the catalog.

On October 28, 1995, Pat Bartinique, with Judy Jordan and Jeffrey Preston, opened a second exhibition, *Kindred Styles: The Arts and Crafts Furniture of Charles P. Limbert*. They chose Gallery 532 on Wooster Street in SoHo, an important Arts and Crafts gallery, and an ideal space because of its 10,000 square feet. Further, the owner, Robert DeFalco, was receptive and supportive of new ideas. When they initially approached DeFalco, they suggested the exhibition might receive a half-page review by Rita Reif in the *New York Times* and a cover story in *The Bee*. DeFalco liked the idea, despite the temporary sacrifice of sales space to display the Limbert items on loan from various collectors. It cannot be overemphasized that none of this would have been possible without the financial backing, hard work, and ingenuity of Robert DeFalco. He has a sensitivity to the arts and art history, and has handled many essential areas involved in putting together an exhibition, such as locating lenders. He also took care of paperwork and many logistical matters.

The opening reception was exciting and packed with people as the Julliard Jazz Ensemble played the music from *Three Penny Opera*. Art historian Roy Pedersen, collector Michael Ottavi, and Pat Bartinique each spoke on an aspect of Limbert design.

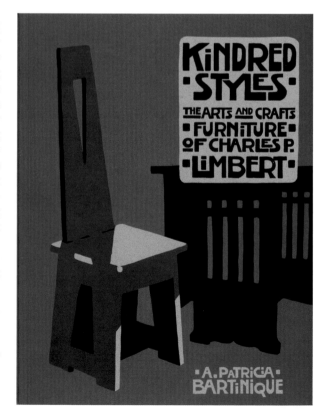

Pat curated the exhibition and again worked with Judy Jordan. The handsome catalog included articles by Ralph Kylloe, Bruce Johnson, Bruce Szopo, Robert Edwards, Roy Pedersen, Jeffrey Preston, and Robert DeFalco and today stands as one of the Limbert primary sources.

Once again, reviews were published in the *New York Times* and *The Bee*. When Pat first contacted the New York Times, Rita Reif's response was that she did not cover more than one exhibition curated by the same person. However, Bartinique's persistent phone calls paid off. In her half-page review, Reif noted that

> *galleries today focus less on Stickley, whose innovative furniture is increasingly rare and costly, and more on his competitors, whose works are more plentiful and less costly. Kindred Styles: The Arts and Crafts Furniture of Charles P. Limbert, an exhibition at Gallery 532 on Wooster Street in SoHo, through Nov. 19, sheds new light on one rival who is unknown today to all but scholars and the most dedicated enthusiasts of the style. Collectors and dealers lent 85 of the 107 pieces on view.*

The exhibition was the first all-Limbert national exhibition. In addition to its SoHo venue, *Kindred Styles* traveled to Toomey Gallery in Oak Park, Illinois in the spring of 1996.

A charter member of The Craftsman Farms Foundation, Pat has been a member of the advisory council and has given talks at the Farms, most recently in June 2012 on "The Tobey Furniture Company: Variations on an Arts and Crafts Theme." She currently serves on the Farms education committee and on the education advisory council.

Pat has written many articles over the years for journals and catalogs, including fourteen for the Grove Park Inn Arts and Crafts Conference catalogs, covering a range of interesting subjects from the 1991 "Walt Whitman: Poet for the Arts and Crafts Movement" to "Meet Me in St. Louis: The Arts and Crafts Meets the Louisiana Purchase Exposition" in 2004.

"Work Worth Doing: A Glimpse at Women of the Arts and Crafts Movement" (1998), "The Making of Beautiful Things: Arts and Crafts Women of the British Isles" (1999), and "The Arts and Crafts Movement and The Progressive Era" (2002), articles Bartinique wrote for the Arts and Crafts Conference catalog, reveal her keen interest in researching the role of women during the Arts and Crafts period. Pat was keynote speaker for the "Symposium of Women in the Arts and Crafts Movement," sponsored by The Arts and Crafts Society of Central New York and The Everson Museum in Syracuse in 2009. Her topic was "Infinite Variety: Women of the Arts and Crafts Movement."

In attendance at the first Annual Grove Park Inn Arts and Crafts Conference, Pat has not missed a single year and actively contributes to the conference. Bruce Johnson, director, understands and appreciates the various ways that Pat is involved in the conference. "She has always been a person who would lead small group discussions, be a seminar speaker, and offer me advice and insight into any aspect of the Arts and Crafts conference. She is one of those people who attends important events and is always ready and willing to help out in any capacity" (Johnson 2012).

Since 2006 Pat has led the Book Club at the Grove Park Inn Arts and Crafts Conference. She chooses titles early in the year so people have time to read them for the upcoming conference. Some that have been discussed are *The Great Gatsby, A Passion for Nature: The Life of John Muir, Spoon River Anthology, Chicago Poems*, and *A Clearing in the Distance: Frederick Law Olmsted and America in the Nineteenth Century*. In addition, Pat leads small group discussions every year on a variety of topics such as "Arts and Crafts Magazines: A Primary Source for Writers and Researchers" and "Living the Arts and Crafts Lifestyle: A Philosophy in Action." On two occasions she has been a seminar speaker. In 1997 she spoke on "The Spirit That Endures: Gustav Stickley and The Craftsman Magazine," and then in 2001 her talk was "1901 and The Arts and Crafts Movement."

Patricia Bartinique wrote the introduction to *The Tobey Furniture Company: A Brief History* in 2012 with Peter Copeland of Turn of the Century Editions/The Parchment Press. The book offers an illustrated history that precedes the reprints of three Tobey furniture catalogs. It is a valuable addition to an area of research that has not been widely studied.

In 2005, Bartinique delivered "The Arts and Crafts Movement—So What's Arts and Crafts About Music?" at a conference of the Community College Humanities Association of which she is a founding member. She has also presented other talks on the Arts and Crafts for the association conferences. Pat is a living recruitment for the Arts and Crafts. She cannot help herself because she feels it so deeply.

Pat's education was in the areas of English and American literature. She is a full professor of literature at Essex County College in Newark, New Jersey where she regularly teaches literature, Shakespeare, and public speaking. Pat became aware in the early 1980s of the Arts and Crafts movement, and it immediately resonated with her through the authors it identifies as its forerunners and, indeed, founders: Morris, Ruskin, and Carlyle in England; Emerson, Thoreau, and Whitman in the United States.

The daughter of a classical musician, Pat has music at her very core. When her father passed away, she used her musical expertise and served as interim music director at his church, both directing the choir and playing organ. Pat jumped in when needed to help out and provided leadership for the music program.

A devoted member of The Masterwork Chorus since 1989, Pat has served on its board since 1995. She served as vice-president for one year, president for four years, and is currently production manager of the chorus. They perform three major concerts a year, including their annual performance of Handel's Messiah in New Jersey and at Carnegie Hall just prior to Christmas.

Pat continues to give talks at conferences and lectures on Gustav Stickley and related Arts and Crafts topics. In 2009 at Craftsman Farms she presented a more developed and revised talk on a topic mentioned previously, "The Story in a New Voice: Music and the Arts and Crafts Movement." She continues to research the music and the role of women in the Arts and Crafts Movement. She is motivated by a love of the Arts and Crafts and expresses that love through her impeccable research. Pat has the rare ability to excel at anything she takes on because she is intelligent and sets extremely high standards for herself. Pat Bartinique has significantly enriched the body of Arts and Crafts scholarship. She is an unspoken hero of the Arts and Crafts revival.

### References

Bartinique, A. Patricia. In interview with Jeffrey Preston. Madison, New Jersey. December 27, 2012.

Johnson, Bruce. In phone interview with authors. June 28, 2012.

Reif, Rita. 1992. Feeling Totally at Home With Furniture by Stickley. *New York Times*. November 29, 1992. http://www.nytimes.com/1992/11/29/arts/arts-artifacts-feeling-totally-at-home-with-furniture-by-stickley.html.

———. 1995. If Stickley Was Hertz, Then Limbert Was Avis. *New York Times*. October 29, 1995. http://www.nytimes.com/1995/10/29/arts/arts-artifacts-if-stickley-was-hertz-thenlimbert-was-avis.html.

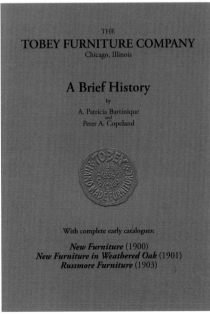

Talking about "Tobey" or "Living the Arts and Crafts Lifestyle" or Walt Whitman, Bartinique is at home with the thinkers, the writers, and the artists of the period.

Michael and Jill, 1982

# 31. Dr. Michael Clark—Jill Thomas-Clark

*On January 1, 2012, Dr. Michael Clark passed away quietly, sleeping in his favorite morris chair. Noted Arts and Crafts author and scholar, Michael was a passionate member of The Arts and Crafts community and will be deeply missed.*

Jill was a Roman art historian and Michael a classics major, each with a secret desire to go to Petra, an ancient city in Jordan. That clinched it. They were married in 1982, and two years later, with a doctorate from University of Michigan, Michael began teaching at Elmira College, in Elmira, New York and Jill was hired by The Corning Museum of Glass.

Michael collected Victorian and Jill liked Art Deco and Modernism, so they frequented auctions and estate sales and discovered an Arts and Crafts chair they both liked:

> *We started to get furniture for the house. We had gone to this really awful auction at Waverly—the kind where they hold up this table and keep saying, "drop-leaf table, drop-leaf table," and the leaf falls off. I mean, it was really bad awful. We got this chair with a partial label, and we wanted to find out what it was. We went to Grove Park Inn the next year, in 1989, and there it was with a complete label that said, "J.M. Young & Sons. Camden, NY."*
> *(Thomas-Clark 2012)*

In an effort to find out more about the chair, in 1989, Jill made some calls and found the local historical society in Cam-

den, New York. Out of pure serendipity, the woman at the historical society had been the owner of the company, J.M. Young, with her husband, and the two of them had run the factory until 1978. The woman described the closing of J.M. Young to Jill:

> *Just before the old Young factory was to be demolished in 1979, she and her husband had retrieved as many of the firm's papers as they could find. They packed them into cardboard boxes and stored them away, hoping that someone, one day, would consider them important. (Cathers 2008)*

Because of the couple's diligence, some of the J.M. Young records were on loan to the Camden Historical Society and some were stored in their basement. It was a goldmine of detailed information, including correspondence, catalogue photos, sales ledgers, shop drawings with measurements and other company documents. It was an unusually complete archive of the history of a manufacturing company that began in 1872.

In their research, the Clarks found something of particular interest regarding Stickley. When L. & J.G. Stickley stopped

Michael in office

At Bouckville antiques show

making Arts and Crafts furniture in 1922, Leopold Stickley contracted J.M. Young to continue production of a limited number of Stickley's most popular pieces of Arts and Crafts furniture. Stickley also sold Young some of their equipment, such as their seat tool. J.M. Young continued their own line and this limited production of Stickley Arts and Crafts into the 1940s.

The Clarks spent a lot of time researching the J.M. Young Company at the historical society in Camden, where Jill went through all the sales ledgers and recorded how many of each piece of furniture was made. (Eventually, the Clarks bought all the company records for five hundred dollars from the previous owners.)

At the 1990 Grove Park Inn conference, Jill discovered that one of the settles at the Grove Park Inn was marked VA. Jill found all the government records that showed the marking was for Veteran Administration hospitals in the 1940s. Previously, no one had thought the Arts and Crafts were produced into the 1940s.

The department of speech and theater at Elmira College approved Michael's topic of J.M. Young for publication, even though it was not related to his department. Michael was even given a sabbatical to complete the research. The

Clarks both liked doing research, and Michael would be able to use this to advance himself in the direction of tenure at the college. In 1994, Jill and Michael Clark published *J.M. Young: Arts and Crafts Furniture*. It was well researched and covered pioneer territory, a topic never before presented, and it broadened the scope of Arts and Crafts knowledge.

Having finished one book, Michael was compelled to hunt down ocean liner records from the time periods that Gustav Stickley was listed as having been abroad. Based on the liner records, they concluded that Gustav did not go to Europe in 1898, a trip he was reported as having taken, because there was no record of his having left the country. There were times he and his brother, Albert, were reported to have been in Europe together, but Michael didn't research other names to see who might have traveled with Gus. Jill thinks investigating this would be interesting.

The next project they planned would be researching second-tier companies. Limiting their research to central New York, they still found over 50 companies that produced a line of Arts and Crafts furniture. They went through years of *Furniture World* and other furniture trade journals, making hundreds of photocopies, and then they visited all the factory towns.

Michael refinishing even-arm settle

At Dalton's with Dave Rudd

Michael really liked talking about the Arts and Crafts with small furniture company families, and he and Jill often uncovered the achievements and identities of their relatives, something the Clarks deeply enjoyed. For example, Gordon Young was quite moved that the Clarks brought recognition to the work of his grandfather and his contribution to the Arts and Crafts movement.

Another example of the Clarks giving honor to a family member through research was with the Plail family. They discovered that Honey Plail had been actively engaged in the business of the Arts and Crafts. She ran the factory and took care of other things generally attributed to men of the time. She broke the glass ceiling. They culled a lot of information about people's relatives and focused on the positive. For Jill and Michael, it was a very human experience that resulted in new friendships with various people in these small companies.

Newcomers to the Arts and Crafts Conference always see the Clarks listed on the conference schedule for tours of the Grove Park Inn. The Clarks humbly and generously share their knowledge with any and all interested parties. In addition, they have led small group discussions, been scheduled

speakers and, in general, have been active and engaged participants in the conference.

In addition to scheduled events, a lot goes on at the Grove Park Inn conference, a crucible of Arts and Crafts ideas. During one of the small group discussions, Jill and David Rago were talking about his magazine, *Style 1900* (at that time it was *Arts and Crafts Quarterly*), and what emerged was a new column. Beginning in 1996 with the third issue of *Style 1900*, "The Best of the Rest" would be a regular feature (title courtesy of Bruce Johnson). In the authors' note, Jill and Michael explain the purpose of the column:

> *After the 1996 Conference in Asheville, it became clear to us that many collectors, dealers, and scholars want more information about lesser-known companies and artists of the Arts and Crafts movement. The purpose of this column will be to examine some of these companies and artists so that the readers may begin to identify their work and assess their merit. In subsequent columns we plan to offer a short history of each company or artist along with an illustration of their work, a description of their shopmarks, and a brief stylistic analysis.*

Michael and Jill regularly presented well-written accounts of obscure companies that would be unfamiliar to most Arts and Crafts collectors. Their articles were usually three to four pages, based on thorough research with at least a dozen footnotes, and accompanied by a few photos. "The Best of the Rest" educated the Arts and Crafts community in areas very few people had researched. They wrote an article for every issue from the end of 1996 through the end of 2000, when work on their planned book consumed them.

Gibbs Smith wanted to publish a book on the Stickley Brothers and, after being turned down by at least one published author, approached Jill and Michael. They accepted but Jill doubted herself as being deserving of such an opportunity. After all, there were others who were well known in the field who had already published on mainstream Arts and Crafts topics. "Why would anybody get excited about a book on the Stickley Brothers by these people who write about other things? (We had done the introduction to the reprint of the 1909 and 1910–11 catalogs of The Indian Splint Manufacturing Co., Geneva, NY for Peter and Janet Copeland, Parchment Press, in 1994.) We weren't specialized—we were just the people who said they'd do it" (Thomas-Clark 2012).

In spite of any feelings of doubt, the Clarks agreed to research and write the book. Gibbs Smith published The Stickley Brothers in 2002, the publisher's first scholarly Arts and Crafts book. "Michael did a beautiful job of writing it, and I lucked into pictures of all five of the brothers. I'm very proud of this book but I would have understood if people hadn't lined up to have it signed" (Thomas-Clark 2012). Readers enjoyed it and learned things they didn't know before. They sold out the 2,500 first-printing copies, putting it solidly into the best-seller category.

Michael had a preference for standard Arts and Crafts, with a particular fondness for bow-arms, while Jill tended more towards pieces with European influences. However, they both very much liked the English influence on early Stickley Brothers and preferred their designs to those of Gustav Stickley. They did like early Gustav furniture but the prices were too strong for their budget.

Albert was more of a furniture man than Gustav. "He didn't publish a magazine or live with Arts and Crafts in his house, and he wasn't beholden to the movement and the philoso-

Jill in her living room with friend

Michael and Jill's home in Elmira

phy and the things Gus espoused" (Thomas-Clark 2012) through his writings in *The Craftsman*.

> But we really liked who he hired to design his furniture and the way he offered a changing variety to the market, like when he hired all the Russian coppersmiths in the teens [1911–1919], and like when he hired all these Japanese to paint his furniture with flowers. He was more the quintessential business person. He was better known than Gustav in the furniture world in Grand Rapids, and he was president of this and president of that. He ran with the big boys—Widdecomb and everybody else. (Thomas-Clark 2012)

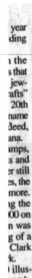

Researching W.B. Brown and Company, a lighting fixture company in Indiana

**Dr. Michael Clark and Jill Thomas-Clark With 1912 W.B. Brown Catalog**

As Gus was the widely accepted standard-bearer for Arts and Crafts furniture, Jill and Michael both felt that Albert was slightly undervalued by the buying public. However, Albert received various awards and was recognized at the 1904 World's Fair for his work furnishing the entire El Tovar Hotel at the Grand Canyon.

Jill wonders where the revival is going and what things will be different at the Grove Park Inn under its new owners. "Michael thought the popularity of the movement wouldn't last as long as it has and always said so. However, he was glad that he was proved wrong and that interest is still going strong. Things have changed but the tenants of the movement are still valid and still draw admirers" (2012). There are some younger people, and dress has become more informal. Everyone now wears jeans, and whereas people never used to attend the lecture and events on Saturday night, now they're pretty much filled.

Michael is missed by everyone in the Arts and Crafts world. However, his careful research and scholarship is not as far outside of the mainstream as it once was because furniture by Gustav Stickley and other mainstream Arts and Crafts furniture designers has become more difficult to find and it is too expensive for a lot of collectors. Jill and Michael wanted to teach people how to look at the furniture and see that there were other furniture makers or companies that produced quality well-designed furniture that were in a different price range than a morris chair by Gustav Stickley. Furniture by J.M. Young, Quaint Art Furniture Company, Harden or Lifetime is far more reasonably priced, so the work of the Clarks has become more relevant, in practical terms, to what many people are now collecting.

**References**

Cathers, David. 2008. "Pioneers." *American Bungalow*. 58. http://www.americanbungalow.com/pioneers.

Clark, Michael, and Jill Thomas-Clark. 1996. Best of the Rest: "The Quaint Art Furniture Company of Syracuse, New York." *Style 1900*. 9 (3): 12–14.

Thomas-Clark, Jill. In interview with authors. Elmira, New York. March 31, 2012.

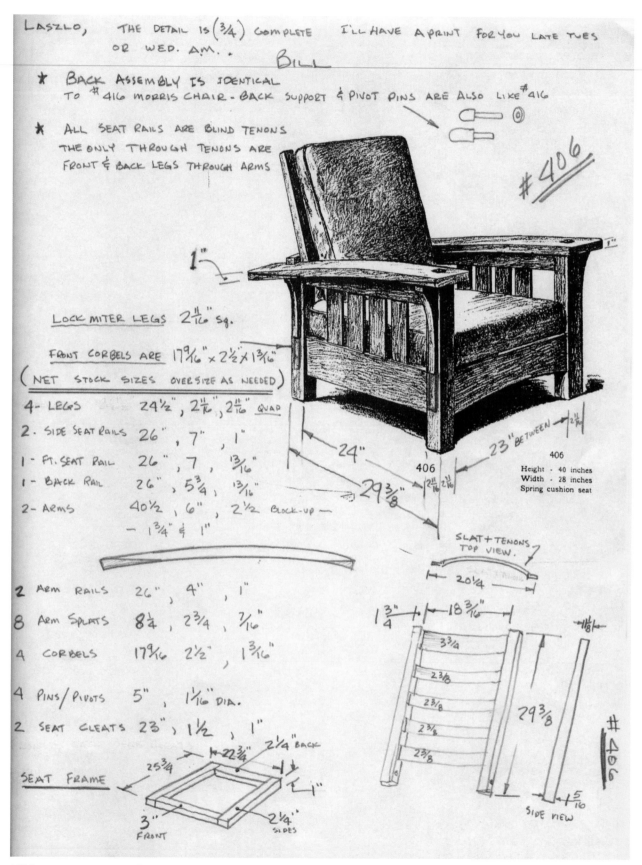

LASZLO, THE DETAIL IS (3/4) COMPLETE. I'LL HAVE A PRINT FOR YOU LATE TUES OR WED. A.M. . BILL

* BACK ASSEMBLY IS IDENTICAL TO #416 MORRIS CHAIR - BACK SUPPORT & PIVOT PINS ARE ALSO LIKE #416

* ALL SEAT RAILS ARE BLIND TENONS THE ONLY THROUGH TENONS ARE FRONT & BACK LEGS THROUGH ARMS

#406

1"

1"

LOCK MITER LEGS 2 11/16" SQ.

FRONT CORBELS ARE 17 9/16" × 2 1/2 × 1 3/16"

( NET STOCK SIZES OVERSIZE AS NEEDED )

4 - LEGS          24 1/2", 2 11/16", 2 11/16"  QUAD
2 - SIDE SEAT RAILS  26", 7", 1"
1 - FT. SEAT RAIL   26", 7", 13/16"
1 - BACK RAIL       26", 5 3/4", 13/16"
2 - ARMS            40 1/2, 6", 2 1/2 BLOCK-UP —
                    — 1 3/4" & 1"

24"

29 3/8"

406

2 11/16 2 11/16

23" BETWEEN    2 11/16

406
Height - 40 inches
Width - 28 inches
Spring cushion seat

2 ARM RAILS     26", 4", 1"
8 ARM SPLATS    8 1/4, 2 3/4, 7/16"
4 CORBELS       17 9/16" 2 1/2", 1 3/16"
4 PINS/PIVOTS   5", 1 1/16" DIA.
2 SEAT CLEATS   23", 1 1/2, 1"

SLAT + TENONS
TOP VIEW.

20 1/4

1 3/4    18 3/16"

3 3/4
2 3/8
2 3/8
2 3/8
2 3/8

29 3/8

1 1/8

#406

5/16

SIDE VIEW

SEAT FRAME

25 3/4    22 3/4    2 1/4 BACK

1"

3"
FRONT    2 1/4
         SIDES

1989 measurement notes for chair by Laszlo Gustav Gigacz

# 32. Aminy Audi

*It was 1989, the Arts and Crafts revival was raging, and prices were spiraling out of control. With their bold business decision to reissue mission pieces, Alfred and Aminy Audi put the lifestyle of the Arts and Crafts movement within reach of a greater number of people by offering newly produced Arts and Crafts furniture at more affordable prices than those of original pieces.*

Alfred Audi; and Aminy with their son, Edward

In the early years of the twentieth century, the five talented Stickley brothers had many furniture-making businesses of varying brother combinations. In 1904, Leopold and John George incorporated what was to become the most successful venture of them all—L. & J.G. Stickley in Fayetteville, New York. In contrast to their brother, Gustav, the two were shrewd businessmen and adapted their products to the demands of the market. Sensitive to the market, they discontinued their line of mission furniture by the end of World War I, replacing it with the more in-vogue colonial revival *Cherry Valley Collection*, which enjoyed success for decades (Stickley 2012).

The other side of manufacturing was the retailing. Fast-forwarding to the 1950s, the biggest retailer of L. & J.G. Stickley furniture was *E.J. Audi, Fine Furniture & Rugs.* In 1960, E.J. was joined by his son, Alfred, fresh from Colgate University, who gradually took over the Manhattan company as his father aged. Some years later, Louise Stickley, Leopold's widow, could no longer manage the Stickley company,

which was still operating in the original factory and had dwindled to twenty-two employees. Louise felt Alfred appreciated the company and its quality more than anyone, and wanted him to buy it. It took them a few years, but in 1974, Alfred and Aminy Audi became the second family to own L. & J.G. Stickley.

Having a large vision, the Audis moved the Stickley operation into a new and much larger manufacturing facility in nearby Manlius in 1985 (Stickley 2012). The family's infusion of new energy into the company paralleled a growing public awareness of the Arts and Crafts movement, and competition for original pieces was becoming intense. Prices for Arts and Crafts furniture were rising quickly; for example, Barbra Streisand bought a Gustav Stickley sideboard for $363,000 in 1988 at a Christie's New York sale (Solis-Cohen 2000).

As part of their vision, the Audis began planning production of pieces originally produced in the early twentieth century by Gustav Stickley and by L. & J.G. Stickley. Alfred Audi selected which mission pieces to reissue and the types of

Laszlo Gustav Gigacz, master craftsman

finishes, with input from company historian Mike Danial, master cabinetmaker Laszlo Gustav Gigacz, and Stickley experts Paul Fiore and Donald Davidoff. (Audi September 2012). The pieces were to look exactly like those produced almost a century earlier, but some construction methods would be updated and hardware would be mass-produced rather than crafted by hand (Stickley 2012).

Aminy Audi attended the second Grove Park Inn Arts and Crafts Conference in 1989. She had taken with her to the conference sketches of the pieces that L. & J.G. Stickley was planning to reissue. She happened to be on the same flight to Asheville as Dr. Marianne Smith (author of the 1983 book, *Gustav Stickley: The Craftsman*) and shared the sketches with her. Dr. Smith was excited about their project and the particular pieces they chose. Likewise, Bruce Johnson supported their project and selection of pieces.

The third weekend of February is when the annual Arts and Crafts conference at the Grove Park Inn takes place and is the epicenter of the Arts and Crafts world—collectors,

dealers, and lovers of the style all come together in an intensely enjoyable crucible of common interest and passion. It's as though real life happens in those few days and the rest of the year is a warm-up period. People bump into each other, meet new people, there's a kind of synergy that leads to unexpected things. For example, Aminy describes what happened as she was leaving the Grove Park Inn at the end of that 1989 conference:

> *I ran into the granddaughters of the founder of the Fulper company. They had recently discovered the secret formula for the Fulper tile in their grandfather's attic. I told them that we wanted to reissue an end table which originally had Fulper tile. I borrowed samples and called Alfred to tell him of my discovery. We immediately decided to add the No. 577 tile-top end table to the original offering. (Audi September 2012)*

Two months later, L. & J.G. Stickley reissued thirty-three pieces of furniture that had been produced in the early part

of the twentieth century, staying true to the original designs and specifications of Gustav Stickley and L. & J.G. Stickley. The Audis had added something new to the marketplace by reissuing original designs.

The Audis realized that their Mission line would be a source of concern for some businesses, but Aminy passionately believed that by popularizing it and making it affordable, they would create awareness of Arts and Crafts as a lifestyle, leading to increased demand and continuity of the style. "It was a huge leap of faith on our part, and it paid off" (Aminy Audi 2011).

Jerry Cohen, involved with buying and selling Arts and Crafts furniture since the 1960s, observed that as prices continued to rise uncontrollably in the late eighties, Stickley collectors were becoming an exclusive set. But when Audi reissued mission pieces in 1989, it helped democratize the revival, making the furniture affordable to a much larger audience. They had taken a style not yet familiar to most people and "exposed it to the population at large" (Saul 2007).

Initially dealers and auction houses felt threatened, but Bruce Johnson, director of the Arts and Crafts conference, believes that Stickley's reissuing of mission pieces actually pumped energy into the revival and brought yet another generation into the fold, one that cares more about the design than the antiquity (Johnson 2012).

Technically, the Audis operate two separate companies: L. & J.G. Stickley manufactures the furniture; and Stickley, Audi, and Company retails it. By careful labeling, as well as new production techniques, Stickley ensures that collectors will readily distinguish between original Arts and Crafts furniture and Stickley reissued pieces (Danial 2011). The Audis took every step to ensure the consumer would be empowered in this way (Johnson 2011).

The experts at L. & J.G. Stickley had carefully developed new construction techniques that are incorporated into some of their reissued pieces, using state-of-the-art technology and specialized machinery (Danial 2011). For detailed explanations of these techniques, see pages 11–12, as well as

Celebrating Thanksgiving together

sidebars for various pieces throughout the Stickley mission catalog online (http://issuu.com/stickley/docs/stickley mission catalog). Walking through the factory, one sees not only impressive high-tech machinery and industry-specific software in use, but also master craftspeople, skillfully applying their art with diligence and pride. Seeing both the latest technology and craftspeople using ages-old techniques is a surprising juxtaposition of the past, present, and future. Aminy Audi articulates the challenge of investing in the best technology while, at the same time, holding on to the best of the handcrafts—"to blend both is a magnificent gift to future generations" (Aminy Audi 2011).

L. & J.G. Stickley occasionally produces custom-order pieces. Edward Audi tells the story of an extra-wide Gustav Stickley Eastwood chair. It was extra wide in order to accommodate the Dalai Lama in a lotus position. In April 2008, the Tibetan spiritual leader addressed students at Alfred and Edward's alma mater, Colgate University. On the auditorium stage, the Dalai Lama began in the lotus position. He got up,

rapped his knuckle on the chair, looked around and said, "This is a chair, a comfortable chair. I may sit down and say nothing at all" (Edward Audi 2011).

The Audi family has a long-held belief that it is their responsibility to educate the public on the construction methods involved in producing their furniture. When Audi began reissuing the Mission line, company historian Mike Danial embarked on a "Stickley Road Show" to present the furniture to the public and teach its history and construction (Danial 2011). Twenty-three years later, Mike still maintains a heavy travel schedule, touted on the Stickley website:

*Join Stickley Corporate Historian Mike Danial for a presentation at Sheffield Furniture on the fascinating history and craftsmanship of Stickley furniture. Mike is an expert in the care of antique Stickley pieces— bring photos of your older Stickley furniture for a free informal appraisal before the presentation. (Stickley 2012)*

A July 4th picnic

There is a strong feeling of community inside the one-story Manlius factory, which is more than 400,000 square feet (Aminy Audi 2011). Executive offices are adjacent to the factory floor, and Aminy and Edward are never far removed from the work that takes place. The annual Thanksgiving dinner served to employees by the executives and managers seems to be everyone's favorite event of the year, based on what this observer heard from several sources. L. & J.G. Stickley's passionate commitment to their workers is evident in not only words and deeds, but by the pride of workmanship displayed throughout the factory.

Stickley's line of mission furniture is a major part of their market today, with many drawn to the contemporary appeal of its structural integrity, simplicity, and beauty of design. The company enjoys strong consumer loyalty, with young couples comprising a significant portion of their expanding market. Aminy proudly tells the story of hurricane and flood victims throughout the years who have written her to say the only furniture in their house that lasted through the dev-

astation was their Stickley. Their dedicated client base from every region of the country often includes generations within one family dedicated to buying Stickley furniture. "Once they buy their first piece, they save for it" (Aminy Audi 2011).

Designing for current needs while preserving the mission style, Stickley creates pieces like queen-sized beds and cabinets for televisions and other equipment. Stickley is sensitive to what retail customers want, and they get feedback. It is rare for a furniture factory to retail its products, but because the Audi family is both manufacturer and retailer, all design is in-house and connects to market demand. Aminy sees this as a significant factor in their success, and because of their success, they have never had to lay off a single employee.

Aminy Audi believes mission design to be transforming and the L. & J.G. Stickley brand to be aspirational, often becoming an important part of people's lives. She maintains that buyers and collectors of their Mission line are just as

The Craftsman workshops, 1902

passionate about the Arts and Crafts as the people collecting the original antiques.

In 1985, in the course of vacating the original factory and moving machinery, shelves, and stockpiles that had been in place for many decades, large stashes of Stickley documents and papers from the original Arts and Crafts period were discovered. L. & J.G. Stickley had been incorporated in 1904. One century later—in 2004—L. & J.G. Stickley established the Stickley Museum in the spacious third floor of the original Fayetteville factory, and today it exhibits many of the long-hidden materials and a historic furniture collection acquired over time (Stickley 2012).

L. & J.G. Stickley began a collaborative program in 2005 with the State University of New York's Cooperstown Graduate Program for Museum Studies. The Stickley Museum has developed significantly as a result of experienced L. & J.G.

Alfred, Aminy, Edward Audi and Carolyn Audi Fischl celebrating with Mike Danial and Mark Koval, 30-year employees

E.J. Audi, Alfred's father, with Leopold Stickley

Stickley staff sharing their knowledge with future museum professionals who, in turn, share their talent, energy, and vision in a hands-on environment under the aegis of L. & J.G. Stickley (Stickley 2012).

The Audi family's passion for the Arts and Craft movement is evidenced by their long-term membership and consistent support over time of the Craftsman Farms Foundation in Parsippany, New Jersey. Since first hearing in 1988 of Craftsman Farms, the home and grounds designed, built, and developed by Gustav Stickley for himself and his family, the Audis have been supportive and actively involved in the foundation. One recent example was an Alfred J. Audi grant Aminy gave to support education programs and continued restoration of the Farms (Craftsman Farms 2008); another recent example was Aminy's fundraising and chairing of the 2011 centennial gala (Craftsman Farms 2011).

The Audi family has received many awards for their leadership, public service, and involvement. Among them, Alfred and Aminy together received the prestigious Laurel Award from the International Furnishings and Design Association in 2004 for "furthering the Arts and Crafts movement in America" (Aminy Audi 2011). Sadly, Alfred died in 2007. Amini and her son, Edward, currently serve on the Board of the National Home Furnishings Industry and both are involved in leadership roles in other areas of the broader community.

In October 2012, the special-order Eastwood chair was on loan again to the Dalai Lama when he spoke at Syracuse University. It is now on display at the Stickley Museum in Fayetteville, its permanent home (Stickley 2012). The Fayetteville Free Library and the Stickley Museum together under the one roof of the original factory site of L. & J.G. Stickley, Inc., offer the community a cultural center based on its rich and unique heritage. In keeping with the Audi tradition of educating the public, the museum is free and open to everyone and, appropriately, sits atop one beacon of democracy—the public library.

### References

Audi, Aminy. Interview by authors in Manlius, NY. September 23, 2011.

——, Aminy. E-mail to authors, September 10, 2012.

——, Edward. Interview by authors in Manlius, NY. September 23, 2011.

Craftsman Farms. "Alfred J. Audi Is Remembered with a Generous Grant." *Notes from the Farms: The Newsletter of the Craftsman Farm Foundation*. Summer 2008, p 9. http://www.stickleymuseum.org/docs/Newsletters/Summer08.pdf.

Danial, Mike. Interview by authors in Manlius, NY. September 23, 2011.

Johnson, Bruce. E-mail to authors. July 9, 2012.

——. Interview with authors in Mountain Lakes, New Jersey. October 15, 2011

L. & J.G. Stickley website. "Our history." August 23, 2012. http://www.stickley.com/OurStickleyStory.cfm?SubPgName=Main&BodyTxt=On.

Saul, Stephanie. "Alfred J. Audi, Who Revived a Furniture Maker, Dies at 69." *New York Times*, online, October 5, 2007.http://www.nytimes.com/2007/10/05/business/05audi.html?_r=1.

Solis-Cohen, Lita. "The Barbra Streisand Collection." *Maine Antiques Digest*, online, February 2000. http://www.maineantiquedigest.com/articles_archive/articles/barb0200.htm.

Stickley Museum website. "About the Museum." September 10, 2012. http://www.stickleymuseum.com.

——. "Dalai Lama Visits Syracuse and Uses Museum Chair." October 10, 2012. http://www.stickleymuseum.com/ExploreStickleyHistory.cfm?SubPg=CuratorsCorner&CuratorsCornerItem=ChipsFromTheStickleyMuseum.

——. "Stickley Roadshow in Maryland." September 10, 2012. http://www.stickleymuseum.com

L. & J.G. factory in Manlius,
New York

Aminy and Alfred Audi; Delivery day

o.p., The Stickley Museum at the site of the original L. & J.G. Stickley factory in Fayetteville, New York; r., Stickley shopmark placed on every piece of furniture; below and on following pages are representative samples of L. & J.G. Stickley reissued Arts & Crafts pieces

Fred Albert, editor-in-chief of Style 1900, with Jennifer Strauss, co-publisher & marketing director and Eliane Talec, chief administrative officer at Rago Arts & Auction Center

# 33. Style 1900

For almost thirty years, David Rago's creation, *Style 1900*, has given the Arts and Crafts world articles, question-and-answer forums, columns, event calendars, and information on anything relevant to the Arts and Crafts. There is always a *Style 1900* booth at the Grove Park Inn with back issues and other publications for sale.

The magazine started in 1986 as *Arts and Crafts Quarterly*, a black and white newsletter. Within two years it was a 32-page magazine that became slicker, more colorful, and longer with each issue. Advertisements became more sophisticated until it was a full-fledged grownup glossy magazine. Various people have had regular columns over the years, such as Bruce Johnson, Dave Rudd, and Jill and Michael Clark. The contributing writers are all experts on the Arts and Crafts, and large amounts of information have appeared in articles written for *Style 1900*.

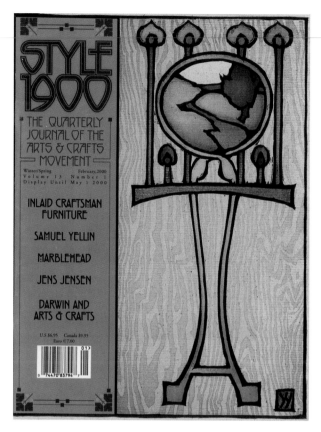

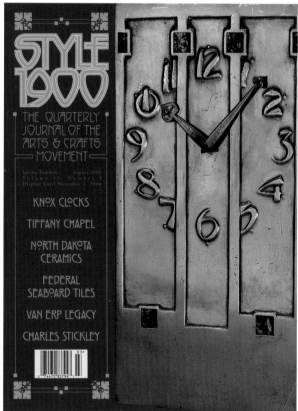

Early publications of Arts & Crafts Quarterly. The name changed to Style 1900 in 1994.

# ||| ARTS & CRAFTS QUARTERLY |||

VOLUME 1, ISSUE 2, JANUARY 1987

## ARTUS VAN BRIGGLE: THE FORMATIVE YEARS

Eugene Hecht

Paris, in the last years of the 19th-century, was the spiritual touchstone of the art world, and everywhere cultured people felt the beckoning call. The pilgrims came, with pilgrims' naïvete, to experience for themselves both the wonderous new and the venerated old; to taste the vigor and excitement, to feel the cutting edge of the nearing century, and come ·back wise and worldly.

Steamships regularly plied the Atlantic from the New World to the Old. And in the summer of '93, among the peregrine students sailing off to the grand academies of Europe, was a young man who would someday found a great pottery (Fig. 1) and become one of America's premiere ceramists. Smiling on a deck in the salt spray, Artus Van Briggle, a tall, slender, delicate fellow, was on his way to Paris, France. Thick

Fig. 1

wavey auburn hair loosely tucked under a jaunty cap, Van—his friends affectionately called him Van—was an artist. Granted he was only 24, but he had been painting since childhood and had already attained some small reputation. At that very moment a Van Briggle picture was on display in the prestigious Salon of the World's Fair back in Chicago[1], and that in itself was no mean accomplishment. Indeed, he even had a patroness, one whose kindness had made possible this voyage to *la ville lumière*.

A freckled, pale, boyish face, dominated by eyes at once dreamy and penetrating, endeared the charming midwesterner to almost everyone he met. Van was high spirited and outgoing, despite the likelihood that he already knew he had been joined in a macabre struggle with tubercular consumption[2]. So many people had the "White Plague," it hardly seemed unusual to be among the unfortunate. About 150,000 Americans alone were dying of TB each year at the turn of the century. That grim debilitating horror, inexorably consuming millions of young souls, was the greatest killer of humankind; but it had always been so. In a strange pathetic way, apathy was the norm[3]. One simply danced with death until the music stopped. The disease, endemic as it was, was part of the nature of things, and would be for almost a half-century more. Van Briggle must have known it was inescapable; and yet, in the beginning at least, it was often slow, often mercifully slow. In the warmth of that July, bound for Paris, confident and determined, Artus still had time.

Only seven years before, he had set out on another steamer, then sailing the river to Cincinnati. Born March 21, 1869, to Eugene and Martha (Bryan) Van Briggle, Artus left the place of his birth and childhood, Felicity, Ohio[4], to

Fig. 2 Artus Van Briggle. Photo from *Rookwood Pottery Potpourri*, courtesy of Duke Coleman.

seek his fortune in the big city. The family, on the paternal side, proudly traced its lineage back to Flemish roots in the 16th-century; to none other than the master painter Pieter Bruegel, the Elder. The "van" was a title added somewhere along the line, and in the mouths of English speakers the "Bruegel" metamorphosed into the more easily pronounced "Briggle." Naturally when Artus showed artistic promise early on (as did one of ' . . . Leona) he was e . . . art as a career. W . . . seventeen, he fou . . . in the Queen Cit . . . wage painting fac . . . a downtown shop . . . had in mind, but . . .

Cincinnati in th . . .

# ||| ARTS & CRAFTS QUARTERLY |||

VOLUME 1, ISSUE 3   APRIL 1987

## THE PHILOSOPHY OF CHARLES ROHLFS: AN INTRODUCTION

Michael James

*"Idealistic renditions in furniture are the poetic expression of hand and brain, and hold within themselves the principle of life."*[1]
—Grace Adele Pierce

There is no doubt that Charles Rohlfs is a magical name among Arts & Crafts scholars and enthusiasts. The rarity of his work in both form and number, with the concomitant prices it demands have given Rohlfs a prominent place in the hierarchies of both design and monetary values. But while his name and work are now more widely recognized, very little is generally known of the man and even less of his philosophy.

Unlike Hubbard or Stickley, Rohlfs did not often engage in proselytizing for his work or philosophy. He did, however, hold passionate, albeit personal, beliefs and ideals which he would expound when pressed. An examination of his statements and writings reveals the mind and soul of a craftsman well within the philosophical scope of the Movement.

According to a journalist who paraphrased one of his talks, Rohlfs summed up the Movement as "a revival of handiwork as a means of individual and hence original expression, the renewal of the art element in labor, and the doing of work for the pleasure there is in doing it."[2] In his own words, art "should be expressive of workmanship that was a pleasure rather than toil that was irksome."[3] This of course differs in wording, but not at all in sentiment from the statements of Morris, Stickley, Hubbard, et al. Rohlfs, as did the others, welcomed and applauded the

*Continued on page 14*

ISSUE NUMBER 30
THE MAGAZINE PUBLISHED
IN THE INTEREST OF
PRESERVING AND
RESTORING THE
MODEST AMERICAN
20TH CENTURY HOME,
THE BUNGALOW,
AND THE RICH LIFESTYLE
THAT IT AFFORDS

# AMERICAN BUNGALOW

RESTORATION
ACCESSORIES
HISTORY
FURNISHINGS
EVENTS
ARTS AND CRAFTS
UPGRADING
PHILOSOPHY
GARDENS
PROJECTS
LANDSCAPING

Display until September 15, 2001

UNITED STATES $6.95 / CANADA $8.95

# 34. American Bungalow

*John Brinkmann lives and works in a bunglaow built in 1914 in the Pasedena area. Once he discovered the architecture was Arts and Crafts, he felt the need to translate the philosophy and lifestyle of the Arts and Crafts movement through the context of living in a bungalow in the twenty-first century. American Bungalow has elevated the humble dwelling and provided leadership to a broader Arts and Crafts audience. The elegant, beautiful and, at times, show-stopping photography has cast the common bungalow in a new light.*

1920s photo of Twycross House, American Bungalow's home and inspiration

John Brinkmann's design office in the 1960s, when he spent two years in Germany, had a cabinet full of European fine art magazines such as Jugend, *Deutsche Kunst und Dekoration, and The Studio*, featuring cutting-edge works of the Wiener Werkstätte, Bauhaus, Art Deco, Jugendstil and Arts and Crafts. John was totally taken by the Arts and Crafts and related movements that had swept across Europe and the United States. It was a period of artistic expression that, in John's opinion, "hit a high and reached a plateau that it has not quite touched again" (Brinkmann 2012). The influence of those magazines stayed with him.

In the 1980s, John Brinkmann owned a successful graphic design firm in what might have been the last old house left on Wilshire Boulevard in Los Angeles. But over a number of years, the art community had migrated off the boulevard and out towards the Pasadena area. John eventually followed. He relocated his business in an old house he bought that happened to be a bungalow—but that meant nothing to him, as bungalows were on every corner, and everybody he knew had been raised in one, including himself.

When John and his design firm settled into the bungalow in 1987, at first it was business as usual for the company. But all types of people, from couriers to CEOS, would come in and comment on seeing genuine rock, wood, and tile. He was struck by the way people were so taken with the authenticity of these materials and started studying the history of the bungalow. He discovered its connection to the Arts and Crafts movement and realized that the embodiment of that connection was its beauty and honesty of construction. What the builder had in mind was visible. It was done by proportion and by grain of wood and joinery. "It's so beautifully honest, that it's hard to ignore. That's what makes it appealing" (Brinkmann 2012). This was a revelation to John, and he wanted to shout it to every person—anywhere—living in a bungalow. The idea for a magazine was beginning to form. He already had a full staff of designers and could recruit a lot of the other talent he would need.

He realized that most people who began moving into old bungalows in the 1970s and '80s did so because they were well built and usually in an affordable part of town. Most people did not live in bungalows out of desire for them.

Twycross House

*We want people who live in these simple little houses, most of which have been painted fifty times over, to recognize that these houses can be beautiful. They relate, not only to an art movement, but to a philosophy that is accessible. What started American Bungalow was the connection between the Arts and Crafts and these common little houses that are in every American town you drive through. (Brinkmann 2012)*

John's grandfather had lived in a bungalow and made his own craftsman furniture, but he didn't know that the style existed elsewhere until he acquired one of Stephen Gray's Turn of the Century publications and looked through it. He realized, "It's Grandpa Brinkmann's furniture. This is just too cool!"

John Brinkmann has bought photography his whole working life and is very familiar with it. During the planning of *American Bungalow,* he happened to see an article illustrated by Alexander Vertikoff's work in the *Los Angeles Times*, and he admired the quality. He arranged to visit Vertikoff in his house in Venice, California, and ended up asking him to do the cover photographs for four issues, the entire first year of *American Bungalow*. Vertikoff agreed to do them. The photography was beautiful and John and Alex worked well together. As it has ended up, *American Bungalow* covers have featured Vertikoff's stunning photography, exclusively, from the very first issue. Brinkmann believes "the quality of Alex's work is one of the reasons the magazine stands out as well as it does" (Brinkmann).

Indeed, *American Bungalow* soon became, among other things, a high-profile showcase for Vertikoff's work, and he has become widely known in the Arts and Crafts world, producing books with notable writers and scholars such as David Cathers and Robert Winter. He has also developed a reputation as a fine photographer outside of the Arts and Crafts, and his work is featured in many magazines and books (http://www.vertikoff.com). His stunning cover photography on *American Bungalow* has caused many a bookstore browser to buy an issue on impulse.

During the early years of the magazine, John had a friend who had begun attending the annual Grove Park Inn Arts and Crafts Conference, the up-and-coming place to learn about the Arts and Crafts, and insisted that John had to go, so he did go in 1992, the third year of *American Bungalow*, and he has attended every conference since.

*American Bungalow* is about the bungalow lifestyle, simple and close to nature. As the cover of each issue proclaims, the magazine "is published in the interest of preserving and restoring the modest American 20th century home, the bungalow, and the rich lifestyle that it affords." The hallmarks of that "rich lifestyle" are beauty, simplicity, authenticity, and the use of natural materials. The type of furniture shown and the articles written portray that lifestyle as authentic, honest, and straightforward. People responded to the bungalow lifestyle as the theme of the magazine, when it first came out, and they still do. What makes it unique to the bungalow dweller is that the focus is on the lifestyle inside these Arts and Crafts houses rather than on collectors.

AMERICAN BUNGALOW

ambungalow.com

In planning *American Bungalow*, John was aware of the realities of advertisers. It was important that the magazine present the Arts and Crafts with sophistication in order to attract and maintain quality advertisers. After the first couple of issues had been published, John was able to write about and present photographs of the lifestyle of some prominent Arts and Crafts collectors, with the support of people like Stephen Gray, David Cathers, and David Rudd. The publication had proved itself by its own high standards. If the bungalow was the neglected stepchild of the old house movement, *American Bungalow* was going to honor it with a journal that looked good enough to display on the coffee table.

Setting and maintaining high standards ultimately translated into more opportunity for the publication. *American Bungalow* soon became a high-end magazine. The high quality photography and presentation appealed to Arts and Crafts scholars and experts. They realized that *American Bungalow*, with its emphasis on lifestyle, could still present collections in a way that few other publications could.

When Brinkmann and Vertikoff approached Stephen Gray about photographing his New York apartment for "Bungalow in the Sky," a 2002 article on Gray's collection (issue 33), Gray kept his involvement to a minimum, but he clearly had his own ideas about photography and lighting. Although Vertikoff requires little direction, the three of them worked together remarkably well. Stephen saw the excellent results, and he championed *American Bungalow* from that point forward. Because of the quality of what they were doing, he helped John and Alex gain access to some outstanding collections.

Once the Arts and Crafts revival got into full swing, the look became mainstream, and soon every discount furniture house had its own version of Arts and Crafts furniture, but something in it was lacking. (Brinkmann remembers a neighbor shopping for a table that was solid wood but was upset because everything was veneered particle board.) It didn't have that "beauty and honesty of construction" that John had discovered when he moved his office into an old bungalow, and that had led him to understand that natural materials are a big part of the appeal of Arts and Crafts in the world of today.

Some people who make Arts and Crafts reproductions produce work every bit as good as the craftsmanship of the Arts and Crafts period. It's handwork, and they're very proud of what they do. It comes through, and though it's not antique, it maintains Arts and Crafts qualities—honesty of construction and design and highly skilled craftswork. These are the companies who advertise in the publication. John selectively accepts advertising from contemporary craftspeople, and the photography in the advertisements is in keeping with the consistent high quality of *American Bungalow*.

John sees the future of the revival as artists and artisans taking the Arts and Crafts work of the early twentieth century a step further, so that new furniture, pottery, houses, textiles—or whatever the medium—maintain the Arts and Crafts aesthetic but manifest the artist's imagination in the context of this new century. He is encouraged by the quality of work of many of the contemporary craftspeople and believes they are essential to sustaining the Arts and Crafts revival.

**References**

Alex Vertikoff website. http://www.vertikoff.com.

Brinkmann, John. In phone interview with authors. November 27, 2012.

ISSUE NUMBER 36
THE MAGAZINE PUBLISHED
IN THE INTEREST OF
PRESERVING AND
RESTORING THE
MODEST AMERICAN
20TH CENTURY HOME,
THE BUNGALOW,
AND THE RICH LIFESTYLE
THAT IT AFFORDS

# AMERICAN BUNGALOW

RESTORATION
ACCESSORIES
HISTORY
FURNISHINGS
EVENTS
ARTS AND CRAFTS
UPGRADING
PHILOSOPHY
GARDENS
PROJECTS
LANDSCAPING

Display until February 28, 2003

UNITED STATES $7.95 / CANADA $11 95

ISSUE NUMBER 51
THE MAGAZINE PUBLISHED
IN THE INTEREST OF
PRESERVING AND
RESTORING THE
MODEST AMERICAN
20TH CENTURY HOME,
THE BUNGALOW,
AND THE RICH LIFESTYLE
THAT IT AFFORDS

# AMERICAN BUNGALOW

RESTORATION
ACCESSORIES
HISTORY
FURNISHINGS
EVENTS
ARTS AND CRAFTS
UPGRADING
PHILOSOPHY
GARDENS
PROJECTS
LANDSCAPING

Display until November 30, 2006

ambungalow.com

348

Barber House in Eau Claire, Wisconsin, built for a lumber baron

# 35. Peter and Janet Copeland

*Due to a job transfer, Peter and Janet Copeland moved to Maplewood, New Jersey in 2000 where they found a Gustav Stickley house which they painstakingly restored over many years. Upon Peter's retirement, they moved back to the Midwest and into a lumber baron's rambling Arts and Crafts house in the forested hills of northern Wisconsin. Recently they moved again, this time into a Frank Lloyd Wright Usonian house in Kalamazoo, Michigan. They collect Arts and Crafts and live in old houses because of their love of history, the same reason they publish Arts and Crafts books and reprint catalogs through their small business, Turn of the Century Editions/The Parchment Press.*

Peter in world headquarters for Turn of the Century Editions/Parchment Press

The Copeland's introduction to the Arts and Crafts was a Stickley Brothers rocker they bought in 1982. They knew nothing about the period or the Stickleys, they just liked the chair. They then began exploring the history and furniture of the early twentieth century, eventually assembling a large and varied collection of Arts and Crafts furniture and accessories.

The Copelands established The Parchment Press in 1993 and reprinted the 1912 Quaint Furniture Catalog, 96 pages with eight to ten pieces on each page. They were picking up on Stephen Gray's idea of creating access to original furniture catalogs through reprints.

The following year, they reprinted the 1909-10 and 1911 Indian Splint Manufacturing Company catalogs in one volume, published in association with the Geneva Historical Society of New York. Their next project was the 1914 Quaint Furniture Catalogue No. 42 with an introduction by Don Marek.

In 2003, the Copelands bought Stephen Gray's Turn of the Century Editions and combined it with The Parchment Press. They offer Arts and Crafts titles, both new and old, including the classic works by David Cathers and the reprinted catalogs of Stephen Gray. Historic exhibition catalogs and important titles published by other houses, such as *Grand Rapids Art Metalwork* by Don Marek and *From Our Native Clay* by Dr. Martin Eidelberg, are also available. Peter fills in the gaps with his own publications, such as The *Lakeside Craft Shops, Sheboygan, Wisconsin* (2005), *Modern Craft Styles by Charles Stickley* (2009), and *The Tobey Furniture Company: A Brief History* (2012), which illuminate important pieces of Arts and Crafts furniture manufacturing history.They have a straightforward and well organized website that makes ordering titles easy: (http://www.turnofthecenturyeditions.com/index.html).

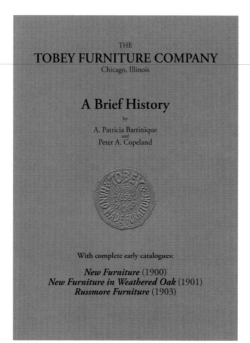

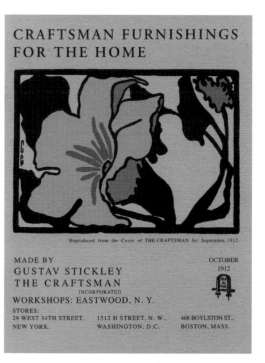

below: The Copelands' former Gustav Stickley home in Mapleton, New Jersey

Turn of the Century Editions/The Parchment Press serves as distributor to a number of Arts and Crafts books published by other houses. They provide a valuable service to the Arts and Crafts community by making such books readily available.

Peter and Janet are longtime members of Craftsman Farms. Peter has served as a Trustee of the Stickley Museum at Craftsman Farms and is currently a member of its Advisory Board. They participate every year at the Grove Park Inn Conference and always have a sale table set up with their publications along with friendly faces that welcome conversation.

### References
Copeland, Peter and Janet. In interview with authors.
    September 25, 2011

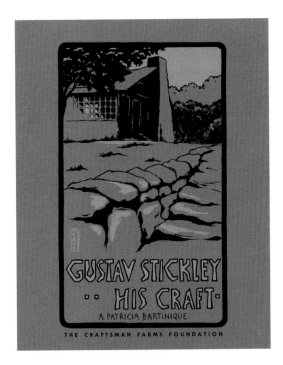

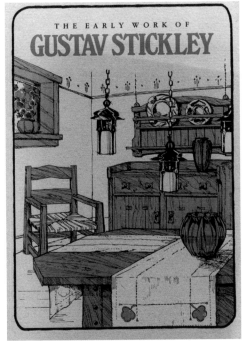

Some of their many Arts and Crafts publications

Peter's favorite
mission oak
rocker

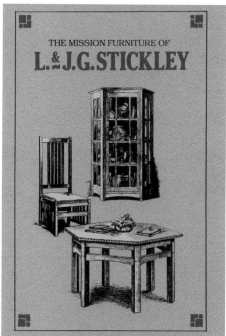

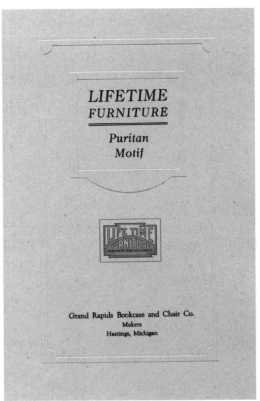

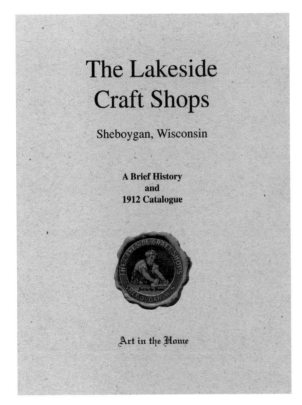

Chest Byrdcliffe Arts and Crafts Colony Woodstock, New York

# 36. Two Red Roses Foundation

*Rudy Ciccarello came to the Arts and Crafts with a uniquely American story, and perhaps later in life than many of the big collectors, but his method in collecting, as in other aspects of his life, is driven by passion, focus, and planning.*

It was just fifteen years ago that Rudy Ciccarello was first attracted to the Arts and Crafts movement when he spotted a reproduction Gustav Stickley bookcase in a dusty antiques shop near his home (Mascolo 2011). His life changed immeasurably as he enthusiastically began collecting furniture and pottery of the period. "I grew to appreciate the historical importance of the movement, the craftsmen and the wonderful pieces of art they produced," says Ciccarello. "I was hooked" (TRRF News).

Ciccarello came to this country from Rome as a young man to work for the Italian Consulate in Boston. He attended college and obtained a Bachelor of Arts from Boston University and a Bachelor of Science in Pharmacy from Northeastern University. He moved to Florida to work in the pharmaceutical

industry. He eventually began Florida Infusion Services (FIS), an innovative and highly acclaimed pharmaceutical supply company (Mascolo 2011) that grew from a small storefront in 1987 in Tarpon Springs, Florida, to the third largest U.S. specialty drug distributor.

*Two Red Roses Foundation* (TRRF) was established in 2004 by Ciccarello for the purpose of promoting awareness and understanding of the American Arts and Crafts movement, and fulfills its mission through exhibitions, scholarship support, and collection development and restoration (Mascolo 2011). The excellent and informative TRRF website (http://71.98.248.87/) gives the viewer a tempting taste of Ciccarello's stunning collection (TRRF News).

"Along Ipswich River" 1893
Arthur Wesley Dow
Color woodblock
9-13/16 x 4-3/8 inches
Ipswich, Massachusetts

Vase with landscape 1909–1910 Marblehead pottery
Marblehead, Massachusetts

Ciccarello has spent the last decade-and-a-half buying both privately and at auction, and his interests include pottery, paintings, and furniture, as well as prints, tiles, metalwork, photography, and lighting (TRRF News). Many auction-goers know that over the last several years, whenever a heart-stopping Arts and Crafts piece would come up at auction, Rudy was usually bidding. And he often succeeded in getting the piece.

> His collection began with furniture by such makers as Gustav Stickley, Charles Rohlfs, the Roycrofters, Byrdcliffe, Greene and Greene, Grueby, Newcomb, and many others but it has grown to include major icons of each art form, ranging from Arts and Crafts pottery to metalwork. He has made it a practice to buy only the best of the best of every aspect of Arts and Crafts work. (Mascolo 2011)

A testament to the broad sweep of Ciccarello's interest in the period is the name he chose for his foundation. William Morris, central to the English Arts and Crafts movement, wrote "Two Red Roses Across the Moon," one poem in a collection of poetry he published in 1858 (Jackson 1996). The poem evokes a dreamy medieval time of knights and ladies, reminiscent of the pre-Raphaelites; a "leaded glass window made between 1900 and 1910 by an unknown art-ist illustrates the poem and exemplifies the focus of the foundation" (Mascolo 2011).

Having amassed a huge collection of Arts and Crafts treasures, Ciccarello found himself wanting to share his holdings with the public (TRRF website). Some big collectors donate to established museums, like Stephen Gray's 2008 promised gift (Gray 2011) to the Wadsworth Atheneum in Hartford and Robert Ellison's 2009 donation of a large Arts and Crafts pottery collection to the Metropolitan Museum in New York (Vogel 2009). Ciccarello has made it clear that his entire collection will be housed and available to the public in a new museum he is building in the Tampa Bay area. The planning and development of the museum, The American Craftsman Museum, is well underway (TRRF News).

Its own museum notwithstanding, Two Red Roses Foundation has made significant contributions to education and awareness of the American Arts and Crafts movement by lending pieces to major shows and creating its own exhibitions in various museums across the country, as listed on its website. Its debut exhibition was in 2006, *The American Arts and Crafts Home: 1900–1915: Selections from the Two Red Roses Foundation Collection*, at the Leepa-Rattner Museum of Art in Tarpon Springs, Florida (TRRF Past Exhibitions).

Linen Press 1904 Byrdcliffe Arts and Crafts Colony Woodstock, New York

Woodblock Arthur Wesley Dow

The foundation has continued to exhibit and lend pieces to other exhibitions, most notably the loan of six pieces of furniture to the Dallas Museum's Stickley retrospective, the loan of fifteen vases and a number of tiles from its collection to the American Art Pottery Association 2009 Convention Pottery Exhibition held in Philadelphia. TRRF will lend five outstanding pieces of Newcomb pottery from its collection to the Newcomb Art Gallery's traveling exhibition, *Women, Art, and Social Change: The Newcomb Pottery Enterprise*, scheduled for March, 2014 through May, 2016 (TRRF Proposal). Other exhibitions include the St. Petersburg Museum of Fine Art and The Flagler Museum.

In addition to the Foundation's commitment to exhibiting its collection to the public, Ciccarello also believes it vital to provide an accurate accounting and cataloging of his collection, as well as a written history of the most important art-

Grueby gourd-shaped Kendrick vase

ists. To accomplish this goal, he sought out and enlisted the help of two of the most well known and respected writers and scholars on the subject, David Cathers and Susan Montgomery. Three manuscripts devoted to furniture, metalwork, and tiles—years in the making—are mostly complete and are being edited for publication in the very near future. Additional catalogs of the TRRF collection of lighting, pottery, and woodblock prints are in the initial stage.

The painstaking collecting of Ciccarello is impressive. The TRRF website has a reference list of "News and Press Releases: Recent News & Media," featuring journal and news articles about new acquisitions. The list is full of superlatives describing the most ever paid for a Nakashima (the Arlyn table), the highest price ever paid for any Arts and Crafts object (a Rhead tile), the highest paid for an example of Newcomb pottery, and the list goes on.

Ciccarello has taken on large projects with some of his acquisitions. For example, with the help of David Rago in 2005, he purchased a set of 1,200 matte-glazed Grueby tiles with iris panels that had originally covered the floor, walls, and ceiling of a bathroom in a turn-of-the-century Cleveland house. A cooperative effort that included the owners of the house, the Two Red Roses Foundation, and two dealers, made possible the careful removal of the tiles. They will be conserved and exhibited in the future. While the Two Red Roses collection already included some major Grueby pieces, this installation was the most complete and included ceramic moldings and fixtures. "The quality and condition of this rare find provides hope to scholars and collectors alike that significant artifacts from the period remain to be found and saved for future generations" (Smith July 2005).

"Supper" Jessie Wilcox Smith
Mixed media on board 28" x 19"

It was only weeks later that Ciccarello acquired, at auction, a large Grueby fireplace surround that supports a nearly six-foot-high mahogany mantel with heavy brackets and moldings. The tiles feature a fifteenth-century cargo ship on a green-glazed field and had been installed in 1903 as part of a renovation of the First National Bank in Auburn, Maine (Smith September 2005).

Rudy Ciccarello not only has the resources to continue developing his outstanding collection but he has the knowledge of Arts and Crafts combined with a keen eye for quality and condition. And to make a classic American story of immigration and enterprise even better, he is giving back to society by ultimately sharing his unparalleled collection in a museum he is paying to build.

Cabinet
Charles Rohlfs
Buffalo, New York

## References

Florida Infusion Services Website. http://www.floridainfusion.com/html/aboutus.asp.

Gray, Stephen. In interview with authors. Avon, Connecticut. July 15, 2011.

Jackson, Vanessa Furse. 1996. "'Two Red Roses Across the Moon': Reconsidering Symbolic Implications." William Morris Society. http://www.morrissociety.org/publications/JWMS/AU96.12.1.Jackson.pdf

Mascolo, Frances McQueeney-Jones. "Rudy Ciccarello And The Two Red Roses Foundation: American Arts And Crafts." *Antiques and the Arts Online.* Aug 2, 2011. http://antiquesandthehearts.com/Antiques/CoverStory/2011-08-02__11-55-09.html.

Smith, David, ed. "Grueby Arts And Crafts Masterpiece Rescued In Cleveland." *Antiques and the Arts Online.* July 26, 2005. http://antiquesandthearts.com/Antiques/Trade-Talk/2005-07-26__14-07-44.html.

———. "Grueby Fireplace Acquired by Two Red Roses Foundation." *Antiques and the Arts Online.* September 20, 2005. http://antiquesandthearts.com/Antiques/Trade-Talk/2005-09-20__12-33-32.html.

Two Red Roses Foundation website. http://71.98.248.87/.

——— website. Press Releases. "Philadelphia chosen to host 2009 Art Pottery convention." January 21, 2009. http://71.98.248.87/News/news_020509.htm.

——— website. News and Press Releases: Recent News & Media. http://71.98.248.87/News/news.htm.

——— website. News. "Beauty In Common Things: American Arts And Crafts Pottery." February 17, 2009. http://71.98.248.87/News/news_0217092.htm.

———. "Museum Proposal. Downtown Tampa Community Redevelopment Area: The American Craftsman Museum, a Public Charity Foundation." September 4, 2012. http://www.tampagov.net/dept_public_affairs_newscenter/information_resources/files/TRRF%20Museum%20Proposal.pdf.

——— website. Past Exhibitions. "The American Arts and Crafts Home: 1900—1915: Selections from the Two Red Roses Foundation Collection" at Leepa-Rattner Museum of Art, Tarpon Springs Florida. 2006. http://71.98.248.87/exhibitions/past_exhibitions/past_exhibitions.htm.

Vogel, Carol. "Major Gift of Art Pottery to Adorn Met's Restyled American Wing." *New York Times online.* January 14, 2009. http://www.nytimes.com/2009/01/15/arts/design/15muse.html?_r=0.

Vase with landscape Rhead potteries 11¼"x 6" Santa Barbara, California

"Camp at Night" 1923 Eanger Irving Couse Oil on board 12" x 16"

"Summer Clouds" Margaret Jordan Patterson Mixed media/paper 9¼" x 11½"

Chest Byrdcliffe Arts and Crafts Colony Woodstock, New York

Inlaid Desk Designed by Harvey Ellis for Gustav Stickley Eastwood, New York

Inlaid music cabinet Gustav Stickley Eastwood, New York

Two views of carriage house, architecture by Edwin Heinle

# 37. Ed Heinle

*Ed Heinle designs houses in a modern aesthetic that resonates Arts and Crafts. An accomplished architect who is fully aware of the history and trends of architecture, his houses should stand for decades or a century, but perhaps of equal importance to his Arts and Crafts legacy is his invaluable work on the Board of Trustees of Craftsman Farms. His expertise as a LEED architect (Leadership in Energy and Environmental Design) has benefited the Farms through his ideas that both conserve the environment and are economical. Ed is engaging a generation of young people in the history of Gustav Stickley and Craftsman Farms through hands-on restoration programs.*

On front stoop of Craftsman
Farms, with Nessa

As a child, the magic of Christmastime always included a trip to Craftsman Farms for Ed Heinle's family. The Farny family, who bought Craftsman Farms in 1917 from Gus Stickley, had a shop on their grounds called *The Silo*. Phyllis and Cyril sold interesting ornaments and decorations and even Scandinavian modern dishes, and they tried unusual things, like operating a restaurant in the dairy barn.

Ed loved to draw and sculpt in clay but a set of old-fashioned blocks, stone blocks from Germany, called "The Little Architect" foreshadowed his career. Growing up in New Jersey and spending time in old towns, Ed became enamored of Victorian architecture, with all its sprockets and turrets and details, and he began drawing his ideas for houses. The furniture within those houses also interested Ed and when he was fifteen, he found a Stickley Brothers Quaint library table with shelves on each end. There was something about the piece that spoke to him. He cleaned and refinished it and carried it with him to Columbia and Yale architecture school.

As a high school student, Heinle could not get enough of the late nineteenth-century aesthetic movement and the pre-Raphaelite painters. He read *Sweetness and Light*, about the aesthetic movement in England, became obsessed with

James McNeill Whistler and drank in the film work of British director Ken Russell on the pre-Raphaelite artists, Rosetti, William Morris, and Burne-Jones.

By the early 1970s, Ed's fascination had evolved to Alphonse Mucha, the Czech art nouveau artist whose iconic style gained affection within the countercultural revolution. That was it—Ed was now completely lost in the curves of art nouveau.

Studying at Yale in the late seventies, Ed had a girlfriend in the drama school who was cultured and sophisticated, and she loved design. One evening, Ed discovered an exhibition catalog on her bookshelf that entranced him, *The Arts and Crafts Movement in America, 1876-1916*, from the 1972 groundbreaking Princeton University exhibition. The proto-modern qualities of the Arts and Crafts appealed to him. His tastes were maturing, and the Arts and Crafts communicated something back to him through what he calls "an artistic experience." Something had moved him.

When Ed was an undergraduate at Columbia, Robert A.M. Stern, head of architecture for undergraduate majors, advised and mentored him. Significantly, Stern introduced

Vice-president of the board of
The Stickley Museum at
Craftsman Farms, at yearly gala

Heinle to the works of Sir Edwin Lutyens, born in 1869. He was *the* English Arts and Crafts architect—very prolific—and designed Munstead Woods as a home for the renowned garden designer, Gertrude Jekyll. Ed was so taken by Lutyens' work that he went to England with his girlfriend after completing his architecture degree from Yale. On a mission to see all of the Lutyens houses, Ed went to the Soane Museum in London, hoping the director could gain access for him to a number of houses that were not public. While she eased entry to some, with other houses, Ed had to rely on his own charm and Yale pedigree to get past the front door. He saw a great deal of the architect's works, and it greatly impacted his developing style as an architect.

Ed immersed himself in the English Arts and Crafts movement and also examined the works of great British designers like C.F.A. Voysey and Charles Rennie Mackintosh. He was captivated by this late nineteenth- and early twentieth-century work. One of his favorite architects, Frank Lloyd Wright, was also very influenced by the English Arts and Crafts movement.

Heinle believes the American Arts and Crafts movement appealed to the countercultural generation of the late sixties and early seventies in the United States because of the rebellious nature of Gustav Stickley and Frank Lloyd Wright and because of its informal, authentic, and natural style. The works produced by Gustav Stickley were the sensual and tactile manifestation of the Arts and Crafts, and his writings in *The Craftsman* magazine explained and elaborated the philosophy behind the works and the lifestyle.

One distinguishing feature of the Arts and Crafts movement and Stickley, in particular, is "how the work acknowledges time through the patina of wear. The finish gets better with age as it acknowledges use over time—leaving actual marks" (Heinle 2012). Ed is drawn to architecture and design that not only mark the passing of time but are enhanced by it. In contrast, mid-century modern design, such as the minimalist chrome furniture of Marcel Breuer, loses its appeal with age and looks best when brand new.

When Craftsman Farms opened in 1989, Ed and his partner, Leslie Brown, began visiting regularly and learned everything they could about Grueby and the "sensual matte green glaze with the velvety quality" (Heinle 2012). They went to as many Arts and Crafts events as they could and attended their first Grove Park Inn conference in 1991. They became solidly hooked on the Arts and Crafts movement.

There is always a tug of war between the cerebral and the sensual for Ed Heinle. His intellect leans towards minimalism, but past a certain point he finds the works are no longer spiritually sustaining. However, while the Arts and Crafts is proto-modern, it has a spiritual quality. The work of Scottish designer Charles Rennie Mackintosh has that spiritual element about it and successfully communicates something. Indeed, the Scots refer to his work as the *spook school*. Frank Lloyd Wright communicates something with "tall-backed chairs and long vertical lines, providing a foil to the incessant horizontality of his architecture. Like the glaze on Marblehead or Grueby, the Arts and Crafts is sensual and tactile" (Heinle 2012).

Ed Heinle in oversized Eastwood chair at the Stickley Museum, Fayetteville, New York. The chair was specially ordered to accommodate the Dalai Lama in a lotus position while on a speaking tour.

The Arts and Crafts aesthetic permeates Heinle's architecture. As a student under Stern, Heinle developed an awareness and appreciation for the American shingle style, a subset of American Arts and Crafts architecture. The shingle style was identified as a uniquely American architectural style by Vincent Scully, mentor to Robert Stern. It emphasized horizontal lines and was leavened by open spaces, such as sleeping porches. Often used for summer homes at the shore, particularly in the eastern part of the United States, it is also found in many other locales, such as Asheville, North Carolina. Frank Lloyd Wright and Gustav Stickley used shingles, a proto-modern architecture, and for the first time there were "sweeping, curving, bending forms created with shingles" (Heinle 2012). The shingle style can be used with other elements to create a look that ranges from formal to casual. Stern revived the style in the Hamptons, adapting it to a modern aesthetic.

Heinle has a talent for designing houses in the shingle style and has created a number of them. Whether it is apparent to the client or not, his buildings reflect Arts and Crafts proportions and features. While many of Heinle's houses are not strictly Arts and Crafts, a lot of his work is tuned that way, such as in his handling of stone, shingle, and copper. "A hundred years from now, people will still love the houses. They serve as landmarks and provide a legacy that appeals to us because of the Arts and Crafts qualities they embody" (Heinle 2012).

Working at the Farms

Heinle believes the plain use of natural materials, forthright design, and lack of pretension are largely missing from our built-up environment and the things that surround us. Much of our contemporary architecture is based on pretense and an obvious effort to ingratiate. The ubiquitous McMansion is the prime example. "Authenticity is difficult to find in life, but it's particularly lacking with residential design, and people lose a reference point for what is real" (Heinle 2012). The legacy of the Arts and Crafts is an alternative lifestyle, an authentic way to be, to see, and to live in this world. Objects are meant to be touched and sat in—an Eastwood chair embraces you. Arts and Crafts objects engage, and in that sense, they provide a satisfaction that is lacking in many modern products.

As vice-president of the board of The Stickley Museum at Craftsman Farms, Ed Heinle has provided leadership. One example of his important work is the selective tree removal program he initiated. In 2008, concerned about possible building damage from fallen trees, Heinle and a team identified Gustav Stickley's original plantings and took stock of the grounds. They found that many of the large trees had been planted by the Farneys. Heinle and his team started selectively removing trees that could endanger buildings during a storm. Remarkably, because many of the large trees had been removed prior to October 2012, there was no building damage from the devastating Hurricane Sandy. An additional benefit is that the views from inside the buildings—looking outside—are now closer to what Gustav Stickley would have intended and enjoyed.

Another of Ed Heinle's ideas was implemented in the spring of 2012. Craftsman Farms established a partnership with the Morris County School of Technology, two miles from the Farms, inviting students to participate in needed restoration work. Beginning with the milk house, under Ed's guidance and based on the historic structures report, students tore off the roof. They cut the "marvelous big chunky rafters" (Heinle 2012) and put them up. Then Heinle showed them how to create the Dutch lap joint for the fascia of the building. Seeing this historic craftswork being passed on is gratifying to Ed. The building was then painted in a color that was historically accurate. The interior, which had been converted to an apartment by the Farneys, was gutted down to the original materials and restored using lumber that had been custom milled to the correct dimensions. This project benefited both the technology school and Craftsman Farms. The partnership will continue with restoration of the calf barn during the fall 2013 semester.

When Heinle proposed the project, he had no idea what to expect. The students arrive at the Farms enthusiastic and happy and when he provides guidance and input, the kids are receptive. Gustav Stickley intended to create a school at the Farms for urban boys where they could learn civic virtues, crafts, and trades. One hundred years later, the students in this partnership are learning the skills Stickley wanted them to learn, and it's happening on his grounds. Heinle finds the whole experience very touching.

The students are enjoying the site, getting involved in the history of the buildings through hands-on work, and absorb-

Designed by Edwin Heinle

ing what they see and hear on the tour. Ed walks them around the site on their initial visit and talks about Stickley—his thinking, his epiphany when he went to England, and his coming back and starting something new that struck a chord with the public. Ed points out how the log house exemplifies what is considered *green* building today because stones from the log house were quarried and dug up on site and the chestnut logs—all seventeen courses—came from trees grown on the property.

Another Heinle stroke of genius has been replacement of the signage. The trees that were taken down on the property were harvested and stored in the dairy barn until a gentleman brought a portable machine to the Farms and milled the trees into usable lumber. The students then took the lumber to the shop at their school and made new signage, based on Ed's sketches. This was Heinle's idea, and it was brilliant.

Ed Heinle is dedicated to Craftsman Farms and has provided outstanding leadership through his good judgment, expertise, and creativity. He is teaching and preparing a new generation to understand and appreciate the work and thought of Gustav Stickley and the Arts and Crafts movement of the early twentieth century, all part of the mission of Craftsman Farms.

**References**

Heinle, Edwin. In phone interview with authors. December 2, 2012.

Mantel clock oak, copper, brass, glass, steel 137/8" x 8³/₈" x 5" c. 1912–1915

# 38. Dallas Museum of Art Exhibition 2010

The 2010-2011 exhibition, *Gustav Stickley and the American Arts & Crafts Movement*, curated by Kevin W. Tucker of the Dallas Museum of Art, opened at the Newark Museum of Art in September 2010 in celebration of the centennial of Craftsman Farms, the home Gustav Stickley built for himself and his family. It traveled to Dallas in February 2011, then went to the San Diego Museum of Art in June. The major exhibition was met with excitement throughout the Arts and Crafts world as it presented the works of Gustav Stickley within the commercial and social context of his production.

*Stickley's seminal contribution was to balance core Arts and Crafts principles that emphasized functional and handmade objects within a factory production system that enabled the sale of his products at reduced costs. To understand his success, both aesthetically and commercially, requires insights into the artistic, financial and social context of Stickley's enterprise, the ideological development of his operation and the formation of the Craftsman home and lifestyle. (Smith 2011)*

The exhibition catalog is a substantial and beautiful book with informative and thought-provoking essays by Beverly Brandt, David Cathers, Joseph Cunningham, and Beth Ann and Tommy McPherson.

### References

Smith, David. Gustav Stickley Exhibition at Dallas Museum of Art. *Antiques and The Arts Online*. March 8, 2011. http://antiquesandthearts.com/Antiques/TradeTalk/2011-03-08__11-21-11.html.

Tucker, Kevin. 2010. *Gustav Stickley and the American Arts & Crafts Movement*. Dallas Museum of Art. Exhibition catalog.

Newel-post lamp, No. 703 Copper, glass Lamp: 21½" x 7" x 7" 1907

Harvey Ellis, American, 1852-1904 Conte crayon, gouache, ink, paper 18³/₄" x 12½" c. 1903

Detail of linen chest

Linen chest Oak, iron 54³/₁₆" x 44⁷/₈" x 20¼" c. 1902–1903

Foxglove tabouret Oak 23³/₈" x 19³/₈" c. 1900–1901

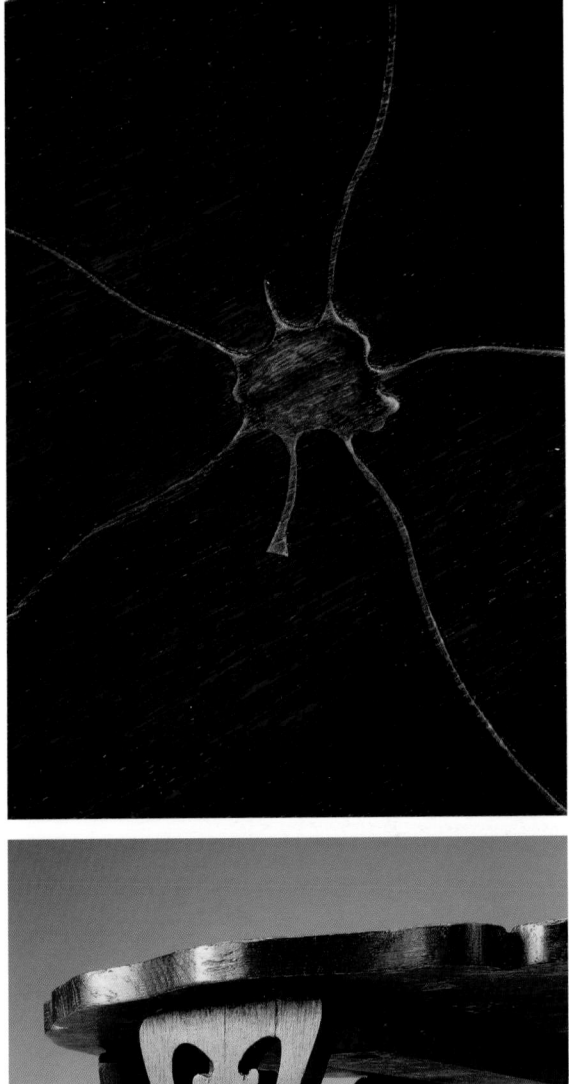

Poppy table Oak 23□" x 19" c. 1900–1901

Tabouret No. 46 Pyrographic floral
decoration added by L. W. Simpson Oak,
earthenware 21" x 19⁷/₁₆" c. 1901-1902

Armchair, Willow, upholstery
(replaced), 42" x 31½" x 31",
c. 1913-1916

Library table, Ash
28³/₄" x 36" x 35" c. 1901

Corner cupboard Oak, iron, glass 72" x 42" x 29½" c. 1902-1903

Reclining chair No. 2340 (No. 336) Oak, leather upholstery 38⅝" x 28⅜" x 36⅞" c. 1901-1902

# Photo Credits

**Chpt. 1:** pp. 1–5 courtesy Don Magner; pp. 6–10 photos by Jeffrey Preston. **Chpt. 2:** pp. 11–12 courtesy Rosalie Berberian; p. 13 photo by Jeffrey Preston; courtesy RagoArts; p. 14 photo by Jeffrey Preston; courtesy Rosalie Berberian; p.15 photo by Jeffrey Preston; courtesy of RagoArts; p. 16 courtesy Antiques and The Arts Weekly, David S. Smith photo; courtesy of Rosalie Berberian; pp. 17–20 courtesy Rosalie Berberian; pp. 21–22 photos by Jeffrey Preston. **Chpt. 3:** pp. 23–25 photos by Jeffrey Preston; p. 26–29 courtesy Bill and Patsy Porter; pp. 30-courtesy Bill and Patsy Porter; photo by Jeffrey Preston; pp 31–32 photos by Jeffrey Preston; p. 33 upper photos by Jeffrey Preston; courtesy Bill and Patsy Porter; p. 34–35 courtesy Bill and Patsy Porter; p. 36 photos by Jeffrey Preston; photo across pond by Bill Porter. **Chpt. 4:** p. 37 courtesy Princeton University Art Museum; p. 38–39 courtesy Berkeley Architectural Heritage Association; p. 40 courtesy Princeton University Art Museum; courtesy Berkeley Architectural Heritage Association. **Chpt. 5:** p. 41 courtesy The Metropolitan Museum of Art, gift of Martin Eidelberg; p. 42 courtesy Martin Eidelberg; p. 43 Collection of Martin Eidelberg, with permission; courtesy Martin Eidelberg. **Chpt. 6:** pp. 45–46 courtesy of Tod Volpe; p. 47 courtesy Everson Museum of Art; p. 49 courtesy Tod Volpe; p. 50, property RagoArts, courtesy Tod Volpe; pp. 51–52 courtesy Tod Volpe; p. 53, property David Cathers, courtesy Tod Volpe; p. 54; courtesy private collector. **Chpt. 7:** p. 55 photo by Jeffrey Preston; p. 56 photo courtesy David Cathers and Dylan Cathers; p. 57 courtesy Dalton's; lower photo used by permission of The Craftsman Farms Foundation, Inc., Parsippany, New Jersey; p. 58 courtesy Turn of the Century Editions; photo of David Cathers used by permission of The Craftsman Farms Foundation, Inc., Parsippany, New Jersey; pp. 59–60 photos by Jeffrey Preston. **Chpt. 8:** p. 61 courtesy Paul Rocheleau; pp. 62–64 photos by Allen Phillips, courtesy the Wadsworth Atheneum; p. 65 courtesy Antiques and The Arts Weekly, David S. Smith photo; courtesy Treadway-Toomey Auctions; p. 66 courtesy Turn of the Century Editions; p. 67 courtesy Bruce Johnson; page 68 courtesy Laura Harris; pp. 69–78 photos by Allen Phillips, courtesy the Wadsworth Atheneum. **Chpt. 9:** pp. 79 courtesy Cathers and Dembrosky; courtesy of Antiques and The Arts Weekly, David S. Smith photos; pp. 80–81 courtesy of Antiques and The Arts Weekly, David S. Smith photos; p. 82 courtesy Robert Kaplan; photo by Jeffrey Preston; p. 83 photo by Jeffrey Preston; pp. 84–89 courtesy Robert Kaplan; p. 90 photo by Jeffrey Preston. **Chpt. 10:** all photos courtesy Jerry Cohen. **Chpt. 11:** pp. 97–104 David S. Smith photos, courtesy Antiques and The Arts Weekly; pp. 105–108 photos by Jeffrey Preston; pp. 106–107 self-portrait courtesy of Antiques and The Arts Weekly, David S. Smith photos. **Chpt. 12:** pp. 109–110 courtesy Richard Caggiano; pp. 111–116 courtesy Derek Danton; p. 117 courtesy Art Accardi; p. 118 courtesy of Peter Smorto; p. 119 courtesy Antiques and The Arts Weekly, David S. Smith photo; courtesy Art Accardi; p. 120 courtesy RagoArts; p. 121 courtesy Richard Caggiano; bottom photo courtesy Derek Danton; p. 122 courtesy Robert DeFalco. **Chpt. 13:** p. 123 photo by Jeffrey Preston; woodblock of Kitty Turgeon by Laura Wilder (www.laurawilder.com); p. 124 courtesy Boice Lydell; p. 125 photo by Jeffrey Preston; courtesy Roycroft Inn; courtesy Martha Augat; p. 126 courtesy Roycroft Inn; pp. 127–130 courtesy Boice Lydell; p. 131 photo by Jeffrey Preston; hanging light courtesy Ted Lytwyn and Cara Corbo; E.Hubbard courtesy Boice Lydell; pp. 132–133 courtesy Nancy Hubbard Brady; p. 134 photo by Jeffrey Preston; courtesy Nancy Hubbard Brady. **Chpt. 14:** p. 135 courtesy of the Dallas Museum of Art; p. 136 courtesy Cara Corbo; p. 137 photos by Jeffrey Preston; u.r., property of Cara Corbo and Ted Lytwyn; p. 138 photo by Jeffrey Preston; lower left, property of Cara Corbo and Ted Lytwyn; pp. 139–141 photos by Jeffrey Preston; p. 142 courtesy Cara Corbo and Ted Lytwyn. **Chpt.15:** pp. 145–148 photos by Jeffrey Preston; pp. 149–150 courtesy of Ed and Kathy Friedman; p. 150 The Craftsman; **Chpt.16:** p. 151 courtesy of RagoArts; p. 152 courtesy Benoit Cortet; p. 153 courtesy Linda Myers; all other photos courtesy of RagoArts. **Chpt. 17:** all photos courtesy of Richie Savoia. **Chpt. 18:** p. 179 courtesy Antiques and The Arts Weekly, David S. Smith photo; p. 180 courtesy Treadway-Toomey Auctions; p. 181 courtesy John Toomey; courtesy Antiques and The Arts Weekly, David S. Smith photo; p. 182 top left, courtesy Don Treadway; other photos courtesy Treadway-Toomey Auctions; p. 183–192 courtesy Treadway-Toomey Auctions. **Chpt. 19:** p. 193 courtesy Skinner, www.skinnerinc.com; p. 194 courtesy Antiques and The Arts Weekly, David S. Smith photo; p. 195 courtesy Skinner, www.skinnerinc.com; p. 196 courtesy Skinner, www.skinnerinc.com; courtesy Jane Prentiss; p.197–205 courtesy Skinner, www.skinnerinc.com;

p. 206 courtesy Antiques and The Arts Weekly, David S. Smith photo. **Chpt.20:** p. 207 courtesy Antiques and The Arts Weekly, David S. Smith photo; p. 208 photograph by Helaine Messer; Courtesy Nancy McClelland; p. 209 photo lower left by Jeffrey Preston; others courtesy Antiques and The Arts Weekly, David S. Smith photos; p. 210 courtesy of Christie's New York; p. 211 courtesy Antiques and The Arts Weekly, David S. Smith photos; p. 212 courtesy Antiques and The Arts Weekly, David S. Smith photo; courtesy Christie's New York; pp. 213–214 courtesy Antiques and The Arts Weekly, David S. Smith photos. **Chpt. 21:** all photos courtesy Christie's New York. **Chpt. 22:** all photos courtesy Dalton's. **Chpt. 23:** all photos courtesy of Michael Adams/Dawn Hopkins. **Chpt. 24:** pp. 239–242 courtesy Bruce Johnson; p. 243 photos by Jeffrey Preston; 2013 conference poster by Laura Wilder www.laurawilder.com, with permission; p. 244 photos by Jeffrey Preston; photo at bottom courtesy Jill Thomas-Clark; pp. 245–248 courtesy Bruce Johnson; p. 249 courtesy RagoArts; top right courtesy Bruce Johnson; p. 250 top left courtesy Jill Thomas-Clark; courtesy Bruce Johnson. **Chpt. 25:** p. 251 photo by Jeffrey Preston; pp. 252–253 courtesy Art Accardi; p. 254 courtesy Art Accardi; photo by Jeffrey Preston; pp. 255–256 courtesy Art Accardi; p. 257 photo by Jeffrey Preston; pp. 258–260 courtesy Art Accardi. **Chpt. 26:** all photos courtesy of Steven Thomas. **Chpt. 27:** p. 265 courtesy Grand Rapids Art Museum; p. 266 courtesy Don Marek; p. 267 courtesy Grand Rapids Art Museum; p. 268 upper left courtesy Don Marek; courtesy Grand Rapids Art Museum; p. 269 courtesy Don Marek; p. 270 courtesy Don Marek; lower right courtesy Grand Rapids Art Museum. **Chpt. 28:** pp. 271–274 courtesy Crab Tree Farm; pp. 275–278 courtesy Crab Tree Farm: photo by Jim Prinz; p. 279 courtesy Crab Tree Farm: photo by Jamie Stukenberg; p. 280 courtesy Dallas Museum of Art; pp. 281–286 courtesy Crab Tree Farm: photo by Jim Prinz. **Chpt. 29:** p. 287 photo by Jeffrey Preston; p. 288 photo by Doug Stivison, used with permission of The Craftsman Farms Foundation, Inc., Parsippany, New Jersey; p. 289 used by permission of The Craftsman Farms Foundation, Inc., Parsippany, New Jersey; photo of house by Jeffrey Preston; p. 290 used by permission of The Craftsman Farms Foundation, Inc., Parsippany, New Jersey; photo at center right by Jeffrey Preston; pp. 291–292 used by permission of The Craftsman Farms Foundation, Inc., Parsippany, New Jersey; p. 293 photo of catalog used with permission of artist, Judith A. Jordan and by permission of The Craftsman Farms Foundation, Inc., Parsippany, New Jersey; other photos by Ray Stubblebine, used with permission of The Craftsman Farms Foundation, Inc., Parsippany, New Jersey; p. 294 photo upper right by Jeffrey Preston; other photos by Ray Stubblebine, used with permission of The Craftsman Farms Foundation, Inc., Parsippany, New Jersey; p. 295 photo of catalog used with permission of The Craftsman Farms Foundation, Inc., Parsippany, New Jersey; other photos by Ray Stubblebine, used with permission of The Craftsman Farms Foundation, Inc., Parsippany, New Jersey; pp. 296–297 photos by Ray Stubblebine, used with permission of The Craftsman Farms Foundation, Inc., Parsippany, New Jersey; p. 298 photo upper left used with permission of The Craftsman Farms Foundation, Inc., Parsippany, New Jersey; other photos by Jeffrey Preston; p. 299 photos by Ray Stubblebine, used with permission of The Craftsman Farms Foundation, Inc., Parsippany, New Jersey; p. 300 photos by Jeffrey Preston; p. 301 photo by Doug Stivison, used with permission of The Craftsman Farms Foundation, Inc., Parsippany, New Jersey; pp. 302–303 photos by Ray Stubblebine, used with permission of The Craftsman Farms Foundation, Inc., Parsippany, New Jersey; p. 304 photo by Jeffrey Preston. **Chpt. 30:** pp. 305–306 photos by Jeffrey Preston; p. 307 upper left and upper center Jeffrey Preston; lower center photo by Patricia Bartinique; catalog cover by Judith A. Jordan, used with permission of The Craftsman Farms Foundation, Inc., Parsippany, New Jersey; p. 308 courtesy Antiques and The Arts Weekly; p. 309 photos 2 and 4, top row, by Jeffrey Preston; others by Patricia Bartinique; catalog cover by Judith A. Jordan, courtesy Robert DeFalco; p. 310 courtesy Antiques and The Arts Weekly; p. 311 courtesy of Jill Thomas-Clark; photo of Pat Bartinique by Sandra Nissen Photography; p. 312 photo by Jeffrey Preston; catalog courtesy of Peter and Janet Copeland. **Chpt. 31:** p. 313–317 courtesy Jill Thomas-Clark; p. 318 photos by Jeffrey Preston; pp. 319–320 courtesy Jill Thomas-Clark. **Chpt. 32:** all photos courtesy L. & J.G. Stickley, Inc. **Chpt. 33:** all photos courtesy Style 1900. **Chpt. 34:** courtesy American Bungalow. **Chpt. 35:** courtesy Peter and Janet Copeland. **Chpt. 36:** all photos courtesy Two Red Roses. **Chpt. 37:** all photos courtesy Edwin Heinle. **Chpt. 38:** all photos courtesy Dallas Museum of Art.